Pastor Thomas M. Hansen
Christ Lutheran Church
150 5th Street
Marine on St. Croix, MN 55047

500
Illustrations

500 Illustrations

Stories from Life for Preaching and Teaching

G. Curtis Jones
&
Paul H. Jones

Abingdon Press
Nashville

500 ILLUSTRATIONS: STORIES FROM LIFE FOR PREACHING AND TEACHING

This book is printed on recycled, acid-free, elemental-chlorine–free paper.

Library of Congress Cataloging-in-Publication Data

Jones, G. Curtis (George Curtis), 1911–
    500 illustrations: stories from life for preaching and teaching/
  G. Curtis Jones & Paul H. Jones.
      p.   cm.
    Includes bibliographical references.
    ISBN 0-687-01545-6
    1. Homiletical illustrations.   I. Jones, Paul H., 1949–   .
  II. Title.
BV4225.2.J659   1998
251'.08—dc21   97-47067
                                                                                       CIP

Scripture quotations, unless otherwise indicated, are from the New Revised Standard Version Bible, copyright © 1989, by the Division of Christian Education of the National Council of the Churches of Christ in the United States of America.

Scripture quotations noted JBP are from *The New Testament in Modern English*, Revised Edition, by J. B. Phillips. Copyright © J. B. Phillips, 1958, 1959, 1960, 1972.

Scripture quotations noted KJV are from the King James Version of the Bible.

Scripture quotations noted NIV are from the *Holy Bible: New International Version*. Copyright © 1973, 1978, 1984 by the International Bible Society. Used by permission of Zondervan Bible Publishers.

Scripture quotations noted RSV are from the Revised Standard Version of the Bible, copyright 1946, 1952, 1971 by the Division of Christian Education of the National Council of Churches of Christ in the USA. Used by permission.

"I Believe in Santa Claus" is reprinted with the permission of the author.

"What About Your Pledge!?!" is reprinted with the permission of the National City Christian Church.

The prayer from Mae Yoho Ward from *The Seeking Heart* is printed with the permission of Christian Board of Publications.

98 99 00 01 02 03 04 05 06 07—10 9 8 7 6 5 4 3 2 1

MANUFACTURED IN THE UNITED STATES OF AMERICA

To Sybil,
Loving Wife and Mother,
Abiding Illustration of Courage and Faith

Contents

Introduction

Our frenetic, demanding society drives us unmercifully. To use George Bernard Shaw's metaphor, deadlines pound us like the insensitive blades of a windmill: By the time we recover from one assignment, another one awaits us. There is no letup!

Preachers, teachers, and other public servants constantly struggle with priorities and schedules, expectations and enjoyments. Very often, in their thinking, writing, and speaking, an illustrative anecdote or historical note can be just what is needed to facilitate the task. We hope that this comprehensive offering of adaptable materials may provide stimulation and assistance to clergy, civic leaders, and others in meeting their professional needs and personal responsibilities.

In a sense, every book is a compendium of contributions, from sources named and unnamed. This volume is no exception. It has emerged from wide reading, experience, and conversations. We have tried to identify and acknowledge copyrighted references, but if there are omissions we apologize. We are grateful to all who graciously granted us permission to include their previously published material.

In addition to the input of family, we are especially indebted to Asa Humphries for reading the entire manuscript, Vickie Mitchell for editorial assistance, Anna Williams for clerical assistance, and President Charles Shearer and Dean James Moseley of Transylvania University for their encouragement. Support from the David and Betty Jones Faculty Development Program of Transylvania University is most appreciated.

A special word of appreciation is extended to Gerry Boyer, whose computer skills and cheerful resolve contributed significantly to the preparation of the manuscript.

We also gratefully acknowledge the support of editors and staff at Abingdon Press.

G. Curtis Jones and Paul H. Jones

Addiction

First, Reform Yourself!

Mahatma Gandhi was one of the most influential men of the twentieth century. His integrity, philosophy of nonviolent resistance, and unflinching courage were as disarming as they were contagious. His disciplines were so well known that he was assassinated at prayer time. The world wept when he died on January 30, 1948.

There are many wonderful stories about this spiritual and political leader, who loved not only his people of India but also all the peoples of the world.

A poor mother and her son once walked all day to reach Gandhi. She had come to ask the great teacher to tell her son to stop eating sugar, which he ate in excess. The compassionate man was silent. Presently he said, "Come back in a week." The bewildered souls obeyed.

At the conclusion of the second visit, the mother made bold to ask why he could not have spoken to the lad during the first trip. The essence of Mahatma Gandhi's reply was: Up until last week I, too, ate too much sugar.

Living with an Alcoholic

Forty-five-year-old Teresa McGovern, daughter of former Senator George McGovern and his wife Eleanor, was found dead in the snow in Madison, Wisconsin, on December 12, 1994. She was an alcoholic. Writing in the February 16, 1995, issue of *Parade Magazine,* Mr. McGovern shares some of the heartbreaking struggles, hopes, and disappointments that are part of dealing with a loved one with

11

an alcohol problem. Like others, the McGoverns discovered that they were powerless to overcome the addiction that was destroying their child. You can assist, says McGovern, advise, agonize, pay, and pray, but you cannot deliver sobriety.

There are many theories about why individuals become alcoholics. The reasons range from genes, chemistry, or a cover-up for personal inadequacies to the environment and personal associations. The only clear pattern seems to be an unquenchable thirst for alcohol, which may be triggered by drinking a glass of wine or a shot of whiskey while in a state of depression. Senator McGovern says of Teresa: She seemed to have been born with a vulnerability to both depression and alcoholism.

This dreadful disease destroys homes and businesses, and creates a sense of shame, anxiety, and stress. Every year, alcoholism and other chemical dependencies claim one hundred thousand American lives.

We are urged not to give up on the alcoholic or on ourselves, but to seek spiritual strength through prayer and to support funding for research and rehabilitation. Yet it is extremely difficult to live with an alcoholic who is a loved one.

Drug-Induced Suicide

No one is immune to the problem of drug abuse in America, but perhaps the children of celebrities are most vulnerable. Hugh O'Connor, thirty-three, son of the actor Carroll O'Connor, took his own life in March 1995 after a long battle with drug addiction. His father writes about the pain in the July 16, 1995, issue of *Parade Magazine* and offers suggestions to stop drug abuse.

"I suppose no death is so hard to accept as this (drug-induced suicide)," writes O'Connor. "The bewilderment, the questions without answers, won't let us grieve calmly: Why did we fail to hear the change of tone, fail to see the darkening of the shadow, fail to discern why our hearts' darling was distant and melancholy, fail at the end to run and hold the angry hands?"

Although billions of dollars have been spent over the last decade to conduct a war on drugs, O'Connor declares it a failure—drugs are readily available and too many lives are still being shattered. He advocates a new approach that includes these suggestions: go after drug dealers, require everyone to carry a national tax identity card, educate parents, and begin immediate discussion of this national epidemic.

Under Control

The key to training Seattle Slew, the only unbeaten horse to win the Triple Crown, was teaching him to contain his brilliance and save himself for the stretch run. "I spent all my time trying to get him under control," trainer Billy Turner recalls of his 1977 Triple Crown winner.

The same could be said for the trainer. A former steeplechase jockey who once won the National Amateur Riding Championship, Turner began losing control of his drinking as the pressures of racing increased. Although riding hard and drinking hard were acceptable ways of life around the track, he soon became a maintenance drinker who required alcohol just to function. After Seattle Slew lost his first race at Hollywood Park in 1977, Turner's drinking problems intensified and he never trained Seattle Slew again. Gradually, owners took their horses to other barns. From 1989 to 1991, Turner's horses won only twenty races.

After he was absent from the track for several days in a row in 1991, friends found Turner at home in bed unconscious and near death. Turner's body had broken down from the abuse of drinking twenty-four hours a day for twenty years. When doctors told him it would be suicide to drink again, Turner quit on the spot.

In 1994, Turner-trained horses won forty-three races, or 20 percent of his starters. His drinking problem now under control, trainer Billy Turner is again ready for greatness.

Computer Addiction

Kevin Mitnick was the world's most celebrated computer hacker. Growing up in Los Angeles with his mother, a waitress, he was so

13

fascinated by cyberspace that he became a computer wizard. His first hack job was cracking the system in his high school's administration office. So far as we know, he did not alter any grades or other information. As a teenager, he had several encounters with the law and was found guilty of stealing technical information from Pacific Bell's computer center. While on probation he accessed computers at a local university. In 1988, he was caught stealing from the Digital Equipment Company. He served a year in prison, where he underwent a twelve-step program for computer addiction. By the time he was released in 1990, he knew as much about the telephone system as anyone in Bell laboratories. Upon his release, he was ordered not to touch a computer, but he could not resist. Kevin Mitnick, the world's most wanted hacker, was finally apprehended by authorities in North Carolina in February 1995. At the time, it was reported that he had one million dollars' worth of stolen data stashed away.

It is frightening to realize that there are individuals capable of interrupting, intercepting, and collecting technical and personal data from the world's most sophisticated networks.

Computer addiction is a growing problem. Be aware of hitchhikers and hackers along the information highway!

When Coaches Need Coaching

The misconduct of three professional coaches, decent and popular men, drew nationwide attention in May of 1995. *Sports Illustrated* (May 15, 1995) carried pictures of the accused on the cover: Gary Moeller, football coach at Michigan; Dennis Erickson, former football coach at the University of Miami and later with the Seattle Seahawks; and Bobby Cox, manager of the Atlanta Braves baseball team.

These highly successful professionals shared a common and costly embarrassment—alcoholism!

Determination

After battling drug addiction and unemployment, and surviving a short-lived marriage, actress Drew Barrymore recaptured her life. She played Holly, a pregnant unmarried mother, in the film *Boys on the Side*. At the end of the working day she now has a light, beautiful feeling.

Reflecting on her downhill spiral, she was quoted in *USA Today* (February 3, 1995) as saying: "If you build your base out of your own stairs instead of people's heads . . . you can't really fall that hard again."

Out of the Rough

Few professional golfers ever win two majors in a career. Even fewer win two majors by the age of thirty. And only John Daly has accomplished the feat by playing out of the rough—both on and off the course.

On August 11, 1991, Daly shot a 12 under par to win the PGA Championship at Crooked Stick Golf Club in Carmel, Indiana, by three strokes. Four years later on July 23, 1995, John Daly won professional golf's most traditional tournament, the 124th British Open, at its most revered site, the Old Course at storied St. Andrews, with a convincing four-hole playoff victory over Italy's Constantino Rocca.

Daly's Open victory, like his struggle with alcohol, his temper, and his personal life, was not easy. He blew a three-stroke lead on the final day and then watched Rocca sink a miracle sixty-five-foot birdie putt from off the green to force a playoff. But unlike the previous year when Daly plummeted from second-round contender to last-place finisher, this time he found the internal fortitude to overcome adversity.

After two failed marriages, temper altercations on the tour, and substance-abuse rehabilitation, John Daly is now sober. In an interview following his 4 under par first round of the 1997 PGA championship, Daly said, "Golf is an addiction and so is alcohol. It's one day at a time with alcohol and one shot at a time with golf."

Tour de Second Chance

While most cycling fans in July of 1995 followed the progress of Spain's thirty-one-year-old Miguel Indurain as he captured his fifth consecutive Tour de France victory, seventy-one-year-old Jewett Pattee and three other over-sixty teammates pedaled in virtual obscurity. Around the clock they rode—in one-hour shifts—to complete the 2,904 miles from Irvine, California, to Savannah, Georgia.

Even more remarkable is the fact that Pattee is a reformed alcoholic who is proof positive that the human body provides second chances. A pharmacist by trade, Pattee's self-professed goal in life was to "show I could outdrink and outsmoke everybody." But after he saw an uncle and a father-in-law die, largely because of their inactivity, Pattee changed his ways at the age of fifty. "They were dying in a heck of a lot more pain than I ever have when I'm blasting up a mountain," he declared. "It hurts me, but I'll take that kind of pain over what they suffered."

Pattee is convinced that his personal Tour de Second Chance is possible for everyone. "The average person looks at a picture of old age, and the common picture is pretty grim," he says. "But it doesn't have to be. I really believe that 75, 80 percent of the things that ail people my age is from sheer inactivity and lousy diet, things that can be corrected from individual effort."

The Great Race

Bands played, flags waved, and people cheered as over one hundred pre–World War II vehicles motored into Lexington, Kentucky, on July 5, 1995, for a lunch stop along their forty-four-hundred-mile, fourteen-day road race from Ottawa to Mexico City. The drivers and their vintage cars, including a Stutz, Marmon, Overland, Velie, Graham, Hudson, and McDowell, were participants in the thirteenth annual $250,000 Great North American Race.

In a road rally each team is given a set of extensive directions with roads to take, turns to make, markers to find, and defined speeds to drive. Although times are assessed at checkpoints every few miles, competitors do not know how they have done until the end of each day. The only instruments permitted in the car are a timing clock and a speedometer that can measure a speed change as slight as half a mile an hour.

Although there is nothing to compare with the Great Race, for Tom McRae, its executive director, the "great race" involves life and not antique cars. Six years before the first Great Race in May 1983 he was in a personal race for his life. In 1976, at the age of 37, McRae was "washed up," addicted to marijuana and alcohol, and in "a black hole so deep I couldn't see any way out."

A year earlier at a friend's home during a Bible study, McRae secretly prayed the "sinner's prayer" and asked God to take alcohol out of his life. Nothing seemed to change. Yet the next summer he miraculously "went straight." He was sober, but broke.

Convinced that he needed psychological counseling, McRae called his family physician for a referral. Instead, Ole Doc Mobley told him to come over. "I'll be your shrink," he said. During the conversation Doc pointed Tom to Jesus and concluded with this observation: "McRae, I've seen a miracle. Medically speaking, it should have taken years of A.A. or psychiatric help for you to get where you are today. God *answered* your prayer." With instructions to read the Gospels, Tom McRae drove out of the pits of personal despair and back into the "great race" of life.

Aging

Persistence

At age eighty-nine, Norman Vaughn scaled the mountain in Antarctica that was named for him by Admiral Richard Byrd. It is about 385 kilometers from the South Pole.

In 1928, Vaughn and two of his Harvard buddies, Edward Goodale and Freddy Crockett, dropped out of school to serve as dog handlers for Admiral Byrd's 1928–1930 Antarctic expedition.

After being obsessed for sixty-five years with the idea of conquering by himself the unforgiving terrain, and after one failed attempt, a plane crash, and expenses of $1.5 million, Norman Vaughn realized his dream on December 16, 1994.

Because of a fused ankle and a knee replacement, he reached the summit only by climbing 7,128 vertical steps chiseled out of the ice by the lead climber, Vern Tejas.

The persistent explorer's comment is worth remembering: "Dream big and dare to fail!"

Profile of a Senior

Who is a senior citizen? What is one?

A senior citizen is one who was here before the Pill and the population explosion. We were here before television, penicillin, polio shots, antibiotics, and Frisbees. Before frozen food, nylon, Dacron, Xerox, Kinsey, radar, fluorescent lights, credit cards, and ballpoint pens. For us, time-sharing meant togetherness; a chip meant a piece of wood; hardware meant hard wear; and software wasn't yet a word. Coeds never wore slacks. We were before panty hose and drip-dry clothes, before ice makers and dishwashers, clothes dryers, freezers, and electric blankets. Before Hawaii and

Alaska became states. Before men wore long hair and earrings and women wore tuxedos.

We were before Leonard Bernstein, yogurt, Ann Landers, plastic, the forty-hour work week and the minimum wage. We got married first and then lived together. How quaint can one be?

Closets were for clothes, not for coming out of; bunnies were small rabbits, and rabbits were not Volkswagens. We were before Grandma Moses and Frank Sinatra and cup sizing for bras. Girls wore Peter Pan collars and thought cleavage was something butchers did. We were before Batman, Rudolph the Red-Nosed Reindeer, and Snoopy. Before DDT, vitamin pills, disposable diapers, Q.E. One, Jeeps. The Jefferson Memorial and pizza, Cheerios, instant coffee, decaffeinated anything, and McDonald's were all unheard of. We thought fast food was what you ate during Lent. We were before Boy George, J. D. Salinger, and Chiquita bananas. Before FM radios, tape recorders, electric typewriters, word processors, MUZAK, electronic music, disco dancing—and that's not all bad!

In our day cigarette smoking was fashionable, grass was for mowing, Coke was a refreshing drink, and pot was something you cooked in. If we'd been asked to explain CIA, Ms., NATO, UFO, NFL, JFK, ERA, or IUD, we'd have said alphabet soup.

We are today's SENIOR CITIZENS, a hardy bunch when you think of how OUR world has changed and of the adjustments WE have had to make!

Centennial Advice

Although Audrey Stubbart was forced to retire in 1960, at the mandatory age of sixty-five, from the publishing business in Independence, Missouri, she did not stop working. The local daily newspaper, the *Examiner*, hired her as a copy editor. Thirty-five years later, still putting in a full day's work, she celebrated her one-hundredth birthday. Her prescription for a long productive life: "I never smoked, I never drank, and I tried to never tell a lie. The last one is the hardest."

Who Are the Aging?

Who are the aging?

"Today's child is tomorrow's elder," replied Bob Blancato, executive director of the nation's fourth and final White House Conference on Aging for this century, held May 2–5, 1995.

And the latest statistics confirm his response. According to national estimates, about six thousand people across the country turn sixty-five every day, and by the year 2000 there will be twenty-six times as many people eighty-five and older as there were in 1990.

How Old Are You?

Jeanne Calment of Aries, France, was born in 1875. *Time* magazine (March 6, 1995) carried a striking picture of her, dressed in colorful clothes. Her kind, intelligent face, with a sharp nose and long forehead, rested smilingly beneath a noble head of white hair.

Like so much of the human condition, longevity seems to be linked to one's genes and disposition. Commenting on her life, the provocative centenarian said, "I took pleasure when I could. I acted clearly and morally and without regret. I'm very lucky." In addition, Jeanne Calment lived an active life; she was often seen riding her bicycle around town until she was one hundred. When she died on August 4, 1997, at the age of 122, she was considered the oldest person in the world.

Not many of us will live to rival her vigor and age. But the U.S. Census Bureau projects that if present demographic trends continue, by the year 2040 there will be at least 1.3 million one-hundred-year-old Americans.

Ralph Waldo Emerson suggested that no one is old until one's soul turned gray!

What Are Seniors Worth?

An elderly woman described her senior years.

"Remember, old folks are worth a fortune—with silver in their hair, gold in their teeth, stones in their kidneys, lead in their feet, and gas in their stomachs. I have become a little older since I saw you last and a few changes have come into my life—frankly, I have become a frivolous old gal.

"I am seeing five gentlemen every day. As soon as I wake up, Will Power helps me get out of bed. Then, I go to see John. Next, Charlie Horse comes along, and when he is here he takes a lot of my time and attention. When he leaves, Arthur Ritis shows up and stays the rest of the day. He doesn't like to stay in one place too long, so he takes me from joint to joint. After such a busy day I'm really tired and glad to go to bed with Ben Gay. What a life! Oh yes, I'm flirting with Al Zymer.

"P.S. I almost forgot. My preacher came to call the other day. He said that at my age I should be thinking of the hereafter. I told him, 'Oh I do, all the time. No matter where I am, in the parlor, upstairs, in the kitchen, or down in the basement, I ask myself—"Now what am I here after?" ' "

Aging Society

The latest statistics confirm the obvious—the eighty-five-and-over age group is the fastest-growing age group in the United States. In 1994, more than three million Americans were eighty-five and over. One in three citizens can now expect to join this elite club one day.

Because people over eighty-five spend more than six times as much as the general population on health care, and since a signifi-cantly smaller workforce will have to support this fastest-growing age group, many experts predict a "growing generational conflict" as the numbers in this age group increase. Trends recognized in the U.S. Census Bureau statistics verify this widening gap. For example, from 1960 to 1994 the eighty-five-and-older population increased by 274 percent while the elderly population in general—everyone over sixty-five—rose 100 percent. During the same period, the total popu-lation grew just 45 percent.

For Ron Crouch, a demographer with the Urban Research Insti-tute at the University of Louisville, these numbers indicate that "this country has one major issue and one major issue alone. That's an aging society and how you adapt to a changing demographic struc-ture we've never before seen in the history of the world."

Options

I asked a friend, who is ninety-two years old, how he was feeling. "Well," he said, "I saw my doctors recently. One said to come back in six months. The other said to return in a year. So, you see, I've got options!"

The Challenge of Age

Those who have the impression that senior citizens should be assigned to retirement communities, nursing homes, or otherwise relieved of their professional and personal responsibilities, should ponder the phenomenal progress of the Church of Jesus Christ of Latter-Day Saints, led by older people such as Ezra Taft Benson.

The late Prophet Benson, secretary of agriculture in the Eisen-hower administration, was president of the Mormon Church from 1985 until his death in June 1994. During his term of nine years, church membership increased from 5.9 million to almost 9 million, with assets of approximately $8 billion. Despite its gerontocracy, the Mormon Church is effective; its networking unexcelled. Today its properties are valued at $30 billion. The church is led by senior citizens.

All of us can learn about the meaning of commitment and courage from this extraordinary American. He met the challenge of age!

White Lie

The mother of President Jimmy Carter, "Miss Lillian," was known for her wisdom and wit. Her character was impeccable. A reporter from one of the networks once came for an interview. Questioning became rather persistent and personal, but Mrs. Carter was more than a match for the media representative. Finally, in desperation, he commented, "Surely, Miss Lillian, you must have told some little white lies along the way."

"Yes, I have," she replied.

"Example?"

"Like when you came for the interview and I said that I was glad to see you!"

Before You Panic

Glenn Cunningham

The unconscious little boy dragged from a burning schoolhouse was not expected to live. He was severely burned. His legs seemed lifeless. Doctors recommended amputation. His parents objected. Through painful persistence, and his mother's faithful therapy, the lad was eventually able to walk. At last he was able to run. At the Princeton Invitational Track Meet on June 16, 1934, Glenn Cunningham established a new world record for the mile: 4:06.7.

Fred Astaire

Initially, Fred Astaire did not receive an encouraging screen test. A 1933 MGM evaluation read: "Can't act! Slightly bald! Can dance a little!"

Albert Einstein

Albert Einstein did not talk until he was four years old; he did not read until he was seven.

Thomas Carlyle

When Thomas Carlyle was almost finished writing *The French Revolution,* a maid accidentally threw the pile of papers in the fire. Carlyle was heartsick and frustrated. But he did not punish the maid nor did he go into mourning for the destroyed manuscript. Instead, he sat down and rewrote the masterpiece, largely from memory.

Leo Tolstoy

Leo Tolstoy, the great Russian writer, flunked out of college.

Henry Ford

Henry Ford went broke five times before establishing a sound, successful business.

Abraham Lincoln

Abraham Lincoln was defeated in his first try for the state legislature; defeated in his desire to become Commissioner of the General Land Office; defeated in the contest for a seat in the United States Senate; defeated for the vice presidency of the United States; and again defeated in an effort to become senator from Illinois. However, despite five political losses, Lincoln was elected President of the United States in 1860.

Thomas Edison

Thomas Alva Edison, an inquisitive youngster, dropped out of school. His teacher in Fort Huron, Michigan, referred to him as being "addled." Eventually, this misunderstood young man revolutionized the world with creations. He patented 6,093 inventions.

Winston Churchill

Winston Churchill flunked the sixth grade. However, at age sixty-two he became prime minister of England.

Richard Bach

Richard Bach's lovely story of a soaring seagull, known as *Jonathan Livingston Seagull,* was declined by eighteen publishers. At last, Macmillan accepted the manuscript. It was published in 1970 and within five years it sold seven million copies in the United States alone.

Bible

"I Want to Read My Bible"

After years of sharecropping and domestic work, after nineteen pregnancies and fourteen children, Ruby Williams—poor, Black, and functionally illiterate—desires only one thing in life: "I want to read my Bible."

Like many of her generation, Ruby Williams was victimized by a "racial caste system" that relegated Black youth to the fields rather than the classroom. Now she wants to read with her own eyes the words that have sustained her for over eighty years.

With assistance from her church, Ms. Williams enrolled in a state-sponsored literacy program. One year later, with her right index finger methodically sliding across the lines of a large-print Bible, she slowly pronounces each word.

"I can read, I can read," she exclaims. "Sometimes I pick up the Bible and read and read and read. I sure do. Glory hallelujah. Thank God."

The Bible

The lead story in the December 18, 1995, issue of *Time* magazine read, "Is the Bible Fact or Fiction?"

The Bible continues to be a controversial book. Each discipline and reader approaches it differently.

To begin with, the Bible was not dropped from the windowsills of heaven. It emerged over a period of fifteen hundred years.

When we turn the Bible into something it is not—a charm or magic wand—we create an idol.

The Bible is not a book about science, though it is prophetic. It is not a book on astronomy, though it refers to the stars. It is not a book on archaeology, though it uncovers truth. The Bible is not a book of jurisprudence, though it describes justice. The Bible does not tell us how to build intercontinental missiles or how to use the Internet, but it does teach persons to be responsible for their actions.

The Bible is a thesaurus of wisdom and guidance. It is a record of the mighty acts of God, containing gifts to God's children and their responses. The Bible is a book about faith. On the whole, the Bible was written by people of faith to arouse and nurture faith. Behind this ageless book stands a person: Jesus the Christ!

Beautiful Before God

I recently visited the Alzheimer's unit of a health care facility. Amid the confusion, the pacing back and forth of ambulatory patients and their irrepressible chatter, sat my ninety-seven-year-old friend in a geriatric chair, slowly turning and patting the pages of her Bible.

What a beautiful picture of faith before God!

The Bible and Culture

At the dawn of the twentieth century, Protestant leaders confidently looked forward to a "Christian century." Now, as the twenty-first century approaches, believers ironically ask whether the new century will even hold a place for Christians.

"Normative pluralism," where all truth claims have equal value, has apparently replaced the perceived Judeo-Christian consensus. As a result, the individual choice to become a Christian is presently made in the face of other religious as well as cultural options.

Situated in this cultural context, the church must pursue an intentional course of faithfulness through the wilderness of secularity where religion is just another "hobby."

It is, therefore, incumbent upon the church to return again and again to Scripture in order to maintain its obedient witness to the gospel. Because the Bible is the church's book and this particular set of writings witnesses to the decisive revelation of God in Jesus the

Christ, it serves as the authoritative norm for church teaching and practice.

Know God Through the Bible

According to Gallup surveys conducted throughout the decade of the 1990s, 95 percent of Americans consistently profess a belief in God or a universal spirit. But where do people learn about God? How do individuals know or experience God?

Not surprisingly, the surveys indicate that 38 percent of the respondents claim that God reveals Godself through the Bible, "which they regard as containing God's actual words and consider to be the absolute truth." While 44 percent of those surveyed consider the Bible as inspired, they do not necessarily believe that it must be interpreted literally.

These surveys not only underscore the prominence of Scripture as a vehicle for the discernment of God's presence in the world, but they also obligate the community of faith to regularly offer Bible-study opportunities.

Digging Up the Dead

Was Ramses II the pharaoh at the time of Moses and the Exodus? Can archaeology lend veracity to the story that the firstborn of Egypt died as a result of the plague told of in Exodus 12:29? Did Ramses II's firstborn son, Amen-hir-khopshef, die prematurely?

The answers to these questions and many more may soon be revealed. Kent Weeks, professor at the American University in Cairo, discovered in February 1995 the thirty-two-hundred-year-old tomb of Ramses II's sons in Egypt's legendary Valley of the Kings.

Ramses II, who died at age ninety-two, was not only one of the mighty pharaohs who greatly expanded Egypt's borders and influence but he was also a tremendous builder. The father of more than one hundred children (over fifty were sons) by twelve wives as well as official concubines, Ramses had this particular tomb built on the grand scale that his numerous progeny deserved. While most mau soleums have no more than ten rooms, Weeks believes this tomb may contain as many as one hundred rooms. "It took Ramses only two or three years to build this tomb," explains Weeks. "It will probably take us ten or twelve to fully excavate it."

Is the Bible Fact or Fiction?

During Hanukkah and Christmas, cover stories for national magazines frequently involve religious themes. The December 18, 1995, issue of *Time* offered a typical yet regrettable example. Accompanying a picture of an angry Moses holding tablets of stone over his head, about to send them crashing to the earth, a headline asked, "Is the Bible Fact or Fiction?"

The cover story, which discussed recent archaeological discoveries in the Holy Land that dramatized the questions of whether Abraham, Moses, and David actually existed and whether the Exodus and the conquest of Canaan actually happened, was fair and balanced.

But the cover portrayal of Moses was not! The posture of this menacing Moses implied that you *either* accept the Bible as fact *or* you reject it as fiction. There is no middle ground.

Unfortunately, this depiction typifies our culture's simplified and dichotomous view of Scripture. The standard questions are more and more framed in dualistic terms: Is the Bible true or false? Is it literal or mythical? Do you or do you not "believe" in the Bible?

To avoid the traditional pitfalls of "fundamentalism" and "liberalism," maybe we need to rethink our questions. Instead of asking whether the Bible is true or false, let's ask whether it is trustworthy as a guide for faith and life. Instead of asking whether we "believe" in the Bible, let's ask whether we choose to "live" within its stories.

Let's move beyond "fact or fiction" to faith!

The Smallest Child

Dr. Digne M. Komp remarked, "The biblical perspective is one where the smallest child knows more than the most enlightened adult."

Know Your Bible

Some people read the Bible as history or as literature. Others learn individual books—their purpose and audience, date and authorship. There are readers who concentrate on the great personalities and stories of Scripture. Still others focus on the Gospels, the life of Jesus, the letters of Paul, or commit beautiful passages to memory.

In referring to the study of Scripture, Harry Emerson Fosdick said, "Read until you stumble upon yourself on its pages."

Children and Youth

Jessica's Legacy

Jessica's dream began at nine thousand feet. "I just like to fly," she exclaimed. "It's like floating."

Her dream turned to nightmare on April 11, 1996, when the airplane she was piloting crashed during a storm just one mile north of the Cheyenne, Wyoming, airport, killing all three aboard.

Seven-year-old Jessica Dubroff, from Pescadero, California, had just taken off on the second leg of her attempt to become the youngest person to fly across the continent. Although she only began flying the previous November and had logged just thirty-two hours of flight, she had hoped to pilot her single-engine Cessna 177 on an eight-day, sixty-nine-hundred-mile journey from Half Moon Bay, California, to Falmouth, Massachusetts, and back.

Media attention that initially focused on Jessica concentrated on questions after the crash: "When should parents push and when should they protect their children?" "Do we expect too much or too little from our children?" "Are our children doing too much too soon?"

In our impersonal culture there is an inordinate amount of pressure on children as well as parents to be noticed, to be recognized, to stand out from the crowd. Do the risks exceed the rewards?

These questions are Jessica's legacy.

Early Commitment

Thirteen-year-old Masoud Karkenagadi of Mission Viejo, California, is a child prodigy. With an IQ of two hundred, he never attended elementary, middle, or high school. Tutored at home, he completed all twelve grades by the time he was seven and graduated from the University of California at Irvine at thirteen.

This young genius has dedicated himself to finding a cure for Parkinson's disease, a challenge that has haunted him since the age of eleven. "I believe my intelligence is a gift from God," he declared, "and I want to use it to the best of my capacity."

Under the direction of neuroscientist Dr. James Fallon, this amazing young man studies from two to five hours a day and does research on rats up to twenty hours per week. Karkenagadi is researching proteins that enhance or destroy brain cells. Professor Fallon is jubilant about Masoud's commitment to conquer Parkinson's and adds, "My God, there's someone who's really going to do it."

God Said Share!

In Jonathan Kozol's book, *Amazing Grace,* Cliffie, a seven-year-old boy from the South Bronx, was sent to the store for three slices of pizza—one for his mother, one for his father, and one for himself. On the way home the lad encountered a man who was so cold he could not speak. The half-frozen stranger pointed to the pizza, whereupon, Cliffie gave him some.

Mr. Kozol asked, "Were your parents mad at you?"

Looking surprised, Cliffie replied, "Why would they be mad? God told us to share!"

Hide and Be Found

When I opened the front door, I knew instantly that something was wrong. Our three-year-old daughter and her friend were returning from an outing to the neighborhood creative playground, and I expected the usual happy reports. But the friend's mother was almost in tears as she insisted, "We have to talk."

Apparently everything was going well until our daughter overheard another group of playmates enjoying the game "hide-and-seek." Without invitation, let alone the knowledge of the supervising parent, our daughter decided to hide as well. One minute she was with her friend and her friend's mother as they made their way to a picnic table for a snack, and the next minute she was gone.

When the woman realized our daughter was missing, she immediately began calling her name. But there was no response. As fear escalated, the mother and daughter scoured the area.

After fifteen agonizing minutes, the woman was frantic. She was experiencing the worst nightmare imaginable to any parent, and it was not even her own child who was lost.

Instinctively she hurried over to another picnic table where a group of parents was visiting, only intending to ask if they had seen the missing child. But as she began to describe our daughter's physical features, tears cascaded down her cheeks and her voice cracked with emotion. She blurted out, "Please help, I've lost a child."

Instantly the parents were on their feet. One mother took charge and asked all the right questions. Soon all the adults were organized into a line that literally swept the playground. Within minutes someone called out, "Here she is!"

The friend's mother ran to the location, reached out her arms and gathered our daughter into a hug of profound relief and joy. Our daughter was all giggles and smiles. Still playing the game, she was basking in the sheer delight of being found.

The Boy Who Knew More Than His Father

"Father, give me the share of the property that will belong to me" (Luke 15:12).

We may assume that he was a nice young man, from a substantial family, who had grown restless and impatient with his father. As was often the practice of the time, the young man asked for his share of the inheritance so that he might strike out on his own.

To his surprise his request was granted.

He took leave. At first all went well. His money attracted many conniving friends. With the erosion of resources, however, his companions fell away. In desperation he decided to return home. He was embarrassed. He dreaded the reception. He anticipated a tongue-lashing and an "I told you so" story. But instead, his father received him with celebration, forgiveness, and love.

The Good and the Bad

A survey by *Who's Who Among American High School Students* reveals mixed news, according to *U.S. News & World Report* (June 26, 1995). The good news is that teenagers in the 1990s are "leading healthier, happier lives" than their counterparts a quarter of a century ago. Marijuana use is down to only 10 percent in 1994, compared to 27 percent in 1972. Although the percentage of sexually active teens is constant, the use of contraceptives has increased from 52 percent in 1971 to 91 percent in 1994. Most important, the survey reports that "happiness at home" has risen to 68 percent, an improvement of nine percentage points.

But the news is not all good. One in every ten teenagers feels unsafe at school, while two in every ten female teenagers have been sexually assaulted. Paul Krouse, publisher of the survey, comments, "Schools have changed so much in the past 25 years that it's like comparing 'The Brady Bunch' to 'The Wild Bunch.' "

Baloney Detection Kit

In a speech delivered to the Pacific Rim Transportation Technology Conference in Seattle on Wednesday, August 2, 1995, the late Carl Sagan told the delegates from thirty-five countries that "our planet is a lonely speck in a great engulfing darkness. . . . We're on our own. We have to help ourselves."

He closed his address by urging all nations to equip children with a "baloney detection kit" so that they will develop healthy skepticism so as not to believe everything that the government and adults tell them.

What's in a Name?

What's in a name?

According to Shakespeare's Juliet, "that which we call a rose / By any other name would smell as sweet" (*Romeo and Juliet*, 2.2.43-44). But is that true for people's names?

According to the book of Genesis, those who have authority to name "others" have responsibility for them (1:28; 2:19-20). Naming a child, therefore, is perhaps the quintessential act of parenthood. Indeed, names subliminally affect us. My brother the doctor is named for his uncle the doctor.

According to a 1994 report from the Kentucky Department for Health Services, Ashley was the name of choice for girls for the fourth straight year, while Austin topped the preference list for boys. And the rest of the list ran the gamut from traditional and creative to the sheer unusual. Some examples: Frona, Hawp, Jeankyrean, Manshell, and Gloryvette. Virtues and values are also in favor: Patience, Harmony, Trust, and Justice. Even cities are popular: Boston, Philadelphia, London, Memphis, Phoenix, Tampa, and Johannesburg.

You name it and you'll probably find a child answering to it.

Multiples

The Triplet Connection's 1995 national convention was held over Memorial Day weekend in New Cumberland, Pennsylvania. There were 195 sets of triplets and seven sets of quadruplets in attendance. One mother, who knew what it was like to change 225 diapers a week, as well as be up every hour and a half around the clock at night, wore a button that read "Once I had time, but now I have triplets."

Don't Disappoint Children

Cal Ripken Jr. signs as many autographs as anyone in professional sports. He is gracious and accommodating. It's not unusual for him to stay for one or two hours after a game affixing his signature (and it has to be perfect) to something important to a child, or to some- thing left in the clubhouse by a member of the opposing team.

One night, the line of autograph seekers was very long. Cal's pen went dry. A mother and her son were next. The boy was in tears. Sensing the disappointment, Ripken turned back from the dugout steps and said: "But how 'bout if I give you my cap? Is that all right?"

Recovering from stunned surprise, the lad exclaimed, "Whoa, Yesss!"

Christmas

Living on Tiptoe!

The Advent season involves waiting, preparation, and expectancy. The miracle of Christmas causes us to stretch, to stand straighter, to step livelier. We expect something to happen. We live on tiptoe!

To You Is Born

Victor Hugo said that nothing is so powerful in this world as an idea whose time has come. Christmas is the perfect consummation of a promise and a person. Through centuries of darkness and doubt, discouragement and disillusionment, hope for the coming Messiah burned in the hearts of humankind. The fulfillment was God's gift of Jesus the Christ. "To you is born this day in the city of David a Savior, who is the Messiah, the Lord" (Luke 2:11).

Christmas Carols

There is nothing like Christmas carols to evoke the spirit of the season. Whether heard in the shopping mall or in the sanctuary, the traditional songs trigger emotions buried deep within our souls.

Because we learn Christmas carols during childhood, they provide an emotional "safe place" in our constantly changing world, as well as fashion a theological portrait of Jesus.

Sister Gillian Leslie, O.D.C., of Norwich, England, offers insight into the theological formation created by Christmas carols when she writes in the November/December 1995 issue of *Living Pulpit*: "What I refer to as the theology of the Christmas carol can, I think, be summarized briefly in terms of four recurring themes. In the infant Jesus four apparent opposites meet together: incarnation with redemption; birth with death; motherhood with virginity; humanity with the divine. It is the paradox of their union in the nativity of this one child that, consciously or unconsciously, we take on our lips in our Christmas liturgies."

This Is No Lullaby!

Although the Gospel of Luke begins with the narrative of Jesus' birth, do not be misled. The first chapter is more than a sentimental story about a baby. It is more than a collection of songs sung by an aging priest, Zechariah, and a young mother, Mary. Her canticle, the Magnificat, is a song of freedom and hope, as well as joy and celebration. As a prophet to the poor, Mary sings a song of liberation that envisions a transformed social order.

"My soul magnifies the Lord, and my spirit rejoices in God my Savior, for he has looked with favor on the lowliness of his servant. . . . He has shown strength with his arm; he has scattered the proud in the thoughts of their hearts. He has brought down the powerful from their thrones, and lifted up the lowly; he has filled the hungry with good things, and sent the rich away empty" (Luke 1:46-48, 51-53).

In December 1985, the apartheid government in Pretoria, South Africa, banned the lighting of candles and the singing of Christmas carols in the vast ghetto of Soweto. The authorities instinctively knew that Mary's song represents more than a sweet Christmas carol. It is no lullaby!

The Flight to Egypt

A Sunday school teacher asked her kindergarten class to listen to Matthew's account of Jesus' birth and then draw a picture.

While the teacher circulated through the class, she noticed that one child was drawing an airplane with four people on board. When she inquired about the identity of the people, the little boy replied,

"I'm drawing the flight to Egypt. And the passengers are Mary, Joseph, and baby Jesus."

"But who is the fourth person?" the teacher asked.

"That's Pontius the pilot!"

I Believe in Santa Claus

In the December 1995 issue of *Visions*, the membership magazine published by the Kentucky Educational Television Foundation, Dick Hoffman, director of programming, explains why he believes in Santa Claus.

Twenty or so years ago, Hoffman had planned a holiday party for his coworkers the Monday night before Christmas. A few days before the scheduled date, a colleague called to ask if he might bring his five-year-old son. Although the party was designed for adults, young Brian was given permission to attend.

Because Hoffman had already purchased gifts for all the adults, he knew that protocol as well as common sense dictated that he provide a gift for Brian. While shopping at a local drugstore for wrapping paper, Hoffman wandered over to the section of children's toys and games. A box sitting on an almost empty shelf caught his attention. As he drew closer his eyes quickly located the inscription that proclaimed, "Suitable for Ages 5 and Up." Pleased with his good fortune, Hoffman picked up the box to examine the contents. It contained a Spirograph set, "plastic geared wheels and colored pens with which to make interesting designs on paper." It was perfect—neither too expensive nor in need of batteries. He purchased the item, wrapped it, and addressed a tag to Brian.

Hoffman continues his story. "Monday night came, and we congregated in our conference room for our party. Brian wasn't there. Having developed a slight cough, he had been left home with a sitter. But another child had shown up, most unexpectedly.

"One of the reporters on the program, John, had a close friend, Mike, who was a newspaper reporter. The two had grown up together and were still best friends. During this time, Mike really needed a friend. His wife was seriously ill in the hospital, fighting for her life. So Mike had asked John to look after his daughter, Ellen, so that Mike could stay at the hospital. John, of course, agreed, and so he and his wife brought Ellen along to the station for the party.

"Ellen was 6 and quite bright—and she knew something was very wrong. It was nearly Christmas, her mother had been in the hospital for weeks, and her father had sent her off to be with friends. She was a sad little girl. John said she had hardly spoken in the three days she had been with him, would barely eat, and had not smiled at all.

"I, of course, had no present for Ellen. But I had one for Brian, who had not shown up. Reasoning that Ellen was close to his age and certainly in need of being included in the celebration, I pulled off the tag marked 'Brian' from the gift and put on another. The tag read 'To Ellen . . . From Santa Claus.'

"When it came time to distribute the packages, I handed Ellen the one with her name on it. She shyly took it, cautiously opened it. When she saw the gift inside, the trace of a smile came over her face.

"For the rest of the party, Ellen sat at the table playing with the Spirograph, making grand designs and occasionally displaying her work to those nearby. John and I were pleased to see her acting much like a little girl should during the holidays. But at the time, neither of us understood the full story.

"About a week after Christmas, I got a phone call from Ellen's father. He told me his wife was greatly improved and the crisis had passed. Primarily, though, he had called to thank me for Ellen's gift—and to tell me that even though he was known as a hard-boiled investigator on a major newspaper, he now believed in Santa Claus.

"It seems that a couple of weeks before Christmas, Ellen had composed a letter to Santa and given it to her father to mail. Mike had stuffed it in a pocket and, in the turmoil surrounding his wife's hospitalization, simply forgot about it. It wasn't until after Christ-mas that Mike discovered the letter in his coat.

"In the letter, in her bold child's hand . . . Ellen had asked Santa for only two gifts, because the first was so big. The first gift Ellen asked for from Santa was for her mother to get well and return home. The other present she requested was . . . a Spirograph set."

Hoffman concludes his story with these words: "There may be some who would call this a coincidence. But I am not so foolish. I realize that Ellen and I were brought together by the Spirit which presides over Christmas. In my heart I know that Santa Claus read

41

Ellen's letter, even as it rested in her father's tweed jacket, and responded in the best way he could."

The Great Pumpkin

During Advent a Sunday school teacher read her kindergarten class a story about the birth of Jesus from the perspective of the animals. Following the scene describing the arrival of Mary and Joseph, she stopped to ask the class who was missing.

Numerous hands shot up and she called on one child. "A cow," the child answered.

"That's a good answer but I was thinking of someone else," responded the teacher.

"How about a horse?" volunteered another child.

Getting exasperated, the teacher rephrased the question, "Who are the animals waiting for?"

After a prolonged period of silence, one brave child declared, "The Great Pumpkin!"

The Bear and the Cat

While preparing an Advent sermon, I read this story in the local newspaper.

In Grants Pass, Oregon, four six-week-old kittens were abandoned at Wildlife Images, a wildlife rehabilitation center. Volunteers caught and adopted three, but one cat eluded them.

A few days later, the lone kitten was seen squeezing through a hole in the fence that corralled "Griz," a 560-pound bear whose mother and sister had been killed by a train. The cat foolishly approached the bear while he was eating from a five-gallon bucket.

"(The cat) was so hungry he walked up and begged for food," explained Dave Siddon, founder of Wildlife Images. "I thought, 'Oh my gosh, it's going to kill (the cat).' "

But to Siddon's surprise, the bear pulled a little piece of chicken out of the pail and dropped it on the ground. The cat walked up and ate it. The two animals are now inseparable.

After reading the story, I immediately thought of Isaiah's vision of a reordered nature in the messianic age: "The wolf shall live with the lamb, the leopard shall lie down with the kid, the calf and the lion and the fatling together, and a little child shall lead them" (Isaiah 11:6).

The Gift of Christmas

Adam Graziano, age ten, of Queens, New York, had suffered massive head injuries in November 1995 in an in-line skating accident and lay comatose in a New York hospital. His mother, Margaret Graziano, kept constant vigil at his bedside and consequently lost her job.

As Advent dawned, Adam came out of his coma. His first word was "Mommy." And then he uttered, "God smiled on me."

Rejoicing over her son's first words, Margaret said, "I'll remember it as my Christmas gift that came early."

Christmas is the time when the world rejoices because God smiled on us and gave the gift of the "new Adam."

Bright Star

In an effort to shore up relations with allies in the Middle East and coordinate military capabilities, troops of several nations participated in a month-long war exercise in 1981. Some four thousand Americans were involved in the maneuvers, planned before Anwar Sadat's death. The code name for the operation was "Bright Star," a symbol of strength and hope.

Unique as was that military deployment, it is in sharp contrast to the "Bright Star" that shone over Bethlehem centuries ago. When Jesus was born, wise men from the East came to Jerusalem asking, "Where is the child who has been born king of the Jews? For we observed his star at its rising, and have come to pay him homage" (Matthew 2:2).

Church

The Perfect Church

When the celebrated English preacher Charles Haddon Spurgeon (1834–1892) was asked by a woman about the perfect church, he replied: "You will not find it, Madam, this side of heaven; and if you do find it, don't go near it; you will spoil it."

The Tyranny of Yeast

According to the latest survey, breadmakers are now standard gifts for newlyweds. The popularity of homemade bread has soared. And that revelation comes as no surprise to bread lovers everywhere. There is nothing more scrumptious—anytime or place—than a fresh-baked loaf of bread, recently sliced and buttered. It literally melts in your mouth.

But there's a problem! Certain breads require "bread starters" that have to be fed each day. And the more you use it, the more it multiplies. Pretty soon you have to give some away in order to keep it going. Before you know it, you are captive to the "tyranny of yeast."

What a perfect metaphor for the church. The more we participate, the more the love of God grows. And out of abundance we pass it on.

Portable Table

As the morning sun filtered through the drawn curtain, I was enthusiastically awakened by our two children bounding upon the bed and serenading me with a rousing chorus of "Happy Father's Day." Breakfast in bed soon followed. What a start to Dad's day!

Like the sunrise, the significance of the moment gradually dawned on me. Food and drink are the staples of life. The basic human drive for physical nourishment calls us daily to the table. But on this day, the table was brought to me. A "portable table" signifies love on the move.

The church is God's "portable table." Jesus shared table fellowship with tax collectors and sinners, and the church is privileged to share the bread of life and the cup of blessing with the world in the name of Christ.

What About Your Pledge!?!

Blessed are church members who pay their pledges before their vacation cometh.

Then they go forth with a light heart.

They wear casual clothing as they wander in pleasant places.

They anoint their bodies with suntan lotion and insect spray;

They sit beside the still waters hoping the fish will bite and the insects will not;

They build a fire of charcoal and place savory meat thereon. They eat thereof and are satisfied.

Night cometh.

They close their eyes in glad tiredness and thanksgiving to God.

And their sleep is undisturbed.

For they know that the good work of their church will not be diminished while they are away.

Remembering Forward

In the novel *100 Years of Solitude,* the author narrates the story of an entire village that experiences amnesia. Everyone is afflicted. People forget their names, their families, their histories; even the words for the simplest things in life—like "chair," "shirt," and "kiss."

One teenage boy, however, still retains the capacity to remember and he decides to label everything in the village before it is too late.

So he proceeds to put a name tag on every object in the village. After completing the task, he erects two signs at the entrance to the village: one sign announces the name of the village; the other sign reads, "God exists."

Every community needs a name. But the community of faith needs more. It must "remember forward" its history and its God!

Your Church, My Homeland

Every Christian should read *In The Service of the Lord* by Otto Dibelius of Germany. Bishop Dibelius was certainly one of the most influential Christians of the twentieth century. We not only admire him for his boyhood struggles and personal accomplishments, but we also salute him for his great courage and faith during World War II.

Hitler denied Dibelius the privilege of preaching and had him watched day and night. Although this man was forbidden to climb the pulpit stairs of Europe, he nevertheless pursued human needs. Imagine, if you can, this scholar, teacher, and preacher precariously moving about Berlin and other communities identifying himself with the rationing of fuel oil and food, greeting soldiers, and leading worship in unsuspected places! No wonder Bishop Dibelius became pastor of the Divided City and eventually one of the presidents of the World Council of Churches.

He concludes his book with a very striking section written in the first person and directed to God. It is a moving confessional and a glorious reiteration of his faith. It is also a confirmation of the compensations of the Christian ministry. Listen to his searching words: "I thank you that despite all changes and upheavals, my life has moved in a straight line. Knowledge and opinions have changed, but my path has remained the same from youth to old age. You have preserved a family for me in which children and grandchildren are one with their elders in their faith in You. You have made Your Church my homeland."

A continuing challenge of ministry is that of making the church of Jesus Christ the homeland of every soul.

True Church on the Edge of Life

On Thanksgiving Day 1995, Glide Memorial United Methodist Church, the most comprehensive nonprofit provider of human services in San Francisco, served more than sixty-five hundred meals. In addition to the traditional turkey and mashed potatoes, Glide also made sure the feeding came with a generous portion of "respect and dignity."

"At Glide, we believe that the true church stays on the edge of life, where the real moans and groans are," said the Reverend Cecil Williams, pastor of the fifty-five-hundred member congregation. "Most church folks settle in, get comfortable, and build doctrinal walls to protect themselves from anyone who thinks or looks differently than they do. . . . The church *has* to be leading the march, and yet it's on the tail end. I decided Glide was not going to be on the tail end, but a beacon light to the nation and the world."

The Church as Commonwealth

In a 1994 interview with the *Blue Grass Magazine,* Wendell Berry, Kentucky farmer and author, proposes that a community is a commonwealth of values. Although there is a lot of sentimental talk about communities these days, Berry observes that building and maintaining communities require tremendous commitment.

"Community in the real sense is a commonwealth. It's a holding in common of many different things of value. . . . It seems to me we belong to each other and God. If that's accepted, there are many practical things you are committed to do. You see that nobody gets hungry, for instance. You see that nobody sleeps in the street. You see that children are taught—not just enough to get them a job or get them a diploma—but taught enough to function as responsible, affectionate members of the community."

The church is God's commonwealth on earth. Sacrificial love identifies its core and servanthood locates its values.

Found: The Perfect Preacher

Finally, the church has called the preacher that suits everybody. What makes him so perfect? His sermons have terrific introductions and fabulous conclusions with only ten minutes in between. Although he preaches against sin, his messages neither offend nor hurt anyone's feelings. He works from 6:00 A.M. to 11:00 P.M. doing all that is necessary, and more. He is an expert in almost every field, specializing in church maintenance and repair. He models for *GQ*, reads the latest books on every subject, has the best behaved family in town, drives a late-model car, gives to every charity, and pledges $100 a week to the church from his $200 weekly income. He just turned twenty-nine and has thirty years of experience. He is tall, short, handsome, and rugged; one brown eye, one blue eye; hair parted in the middle—the left side is blond and straight, while the right side is dark and wavy. He puts in extra time with the youth but he spends all his time with the older adults. He smiles all the time with a straight face, because he has a good sense of humor that keeps him seriously dedicated to the Lord's work. Although he has a glowing personality with thick skin and nerves of iron, he is always sensitive to everyone and tolerates everything. In short, he is the perfect preacher.

God's Movable Feast

In 1950 Ernest Hemingway included these words in a letter to a friend: "If you are lucky enough to have lived in Paris as a young man, then wherever you go for the rest of your life, it stays with you, for Paris is a movable feast."

If you are so fortunate as to have been reared in the atmosphere of the church, embraced her teachings, sung her hymns, absorbed her Lord, then, wherever you go for the rest of your life, she stays with you, for the church is God's movable feast.

Communication and Computers

Wallpaper

According to Alvin Toffler in *Power Shift* (1990), the United States turns out 1.3 trillion documents—both paper and computer files—in a year. That is a sufficient quantity to "wallpaper" the Grand Canyon 107 times.

On-line Ethics

As more and more computer users go on-line, the need for legal and ethical standards on this exciting form of communication increases dramatically. What privacy rights do computer users have when they are connected to the World Wide Web and other large networks? Can they access private files at whim? When is copyright an issue?

"Computer technology is the most powerful and the most flexible technology ever developed," declares Terry Bynum, who chairs the American Philosophical Association's Committee on Philosophy and Computing. "Even though it's called a technical revolution, at heart it's a social and ethical revolution because it changes everything we value."

New Words

According to the Dictionary Society of North America (*U.S. News & World Report*, July 24, 1995, p. 14), twenty-five thousand new words enter the American language each year. Although new vocabulary develops most frequently in the fields of computer science, health, science, and politics, national events also spawn new words. For example, the O. J. Simpson trial is responsible for the appearance of the word "criminalist" in the 1996 *Webster's New World Dictionary*. A "criminalist" is defined as "an expert in the use of scientific methods to investigate crimes, specifically by collecting and analyzing physical evidence."

Because lexicographers consider common word usage, frequency of citation in publications, and anticipated durability before proposing a new word or meaning for the dictionary, only 4 percent of new words make the cut. Some dictionary-approved words of the '90s include: Afrocentric, cyberpunk, glass ceiling, global warming, Internet, killer bee, managed care, microbrewery, PCs, Prozac, sunblock, and taxol.

Cyberporn

Computer pornography: it's popular, it's profitable, it's perverse, and it's playing on your personal computer.

In an eighteen-month study of on-line erotica conducted by Carnegie Mellon University (*Time*, July 3, 1995), researchers surveyed "917,410 sexually explicit pictures, descriptions, short stories, and film clips." The results are twofold: Cyberporn is popular and profitable. According to the report, trading in sexually explicit material is now "one of the largest (if not the largest) recreational applications of users of computer networks" and the top five adult-oriented computer bulletin board systems generate annual revenues over $1 million. However, the popularity of computer pornography needs to be put into perspective. On-line erotica represents "only about 3% of all the messages on the Usenet newsgroups" which in turn represents "only 11.5% of the traffic on the Internet."

Nevertheless, this report highlights a unique challenge for both society and family. The information superhighway, which represents "the most democratic of media," is heavily traveled by young computer experts who can, and often do, steer into the ditch. Yet most parents are unqualified to give driving lessons to Internet cruisers, or even supervise them.

Share the Secrets

Dale Carnegie moved from Missouri to New York City in 1912. He found employment teaching public speaking to night students at the 125th Street YMCA.

Because his course was unstructured, Carnegie had ample room for experimentation. Although speaking with clarity and poise was his primary focus, developing human skills—how to get along with people—was equally important. So, after years of creative involvement in personal communications, he produced from notes the popular book, *How to Win Friends and Influence People.* It sold thirty-six million copies! This best-seller was followed by two other volumes: *The Quick and Easy Way to Effective Speaking* and *How to Stop Worrying and Start Living.*

Although Dale Carnegie died in 1955, his message and methods continue to spread because "he taught others how to teach his course." Today his classes are available at more than one thousand American locations. And it all began when one man discovered and shared the secrets and power of effective communication.

Something Wonderful to Contribute

When Admiral Richard Byrd explored the South Pole, the Columbia Broadcasting System had a contract to carry all of his reports from the expedition. On the day of the initial radio broadcast, the country was practically tingling with excitement. One of the engineers from CBS named George went home for lunch. While eating, the telephone rang. He answered it hurriedly and, anticipating the program, forgot to hang up the receiver. Admiral Byrd came on but the reception was poor. This particular engineer was needed! The studio telephoned him but, of course, the phone did not ring because the receiver was off the hook.

Guessing the nature of the problem, CBS radioed Byrd at the South Pole asking him to tell George to please hang up the receiver. It was done. Then the studio called George, who returned and corrected the difficulty.

Not only was the shortest distance from the studio to George's home—only a few blocks away—by way of the South Pole, but George was also the only person who could solve the problem.

In the realm of adventure Byrd was in a class by himself. But the engineer, perhaps a man who had never left the continental United States, was essential if Byrd was to be heard!

This is the continuing parable of life. Every person has something distinctive and wonderful to contribute to the reign of God. Like the master who entrusted his servants with differing amounts of money, so God gives us skills and gifts to be used to forge a more excellent way.

Electronic Tracking

Over a period of some twenty years, hunters in the Pensacola area of Florida have often had their dogs mysteriously disappear. Own-ers assumed they were stolen, but their assumption was incorrect.

In August 1995, Rufus Godwin was searching for Flogo, a $5,000 walker hound, in Blackwater River State Forest, forty-five miles northeast of Pensacola, when he heard a faint signal from Flogo's electronic tracking collar. The signal led the pursuers to a "gator hole," deep in the swamp.

The Florida Game and Fresh Water Fish Commission dispatched authorized trappers to the scene. Eventually, a ten-foot-eleven-inch, five-hundred-pound, fifty-year-old bull alligator was captured. In his belly was Flogo's tracking collar and at least six additional dog collars, one dating back fourteen years.

What a Day

On September 3, 1833, a twenty-three-year-old printer by the name of Benjamin Day launched the *New York Sun* and began what we now call the information explosion.

Although the population of New York City in 1833 was over two hundred thousand, the circulation of the largest daily newspaper was only forty-five hundred subscribers. And because it sold for six cents a copy, most urban workers could not afford a paper on an average wage of seventy-five cents a day. Furthermore, newspapers were printed on handpresses that could produce only a few hundred copies an hour.

But Day quickly revolutionized the newspaper industry. On that September day he sent a horde of newsboys into the streets to sell his paper for only one cent a copy. In addition, he hired another printer for $4 a week to "report" police cases. Within four months the *Sun* had the biggest circulation in the city. Two years later Day purchased the latest technology—a steamdriven press—and the readership of the *Sun* soared to twenty thousand.

Benjamin Day had invented the popular press.

Wonderful Words

In his fascinating book *The Magic and Mystery of Words*, J. Donald Adams asserts that neither great poetry nor excellent prose "can be fully savored unless it is heard as well as seen." He reports that Harvard Professor Charles Townsend Copeland required his students to read their work aloud to him.

"A word fitly spoken is like apples of gold in a setting of silver" (Proverbs 25:11).

Community

Paradise Restored

On July 1, 1978, his first day as president of Yale University, A. Bartlett Giamatti issued this memo:

"To the members of the University community:
    In order to repair what Milton called the ruin of our grand-parents, I wish to announce that henceforth, as a matter of University policy, evil is abolished and paradise is restored.
    I trust all of us will do whatever possible to achieve this policy objective."

Born or Naturalized Citizen?

Have you ever attended a naturalization ceremony for American citizenship? I found it to be a humbling and enlightening experience. There were 111 applicants in the class; many had worked for years to qualify. They had passed a comprehensive examination on the history, privileges, and responsibilities of citizenship.

At one point in the proceedings, the immigration officer called out a name, saying, "Stand up and say, 'Freedom!' " The applicant obeyed. Then he encouraged the second and the third person to stand and exclaim, "Freedom!" This was followed by the entire class standing and shouting "Freedom!" At last, everyone was asked to add his or her voice to the tumultuous crescendo.

The presiding officer used this dramatic and powerful example to emphasize the importance of voting. A single vote seems insignificant, but when added to others it becomes a powerful voice.

I came away feeling that many of these "new" Americans were better equipped to serve our country than some who could trace their footprints to Jamestown or Plymouth Rock.

Corporate Compassion

Corporate downsizing and mergers are all too common these days. So common, in fact, that between 1991 and 1995, 2.5 million workers lost their jobs. New technology, along with an insatiable appetite for burgeoning profits, has enabled companies to shed more and more workers. The trend toward downsizing raises critical economic, social, and moral issues.

A refreshing contrast to prevailing managerial policy and practice was demonstrated by Aaron Feuerstein of Methuen, Massachusetts. During the Christmas season of 1995, Malden Mills, a family-owned textile factory, burned to the ground. Seventy-year-old Feuerstein informed his three thousand employees that they would receive pay for thirty days and benefits for ninety days. Then, on January 11, 1996, the owner announced that workers would not only receive wages for an additional thirty days, but that the mill would be rebuilt and the current employees rehired.

When Mr. Feuerstein was asked to comment on his corporate compassion, he simply said, "It was the right thing to do."

Against the Rules

From Joseph Campbell's admonition to "follow your bliss," in *The Power of Myth*, to Pocahontas's dream to "choose your path," in the Disney movie, Americans are routinely encouraged to break communal rules. Now corporate business has joined the assault on the traditional values of loyalty and respect. Our society's insatiable appetite for individual self-fulfillment and our unquenchable thirst for change have convinced American business to not only embrace but to profit from the symbols and language of the "counterculture."

The following television advertising slogans are ubiquitous: "Find Your Own Road" (Saab); "Sometimes You Gotta Break the Rules" (Burger King); "Just Do It" (Nike); "There's No One Way to Do It" (Levi's); "This Is Different. Different Is Good" (Arby's); "The Line Has Been Crossed. The Revolutionary New Supra" (Toyota); and "If You Don't Like the Rules, Change Them" (WXRT-FM, Chicago).

When contemporary American business culture endorses the "counterculture" values of rule-breaking, convention-smashing, and tradition-bashing, community building is against the rules.

Cars and Community

Americans are in love with the automobile. That's nothing new. But that infatuation has turned into a major "addiction," according to George F. Kennan in his book *Around the Cragged Hill*.

Because the automobile allows us to worship as well as work at great distances from our homes and to live even greater distances from our birth families, Kennan declares that the car "has turned out to be, by virtue of its innate and unalterable qualities, the enemy of community generally. Wherever it advances, neighborliness and the sense of community are impaired."

The New Elite

There is emerging in America an elitist group known as the "overclass." They are, for the most part, graduates of prestigious schools. These front-runners are young, smart, rich, manipulative, energetic, tireless workers, who embrace the ideology of "merit." The word "failure" is not in their vocabulary. They establish self-defined parameters. Their lifestyles are distinctive and expensive. Their children go to the best private schools.

The "overclass" help to perpetuate a two-tier society. Although they avoid mixing with other classes and individuals as much as possible, they reach those in power, those who can foster their objectives.

Newsweek carried an elaborate story on the "overclass" in its July 31, 1995, issue—complete with names, pictures, and employers of the top one hundred American elite. "They are among the country's comers, the newest wave of important and compelling people."

Who Defines Justice?

Just three doors down the hall from the courtroom where the O. J. Simpson criminal trial was taking place, Ernest Dwayne Jones was on trial for a gruesome murder. He was accused of killing Julia Miller with kitchen knives.

Although it was a death penalty case, it proceeded with one prosecutor and one defense attorney. There was precious little media attention. No "dream team" of experts, no computer monitors, no huge video screens were involved. Pictures of evidence were attached to a bulletin board.

During a one-day DNA hearing, two expert witnesses were called. Jones even took the stand in his own defense.

After twelve days of trial testimony, he was found guilty of "first degree murder with special circumstances." Although sentencing was delayed, jurors in the case returned to their regular lives in less than one month.

When you are poor and not rich, who defines justice?

Five Third-Class Tickets

Our pastor used the passenger classification of the early American stagecoach operation—first-, second-, and third-class riders—to profile communal life. In those rough and romantic days, in case of accident or a breakdown, first-class passengers could remain in place. Those occupying second-class space were expected to leave the coach, but not to work. Third-class travelers were not only expected to leave the stage, but also to help with repairs, or to lift the vehicle out of the mire and mud.

Following the sermon, our church sings a hymn of consecration and invitation, which offers an opportunity for anyone to identify with Christ and the church. On this Sunday morning, a family of five walked down the aisle. The man said to our pastor, "We would like five third-class tickets."

A Sense of Shame

In his autobiography, *My American Journey*, General Colin Powell identifies an ironic feature of our society. Although our culture is presently preoccupied with "correctness," we have apparently lost our sense of shame.

"A sense of shame," he writes, "is not a bad moral compass. I remember how easy it was for my mother to snap me back into line with a simple rebuke: 'I'm ashamed of you. You embarrassed the family.' I would have preferred a beating to those words."

Character of the Underclass

In his autobiography, *All Rivers Run to the Sea*, Professor Elie Wiesel of Boston University, a survivor of Hitler's concentration camps and the 1986 Nobel Peace prize laureate, reflects on the Nazi years. Like other communities with a large Jewish population, his hometown of Sighet, Transylvania, lived under constant surveillance and cruel demands.

Denied basic rights and daily staples, Professor Wiesel praises the conduct and character of their housekeeper, Maria. This courageous, uneducated, Christian woman continued her service to the family. She not only took great risk by bringing them food but she also offered to hide them in her mountain cabin. Her loyalty was humbling.

Reflecting on those difficult and dangerous days, the author concludes that help came not from the intellectuals, dignitaries, or community leaders; it came from a peasant woman. Against such a background, this distinguished world citizen raises a troubling yet pertinent question: "Of what value was their faith, their education, their social position, if it aroused neither conscience nor compassion?"

Courage

To Maximize Memory

In 1991, Grace Jacobian lost her eyesight. This once successful fashion designer contacted the Braille Institute to teach her to read by touch. While there, she discovered a heretofore unrealized talent—painting! At age ninety she is totally blind, and paints from memory. Her work has hung in a Los Angeles City Hall gallery. She is recognized as "a genuine folk artist of Southern California."

"Remembering," she says, "isn't the same as seeing." But it is all she has left, and she maximizes her memory.

A Survivor!

Thirty-three-year-old Mike Goodell, a canoeist from Mount Morris, New York, became disoriented in the Okefenokee Swamp while trying to photograph a woodpecker. The odyssey began on February 4, 1996; he was rescued forty-one days later. Though he lost fifty pounds, this courageous man survived the harsh and dangerous environment by living on leaves, berries, bugs, and swamp water. During this time, according to weather reports, it rained thirteen times and the temperature ranged from thirty-six to eighty-four degrees.

All the while, a massive manhunt wrongly focused on Billy's Island, an eight-square-mile area near the west entrance to the Okefenokee Wildlife Refuge. After combing the island with rangers, volunteers, dogs, and helicopters four separate times at an expense of $35,000, the search was terminated.

Subsequently, a group of college student volunteers, who were clearing a trail in the dense jungle, stumbled upon Goodell. He was dehydrated and suffered from cuts, bug bites, and bruises.

When asked how he made it, the weary survivor forced a weak smile as he replied, "Just perseverance."

Good as Gold

Dan Jansen of the United States was one of the most powerful speed skaters in the world. Yet unbelievable adversities—including the death of his sister, Jane, during the 1988 Winter Olympics in Calgary—plagued him, denying him a medal.

At the 1994 Winter Olympics in Lillehammer, Norway, Jansen was once again the overwhelming favorite to win the 500-meter race, but he slipped and finished a disappointing eighth. In seven races through four consecutive Winter Olympiads, he had failed to earn a medal.

But Jansen refused to quit! In his last event, the 1,000-meter race, he brought home the gold in a world-record time of 1:12.43.

Finally his global admirers could celebrate. But it was the announcer in Hamar's Vikingskipet skating hall who captured the moment: "I remember your poet, Robert Frost. He said, 'Nothing gold can stay.' But you who know what it means to have lost, can really stay gold today."

The Courage of Care

While classmates in Myrtle Beach, South Carolina, Susan Benner and Bennett Scott shared many honors. In seventh grade, both were voted "most likely to succeed." In high school, both were voted "most talented." They even had the same piano teacher. Now they "share" a kidney.

After being out of touch for years, Benner and Scott were reacquainted at their thirty-third high school reunion in August 1995. Yet Scott just barely made it because diabetes had destroyed his kidneys the previous year. Although he was on a waiting list for a transplant, a donor had not been found.

Benner, blessed with excellent health and two good kidneys, made her offer of kidney donation during the reunion. Scott eagerly accepted. Remarkably, their blood samples were a close match.

"They said it was coincidental, that the odds are very low for two (unrelated) friends (to match)," explained Benner. "(But) I was expecting it. I think this is very God-directed."

Donating a kidney involves major surgery. Although there exist no long-term negative effects from having only one kidney, the five-hour operation requires six weeks of recuperation.

"She's as gutsy as can be," Scott declared. "I'm scared of this surgery, and there she is, totally well, totally able to do anything. Yet, she's . . . getting ready for surgery she doesn't need."

Dr. Alan Hull, president of the National Kidney Foundation, put Benner's donation in perspective. "Most people, while they really care about people, don't care *that* much."

Brie

I met Brie when she, her sister, and grandmother sat next to us at a McDonald's. Instantly I knew that she was special. Although she was smaller than her four-year-old sister, Brie's new front teeth suggested the reverse birth order. We soon learned that tomorrow was Brie's eighth birthday. She suffers from spina bifida and has endured numerous operations. Because her parents are divorced, both children live with their grandparents.

As the grandmother told us about Brie, my heart ached. "She is the happiest child I know," she informed us. "If she is sad it lasts for only a moment."

When we said good-bye, my eyes teared. Although I had known Brie for only a few minutes, she had made a lasting impression. Her quick smile and cheerful spirit proclaimed a courageous lust for life.

The Last Marathoner

Champions are honored; losers are forgotten. This axiom applies particularly in sports.

When reporting the results of the 1995 New York City Marathon, headlines of *The New York Times* read: " '94 Winners Do It Again." The accompanying story focused on the second straight victories for the men's champion, twenty-seven-year-old German Silva from Mexico, and the women's champion, twenty-two-year-old Tegla Loroupe from Kenya. Details of their successful title defenses and even the weather—it was the coldest marathon ever, forty degrees with winds blowing up to thirty-two miles per hour and a wind chill of eighteen degrees—were mentioned.

Conspicuously absent was the story of the last marathoner. One full day after the winners crossed the finish line, and twenty-six hours after she started the 26-mile, 385-yard race, Zoe Koplowitz reached the tape—the last of some 29,700 competitors. It was the eighth time the forty-six-year-old multiple sclerosis sufferer had finished the race on her aluminum crutches. She calls herself the "world's slowest woman runner."

Darkness to Light

After digging for more than two weeks in the rubble of the collapsed Sampoong department store in Seoul, South Korea, in July 1995, An Gung Wook, a rescue worker, was exhausted. Although the death toll had reached 323 and hope was fading that any of the remaining four hundred people believed trapped would be found alive, An squeezed his way through a hole not much bigger than his head and shined his flashlight into the darkness.

He thought he heard sounds. Burrowing with his hands through steel wires and cement fragments, he called out for someone to respond to the beam of light. Suddenly a faint voice was audible. Miraculously Park Sung Hyon, nineteen, who had been buried face down for sixteen days in a space no larger than a coffin, was alive.

When she inquired about the day's date, Park was amazed to learn she had been trapped for so long. She thought only five days had passed.

Although doctors do not know how she survived sixteen days without water, some speculate that the darkness that caused her to lose track of time might have also caused her body functions to slow down. Regardless, Park Sung Hyon was in stable condition with only a scratch on a leg and mild kidney problems.

The darkness of her momentary tomb has shed new light on how long rescuers should persist in searching for survivors of natural disasters and building collapses.

Man Versus Machine

While many Americans in February 1996 were enduring a blizzard of rhetoric from presidential candidates, Garry Kasparov was quietly battling the IBM-programmed chess supercomputer, Deep Blue. Although Kasparov was the world chess champion, he lost the first game of the best-of-six contest in thirty-seven moves. He was devastated. But consider this comparison: Deep Blue can evaluate two hundred million moves per second, while Kasparov evaluates two moves per second.

Although the "man versus machine" match was close, Kasparov's creativity and cunning overcame raw processing power, four to two. According to Kasparov, the quality that separates humans from machines is intuition: "(Deep Blue's) computational power was not enough to overcome my . . . intuitive appreciation of where the pieces should go."

Even though Kasparov was defeated by the same computer in May of 1997, he remains the human "king of chess."

All in an Afternoon

On Friday afternoon, January 26, 1996, Dewayne Ward and a friend were driving to Highlands-Cashiers Hospital, in North Carolina, to witness his comatose grandmother's separation from her sophisticated life-support system. The weather was miserable. Near-freezing temperatures and rain made driving treacherous. West of Sapphire Valley, on U.S. 64, a Ford Mustang traveling east began to slip and slide, eventually ending up in Horsepasture River. Seeing what happened, Ward, without hesitation, leaped from his truck into the frigid, fast-moving water and rescued nineteen-year-old Chad Vincent Wood, who was trapped inside the car.

Subsequently, the humble hero resumed his mission to the hospital to see his grandmother's life-support equipment turned off. She died within forty-five minutes.

Towering Courage and Trust

World citizen and contagious Christian Terry Waite entitled his autobiography *Taken on Trust.* In it he recounts his horrendous experience as a hostage in Beirut prisons for 1,763 days, almost four years of which were in solitary confinement. His first cell, underground, measured seven feet by ten feet. The height varied between six feet and six feet nine inches. Because he is six feet seven inches tall, Waite had difficulty standing erect. He learned to sit in a lotus position. Although living in cramped quarters, he made himself walk. Some days he estimated he walked seven miles. Day and night were indistinguishable. He was led to the toilet once a day.

Early in his "detainment" Terry Waite vowed that his captors would not capture his soul. "Whatever is done to my body, I will fight to the end to keep my inner freedom."

He discovered that fasting increased his spiritual strength. His prayer life was consistent and beautiful. From memory, he would go through the communion service as recorded in the *Book of Common Prayer*, without the visible sacrament, of course.

This man, who served as envoy for the Archbishop of Canterbury for many years and who had personally negotiated hostage releases for six years, had at last become a hostage himself. Painful as was his condition, he accepted and recited his mantra: "No regrets, no sentimentality, no self-pity."

Death and Grief

Ready to Die?

When Socrates was told to prepare to die, he replied, "Know ye not that I have been preparing for it all my life?"

Dying with Dignity

Norman Vincent Peale, eminent preacher and author, died at his home on Christmas Eve 1993. This advocate and practitioner of positive thinking departed this life as he had lived it: with dignity, love, and peace. His family, standing in solemn gratitude for a contagious Christian life, transformed a bedroom into a sanctuary of rare beauty and faith.

The Ultimate Dropout

Timothy Leary, the former Harvard psychologist and counterculture celebrity, is best known for having urged the college generation of the 1960s to "turn on, tune in, and drop out." After learning at the age of seventy-four that he had terminal prostate cancer, he prepared for the "ultimate dropout."

"How you die is the most important thing you ever do," he contended. "It's the exit, the final scene of the glorious epic of your life. It's the third act, and you know, everything builds up to the third act."

Because he was afraid of losing his dignity as well as his mental agility, he formulated a personal, "quality of life" document that specified when he considered life not worth living. "I like options," he declared. "You're as young as the last time you changed your mind."

Timothy Leary died on May 31, 1996.

Date with Death Moved Up

Over five hundred people died in Chicago of heat-related causes during the blistering days of July 1995. Mayor Richard M. Daley and his colleagues were criticized for the manner in which they responded to the crisis.

Referring to the heat-related deaths, Edmund R. Donoghue, medical examiner for Cook County, said, "Many were probably very near death and their date of death was just moved up by the heat."

The Price of Gold

More than one hundred gold miners were killed on the job in an elevator accident in Orkney, South Africa on May 22, 1995. The cable on the metal, two-floor cage snapped, and the cage carried the men to their deaths. The cage fell 1,650 feet to the bottom of the 1.4-mile-deep mine. Apparently, a thirteen-ton locomotive entered a tunnel that was supposed to have been closed, crashed through the barriers, and cut the cable.

Commenting on the horrible accident, Minister of Energy and Mineral Affairs Pik Botha said, "The locomotive could not have moved as it did, had it been properly controlled."

President Nelson Mandela declared a national day of mourning following the Orkney accident.

The Deathbed of Your Spouse

Dr. Sheldon Vanauken was a distinguished professor at Lynchburg College in Lynchburg, Virginia. He published a number of best-sellers. In *A Severe Mercy*, he relates the story of his happy marriage, his wife's long, terminal illness, their prayers and hopes. The professor watched his wife's ongoing struggle for life until one morning about three o'clock, when the hospital called to say his wife was drifting away.

Although time was critical, the professor bathed and shaved before going to her bedside. By way of explanation, he said, "But I had to come to her—I had to face what must be faced—clean."

Died on a Treadmill

George Romney, born in Mexico in 1907, was a crusader, innovator, business executive, politician, and an ardent member of the Mormon church.

While chairman of American Motors, he envisioned production of smaller cars to compete with the gas guzzlers. The Rambler is an example.

His community involvement, business skills, and labor connections catapulted him into the governorship of Michigan for three terms. His campaign for the presidency in 1968 never recovered from his unfortunate remark that he had been "brainwashed" by the military and diplomatic corps into supporting the Vietnam War. Mr. Romney retired from active politics in 1972, although he was President Nixon's housing secretary for a brief time.

Governor Romney was a "fitness buff," and always looked robust, as if he had been chiseled out of granite; an athlete in the peak of condition. Ironically, he died July 26, 1995, in Bloomfield Hills, Michigan, on his treadmill.

Turn for Home

Tom Lane believes in exercise. Born on June 21, 1894, he works out twice a week in a San Diego pool and holds virtually all the records for swimming in his age category. To exercise his brain, he memorizes poetry. On the occasion of his 101st birthday, he recited his own poem, "A Sail in San Diego Bay."

> I looked upon the stars
> Throughout the heaven known.
> Each one a sun, some of them
> Much larger than our own. . . .
> And now it's time to turn for home.

67

The hour's getting late.
We slack our sheets to sail back in
That glittered silver gate.
(*U.S. News & World Report*, August 28/September 4, 1995)

Facing Death

Socrates, the fifth-century B.C. Athenian philosopher, heard the reading of his death verdict. The charge? Heresy. Those in authority claimed that the scholar refused to acknowledge the gods of Athens. The panel of 501 judges had voted: 281 affirmed the charge while 220 favored acquittal.

Socrates was given an opportunity to escape. He refused, saying that no one knows "whether death is not the greatest of all goods that can come to man."

The condemned philosopher was so magnanimous that, despite the vote, the court was moved to free him, if he promised to abandon his search for truth "and follow wisdom no more."

"Men of Athens, I thank you, and I am grateful to you. . . . I would far rather die after that defense than to live upon your terms."

The great Athenian spent the last hours of his life discussing immortality. Finally, he drank the fatal hemlock.

Embarrassing Moment

A relative from Florida en route to Connecticut stopped off in Richmond, Virginia, for a visit. As I was loading her luggage into the trunk of our car, I noticed that one bag was shaped differently and was heavy. Jokingly, I asked, "What do you carry in this one, your money?" "No," she softly replied, "my mother."

What was said in jest produced tears. She was taking her mother's ashes home.

Discipleship

A Christian!

The Des Moines Tribune (December 5, 1968) reported an amazing event that occurred in South Africa. Two businessmen, Mr. Rumbold, and his colleague, Mr. Samuel, hung their coats over chairs while they had lunch in Luska, in the "copper country." Afterward, Mr. Rumbold missed his wallet; it contained cash and coupons for gasoline.

Three days later, while driving back to Johannesburg, a middle-aged African, dressed in shorts, waved them down. "Are you going to Johannesburg?" he asked. The travelers replied in the affirmative. Whereupon, the Black man took a wallet from his pocket and said, "Would you please try and find a Mr. Rumbold there and give him this wallet? I found it in the street three days ago."

Rumbold was inarticulate. Showing the African his identification, he examined the wallet. Everything was intact. The poor, humble man refused a reward, saying, "No, sir. I do not need to be rewarded for not stealing. I am a Christian."

Confidence in Our Preparation

In the last six minutes of the University of Kentucky's 1996 national semifinal men's basketball victory over the top-ranked University of Massachusetts, Mark Pope—Rhodes scholar candidate and senior—calmly sank all six of his free throws. Twice he stepped to the line with Kentucky clinging to a three-point lead. Pope did not miss.

Putting to rest the speculation that Kentucky would wilt in the national spotlight, Pope remarked after the game, "We go through those exact situations every day in practice. That gives us all confidence in ourselves because we have confidence in our preparation."

Victory for All

From the locker room to the classroom, our culture's operative slogan is "winning isn't everything, it's the only thing." We seldom compete just for the sheer enjoyment of the game. Anything less than victory is perceived as failure.

But the motto of the Great North American Race—the cross-country race of pre–World War II vintage cars—is different: "To Finish Is to Win." And to honor the slogan, $25,000 of the quarter-million-dollar prize money goes to the driver of the oldest car that completes the race.

In 1983, the inaugural year of the race, two days from the finish line, it appeared that Dr. Robert Fuson in his 1912 American La-France Firetruck would earn the oldest car prize. His closest competitor, Tom Lester, in a 1909 Mercedes, had just been towed into the overnight stop.

Instead of going to sleep and turning out the lights on Lester, "Doc" spent the night helping to repair the Mercedes. The next morning, Lester and his car started on time and went on to collect the oldest car trophy.

When asked to explain why he assisted his competitor, Doc replied, "Taking home the trophy would have been a victory for me, but helping him finish was a victory for all of us."

That year Dr. Robert Fuson also took home a prize: a trophy named in his honor. And each year since, one Greatracer is awarded the "Doc Fuson Spirit of the Event" Trophy that honors "his determination, enthusiasm, and selflessness."

Annual Remudding

A visitor to the Southwest cannot help noticing the predominance of adobe architecture; from "hornos" (the round adobe bread-baking ovens) to houses, commercial buildings to contemporary churches. Although adobe is labor intensive—bricks are created from a mixture of clay and straw, which then require a coat of mud plaster—its beauty as well as its ability to retain heat in the winter and remain cool in the summer make it a popular and practical natural building material.

However, inclement weather necessitates annual remudding. This is especially true for preserved adobe churches. The parishioners at the San Francisco de Asis Church (founded circa 1615) in Ranchos de Taos, New Mexico, remud the church each year. By working together to recoat the exterior walls of the church, the members reconstitute the interior and spiritual walls of their community of faith.

Willing to Lose

After a grueling racquetball match, my opponent asked me how I developed such a strong backhand shot.

Without hesitation I replied that several years ago I made a conscious decision to hit a solid return on every backhand shot, even if it meant losing the point. Because I was once willing to lose, I am now in a better position to win.

My comments recall the paradoxical truth of Jesus' saying: "Those who find their life will lose it, and those who lose their life for my sake will find it" (Matthew 10:39).

Don't Flunk the Course

Richard N. Johnson, author of *Life As It Ain't Yet,* shares a story that originated at Central State University. A coed called the Spanish teacher on behalf of her roommate, who had not attended a single class all semester, to find out if there was any way the roommate could "make up" the semester's work in the final two weeks. The teacher replied, "Inform your roommate she has flunked the course."

We see ourselves in this drama. Like the delinquent student who learned that a semester's worth of work cannot be accomplished in the final two weeks, we frequently procrastinate, put off things we promised to do, until the opportunity is gone.

We cannot pass the course in two weeks! A commendable, conta-gious life requires a lifetime of daily effort.

Brother in Christ

While serving as a deacon in a large urban congregation, I ap-proached a visitor who was having difficulty holding her small child and negotiating the bulletin at the same time.

"May I help?" I inquired, reaching for the child.

"No," she sternly replied, "I don't trust strangers!"

Mentally I rejoined, "I am not a stranger but your brother in Christ."

Nothing Free in Free Throws

The pivotal moment in the National Basketball Association's 1995 Championship Series between the Orlando Magic and the Houston Rockets came with 10.5 seconds left in the first game, and Orlando up by three points. Nick Anderson of the Magic stepped to the free throw line for two shots. He missed the first and "stiff-armed" the second. Remarkably, the rebound wound up in his hands and he was instantly knocked to the floor. He was awarded two more free throws. But again, he missed them both.

What was it like to miss not one, not two, not three, but four free throws that would have iced a game that his team eventually lost?

Neither pointing fingers nor making excuses, Anderson intimated that maybe, just maybe, he "did choke." But failure is part of the game. "The bad comes with the good," he said. Yet four missed freebies in that pressure-packed situation are not about to haunt him forever.

"When your best friend gets shot up on the street, that's some-thing you never forget," Anderson related. "That's tragedy." Out-side Simeon High School on Chicago's South Side, Ben Wilson, age sixteen, Anderson's friend and teammate, was senselessly shot to death. Anderson has worn Wilson's number 25 ever since.

Be Your Pieces

At the age of two, Elliott Fleming had memorized all fifty-six lines of the poem " 'Twas the Night Before Christmas."

At the age of three, he could add numbers in the thousands in his head.

When he was four, he learned to play chess.

At the ripe old age of nine, Elliott was a "chess monster," defeating most classmates and the teachers, too. Indeed, he challenged adults with this line: "C'mon, let's play. One minute." This means that both players set their respective clocks at one minute; each person has sixty seconds to make all the moves in the game or lose on time. In other words, you play an entire game of chess in about the same amount of time that it takes the horses to run for the roses in the Kentucky Derby.

Two years later, as a fifth grader, Elliott Fleming won the Kentucky elementary school chess championship. Here is Elliott's secret: "You have to *be* your pieces. You have to see the squares the same way your pieces see them."

"It's Work"

Susan Sarandon won the 1996 Academy Award for Best Actress for her portrayal of Sister Helen Prejean in the movie *Dead Man Walking*. In the movie, based on actual events, the nun becomes spiritual adviser to Matthew Poncelet, a convicted murderer on Louisiana's death row, played by Sean Penn. Although Prejean has personal doubts about her work and is repeatedly confronted by the victims' enraged parents, she draws upon inner strength to sustain her ministry. At the end of the movie, immediately after Poncelet's funeral, the father of one of the victims comments that he wishes he had her faith. Instantly, Sister Helen Prejean replies, "It's not faith. It's not that easy. It's work."

Easter (Crucifixion and Resurrection)

"Tomorrow Today!"

A five-year-old boy was making his first transcontinental railroad trip. When the train sped into a tunnel and darkness enveloped the coach, the lad gasped in fear. The train quickly cleared the tunnel and there was daylight again. Instantly, the relieved youngster exclaimed, "It is tomorrow today!"

This is the quintessence of Easter!

He Leads the Way

Jesse Hilton Stuart (1906–1984), native Kentucky educator and author, tells in one of his books about his first teaching job. Although the school was not far from his home, he had to walk through a field of weeds to reach it. On opening day, Stuart noticed that the high weeds were dripping with dew. To walk through the wet weeds would surely ruin his trousers. But his father, seeing the problem, volunteered to walk ahead of his son. The father trampled down the weeds, thereby making a path and absorbing much of the dew onto his own pants.

A Collision That Changed the World

Whatever the ancient Palm Sunday entrance into Jerusalem meant, it provided a collision between love and hate that shaped itself into a cross. And that which lifted it from grotesqueness to glory was the presence and power of God.

Herod the King

After looking at a picture of Prince de Talleyrand, the most influential French public official during the French Revolution, Gilbert Stuart, portrait painter and student of facial expression, remarked, "If that man is not a scoundrel, God doesn't write a legible hand."

God writes plainly, and there is little heroism in the countenance of Herod Antipas. Like all the Herods, he was handsome, fastidious, and extravagant. He was a sensual man, fond of good living. In many ways he wanted to serve people, but always overriding their needs was the desire to serve his own purposes.

Herod was not altogether irreligious. He was irresponsible, sentimental, and hopelessly weak. He relied on craftiness rather than the power of clear purpose. Religion touched his emotions, but not his will.

The Pharisees once warned Jesus that Herod wanted to kill him. He replied, "Go and tell that fox . . ." (Luke 13:32).

The Necessity of the Cross

The Lenten journey of Christians from Palm Sunday to Good Friday to Easter is fraught with danger. We enthusiastically wave palm branches to celebrate Jesus' triumphal entry into Jerusalem. We vicariously identify with Jesus as he overturns the tables of the money changers in the Temple. And we confidently point to the Resurrection as validation of Christian truth. But seldom do we tarry at the cross. The sorrow and judgment of the Crucifixion are too often ignored.

But Palm Sunday 1995 coincided with another solemn occasion that underscored the necessity of the Cross. Fifty years before, on April 9, Dietrich Bonhoeffer was hanged by the Nazis at the Flossenburg concentration camp in Bavaria for participating in a failed attempt to kill Hitler.

Although Bonhoeffer was by no means the only Christian clergyman to be killed by the Nazis, the dramatic example of his life and the broadly ecumenical appeal of his thoughts make him an exemplary theologian and pastor.

Born in 1906 and educated at the University of Berlin, Bonhoeffer opposed from the start Nazism and Hitler's anti-Semitic laws. In 1935 he returned from a two-year pastorate in London to administer the seminary of the German Confessing Church, which opposed the pro-Nazi "German Christian" movement.

While on a lectureship at Union Seminary in New York City in 1939, Bonhoeffer cut short his stay to return to Germany. He explained his decision, made over the protest of his American friends, in these words: "I will have no right to participate in the reconstruction of Christian life in Germany after the war if I do not share the trial of this time with my people."

Gave It Up for Lent

A woman walked into a doughnut shop and ordered three rounds of hot chocolate and three chocolate eclairs, and finished them all. The server didn't think anything of it until the woman appeared again the following day at the same time and then the next day and so on for several weeks.

Finally, the server's curiosity got the better of him. When the woman walked in the next time and ordered three hot chocolates and three chocolate eclairs, he introduced himself.

"My name is John," the server said, "and what is your name?"

"Sue Smith," she said.

"Would you please tell me why you always order three rounds of the same food and drink each day?" the server inquired. "I'm really curious."

"Well, you see, my two sisters and I were always close, but now our work has taken us to different parts of the world," Ms. Smith replied. "This is sort of a family thing where we promised to eat and drink to one another every day until we meet again."

The server thought that was admirable and told her so.

Several weeks passed. Then, one day the woman walked in and ordered one less round than usual.

"Oh, I'm so sorry, Ms. Smith," the server said. "How did it happen?"

"How did what happen?"

"That you lost a sister."

"Who said anything about losing a sister? I gave up chocolate for Lent."

Non-Christians and the Resurrection

According to "Harper's Index" (*Harper's,* March 1995), 52 percent of non-Christian Americans say they believe in the resurrection of Christ.

The Search for Jesus

Newsweek, Time, and *U.S. News & World Report* all carried a picture of Jesus on their April 8, 1996, covers. Each magazine featured an informative yet controversial article on the life, death, and resurrection of Christ.

Most of the debate focused on the historical reliability of the New Testament resurrection narratives. As Paul correctly asserted, this affirmation identifies the heart of the gospel: "If Christ has not been raised, your faith is futile and you are still in your sins" (1 Corinthians 15:17).

The power of the Resurrection so captivates the human quest for meaning that during Lent and Easter, even money-driven magazines join the search for Jesus.

He Could Not Save Himself

In July of 1944, the Swedish Foreign Ministry sent Raoul Wallenberg, student of architecture as well as banking and international trade, to Budapest in order to help protect more than two hundred thousand Jews who were left in the Hungarian capital after the deportation of 437,000 Hungarian Jews to Auschwitz. By issuing thousands of "protective passports," by removing persons from concentration camp–bound trains, by establishing special hostels that formed the "international ghetto" separate from Budapest's main Jewish ghetto, and by foiling a plot to blow up the ghettos before the city's impending liberation, Wallenberg is credited with saving an estimated twenty thousand to one hundred thousand Jews from the Nazi Holocaust.

When the Soviets occupied Budapest, Wallenberg attempted to negotiate with them on behalf of the Jews. However, the Soviets were highly suspicious of the Swedish mission and charged its staff with spying for the Germans. Wallenberg was requested to report to the Soviet army headquarters in Debrecen. He complied, believing that he would be protected by his diplomatic immunity. On January 17, 1945, Wallenberg returned to Budapest and was overheard to say that he did not know whether he was a guest of the Soviets or their prisoner. That was the last time Wallenberg was seen in public.

Responding to Swedish demands, Soviet authorities announced in 1956 that Wallenberg had died in prison in 1947. Although con-flicting testimonies have surfaced, there is little hope of finding definitive evidence, since most of the relevant documents have apparently been destroyed.

The man who saved others could not save himself.

The Candle of Light

During my ministry with Edgar DeWitt Jones (no relation) in Detroit, he shared this story. A boy by the name of John Todd lost his parents when he was six years old. Young Todd was sent to live with an aunt. He thrived under her loving care and stayed with her until he was a young adult and became independent. In her later years, as her health declined, she wrote to him for comfort. This is his reply.

"It has been almost 40 years since I was left alone in the world. When my mother died, you sent me word to come to your home, and that you would be a kind mother to me. I remember the long journey and my fear of your servant whom you sent to meet me. And I can still remember my anxiety as, perched on your horse and clinging tightly to William, your servant, I started for my new home, riding toward the sunset.

"Night fell before we finished the journey, and as darkness deepened, I began to be afraid. 'Do you think she'll wait up for me?' I asked William. 'She'll surely wait up,' answered William. 'When you turn the next corner, you'll see her candle in the window for you.'

"Soon we turned the bend in the road, and there, sure enough, was your candle shining in the window. I remember you were waiting at the door, that you put your arms around me, and lifted me, a tired and bewildered little boy, down from the horse. There was a fire on the hearth and a warm meal awaiting me.

"After supper, you took me to my room, heard my prayers, and then sat beside me until I dropped off to sleep. You are probably wondering, my dear Aunt, why I am recalling all these things. Some day soon God will send for you. Don't fear the summons, the strange journey through the darkness. At the end of the road you will find love and a welcome as you enter the father's house. As you turn the road, you will see the candle of his love shining for you."

Education

Thomas Jefferson on Education

In 1785 Thomas Jefferson wrote to his fifteen-year-old nephew concerning the role of the classics in the development of the total person. Three attributes were mentioned: an "honest heart," a "knowing head," and a "strong body."

These qualities, declared Jefferson, shape the student into a "useful" person both for oneself and for society. At the center is the "honest heart," which can discern what is honorable from what is base. "Give up money, give up fame, give up science, and give up the earth itself, and all it contains," exhorted Jefferson, "rather than do an immoral act."

The fundamental purpose of reading the classics, concluded Jefferson, is to acquire the "knowing head" that will govern the "honest heart" and "strong body."

Sculpting a Sculptor

While on vacation in New Mexico, I met Doug Scott, a gifted and self-trained sculptor. When I asked how he became interested in sculpting, he indicated that his grandfather was the only family member who carved. Then he told me about an elementary school event that shaped his life.

"In fourth grade, I carved a couple of seals for 'show-and-tell' and the teacher expressed doubts—out loud to the class—that someone my age could have done them. After three separate inquiries, my tears finally convinced her of my honesty. She then made amends. She placed the seals on opposite ends of her desk and asked the class to come up and inspect them. Then she announced to the class, 'One day, Doug will be famous.'

"That incident made a big, a very big impression."

On February 3, 1996, Doug Scott's twenty-five-hundred-pound white marble statue of Roy Rogers and Dale Evans, *Till Death Do Us Part,* was dedicated at the Roy Rogers Museum in Victorville, California. The marble used for this piece was "rubble" from the Colorado marble used for the construction of the Lincoln Memorial in 1928. Doug Scott is now famous.

Get an Education

Born in 1891, just miles from the site of the Little Bighorn battlefield, May Childs is believed to be the oldest living Crow Indian. She lived in a tepee until she was five years old, attended a Catholic boarding school, and appeared in numerous movies for Paramount Studios.

When asked to comment on the discrimination that Native Americans have faced, she quoted Chief Plenty Coups, a revered Crow leader, "Learn to associate with the white man, learn his ways, get an education. With an education you are his equal; without it, you are his victim" (*U.S. News & World Report,* August 28/September 4, 1995).

Committed Crusader

The "politically correct" community refers to him as "the right hand of God." Ralph Reed, brilliant strategist, articulate communicator, and powerful politician, is the former executive director of the Christian Coalition. He had the support of at least sixteen million active members and a budget of $14 million. Statesmen and politicians still seek his counsel.

In commenting on the future state of the country, Reed said, "The future of America is not (shaped) by who sits in the Oval Office, but by who sits in the principal's office."

Disorientation to College

It had been a long day. Up at 6:00 A.M. A trip to the airport with tearful good-byes. Two flights totaling five hours and twelve hundred miles. Then a two-hour car ride.

Fatigued, yet buoyant of spirit, the lone figure trudged the last mile on foot—weighed down by a suitcase in each hand and a case of nerves in his stomach.

As the individual made his way through the arched entryway to the beautiful old campus, his eyes fixed on the bold letters "SDS." Though tired, his mind was still alert. Quickly he deciphered the letters to mean "Student Directory Service." He approached the table and requested his room assignment.

But to his utter dismay, he received instead a lecture on the evils of capitalism. SDS, he later found out, stood for "Students for a Democratic Society"—the most radical political group on campus. It was 1968 and the Vietnam War was at its peak.

I was that student. And that was my disorientation to college.

Do You Know Me?

Carl Hurley, America's funniest professor, told the following story about his days in the classroom.

My reputation as a "tough professor" was well deserved. I not only insisted that students work to their potential, but I also demanded that they complete their assignments on time.

On the occasion of an in-class exam, I gave the usual pretest statement that reviewed the instructions as well as my intention to pick up exams at the end of the class period.

When the bell sounded, I immediately asked everyone to stop writing and turn in their exams. I scooped up the papers and headed for my office.

After setting the exams on the corner of my desk, I began to sort through my mail. Then there was a knock on my door.

Upon answering the door, I was greeted by a huge young man who held an exam in his hand.

"Here's my exam," the student declared.

"Excuse me," I began, "but you know the rules. I do not accept late papers."

Standing perfectly erect, the student inquired, "Do you know who I am?"

Bristling, I shot back, "No, I do not!"

"Good," the student exclaimed, as he reached for the pile of papers and placed his right in the middle.

Be Bold!

George Bush, forty-first president of the United States, gave the commencement address at the College of William and Mary on May 14, 1995. He was popular with the students, partially because he arrived early and fraternized with them and partially because he had just resigned from the National Rifle Association because of their use of offensive language in a fund-raising letter.

Toward the close of Mr. Bush's address he challenged the gradu-ates to "be bold in your dreaming, be bold in your living, be bold in your caring, your compassion, your humanity."

Accession

In *Just As I Lived It*, Lester G. McAllister shares a fascinating historical fact concerning Transylvania University in Lexington, Kentucky. The school was founded in 1780 and was very cognizant of world affairs. During the French Revolution, Transylvania sent a professor to Paris with $5,000 in gold to acquire scientific equipment and books. Dr. McAllister reports that "somehow the books pur-chased in the long ago had never been accessioned by the library."

A Mind Stretched

While visiting in the home of a retired schoolteacher, our host escorted us downstairs to see his study. As he identified memorabilia, he stopped in front of a large sign on the wall and remarked, "I used this motto in the classroom for forty years."

The sign read: "A mind stretched by a new idea can never return to its original dimension."

Environment and Ecology

Roots & Shoots

In 1960, at the age of twenty-six and under the tutelage of paleon-tologist Louis S. B. Leakey, Jane Goodall began her study of chim-panzees at what is now Tanzania's Gombe National Park. What was anticipated to be a three-year—and surely no more than a ten-year—project has turned into the longest field study of animals in the world, spanning three chimp generations.

Like her initial study, Jane Goodall's interests have also expanded to include animal and environmental conservation. In 1991 she started an environmental education program for children called "Roots & Shoots." This program for young naturalists now includes over 250 Roots & Shoots groups in over twenty countries, including the United States, Canada, Germany, and Japan.

"Teaching (children) to care for the earth, and each other, is our hope for the future," Goodall says. "And if we can't give our children hope, we really might as well pack it in."

"Bee-ware"

You know them as the flying critters that build hives, tend flowers, invade picnics, and disturb summer naps.

But did you know that bees are the main pollinators for 60 percent of U.S. produce, including apples, plums, cranberries, blueberries, citrus, sunflowers, and almonds?

Yet the bee population is dwindling at an alarming rate. In 1947, there were nearly 6 million managed bee colonies in the United

States. Fifty years later, the number had declined to 2.6 million. Nationwide, one-fourth of beekeepers' managed hives have died in the last five years. North America's three thousand varieties of wild bees are also threatened. In some areas, three out of four hives have recently died. The major reasons are the heavy use of pesticides, imported parasites, and development.

The precipitous decline in the bee population is devastating not only for the bees but also for humans. In the spring of 1996, almond growers in California had to import bees from Texas and the Dakotas in order to pollinate their groves.

Experts worry that the bees' decline will lead to smaller crops and higher prices for an assortment of basic foods. "If we'd lost a fourth of any other resource, people would be going nuts," commented Gary Nabhan, science director of the Arizona-Sonora Desert Museum. "And yet people still don't get the connection that we're really dependent on bees for the stability of the food supply."

Wayward Feet

In her popular book *A Guide to Wildflowers & Ferns of Kentucky*, Mary Wharton, teacher and environmentalist, warns about indiscriminate picking of blooms, lest some species disappear. Yet her sternest warning is directed to the lower extremities. She writes: "Some of the most 'unkind' treatment that wildflowers experience is executed not by the human hand but by the human foot." Watch where your wayward feet walk!

Polluted Runoffs

The February 1996 issue of *National Geographic* reported that 80 percent of the degradation of U.S. waters is due to polluted runoffs from parking lots, farms, and ranches. Rain sweeps grease and litter from lots and streets into water supplies. In addition, the use of chemicals and raw manure indicts current agricultural practices as a major source of pollutants. Forty-four states report groundwater contamination, and half of the nation's wells contain excessive nitrates.

Reducing harmful water runoffs is not only a national goal, it is also a personal challenge.

When Nature Says "No"

The June 1995 launching of the space shuttle *Discovery* was postponed, not because of inclement weather, not because of mechanical malfunctions, but because woodpeckers drilled 135 holes in the skin of a fuel tank.

Ecology and Extinction

According to *National Geographic* (September 1995), one thousand kinds of creatures that once enjoyed Hawaii's lush landscape have vanished in the last fifteen hundred years. Native species were not equipped to handle the consequences of the Polynesian and European explorers. Later invasions compounded the ecological problems.

Below the Sea

Writing in the January 1996 issue of *Smithsonian*, Cheryl Lyn Dybas reported that "the bottom of the sea throbs with life." There is bizarre yet beautiful, frightening yet exotic sea life found twelve thousand to twenty thousand feet below the surface of the water.

"The key to the ecological web of life in the deep," Dybas said, "turned out to be marine snow; the never-ending precipitation of bits of plants and animals falling from above."

Nature continually recreates in this magical environment. As stewards of the planet, we must both respect and protect the ecological balance, wherever it occurs.

Fabulous Fish Story

One does not normally associate fishing with Yale University. Yet in its diverse class of 1997, filled with overachievers, there is an undergraduate named James Prosek, who is an authority on trout. According to the April 1996, *Yale Alumni Magazine,* the young man has "gone fishing" since he was nine years old. Although he has caught over five thousand trout in streams from Connecticut to Alaska, he, like many fishing enthusiasts, threw most of them back.

Because anglers are usually more interested in trophy-size fish than preserving the diversity of trout, many native strains are cur-rently endangered. In particular, the practice of dumping big, non-native trout into lakes populated by native fish jeopardizes the indigenous trout. Prosek's book *Trout: An Illustrated History,* pub-lished by Knopf, appeared in the spring of 1996. In it, he writes that there are believed to be seventy different varieties of North Ameri-can trout and he provides a history and description, as well as an illustration, of each one. Prosek's work is being compared favorably with the bird paintings of Audubon. He hopes that the book's publication will increase awareness of the plight of indigenous trout and raise money for preservation projects.

Even though an English major, Mr. Prosek says, "I've become a P.R. agent for trout."

A Glimpse of Compassion

A friend was critical of the American Red Cross. So I did a little research and discovered some startling statistics from the organiza-tion's materials detailing recent disasters.

Sometimes there are as many as eight thousand national disasters in a year. Here are a few well-remembered ones:

Hurricane Emily, August 1993, left 3 dead, 2 hospitalized. The Red Cross served 45,260 meals and contributed $736,950 in relief.

The Missouri and Illinois floods, September 1993, left 3 dead with 2,023 families affected. Red Cross relief totaled $8,938,000.

The Texas floods of 1994 affected 9,825 families. Some 1,031,000 meals were served and 57 shelters were opened. The Red Cross provided $14,600,000 in relief monies.

The southern California earthquake, January 1994, left 59 dead, 1,500 hospitalized. The Red Cross served 1,730,286 meals and donated $36,924,084.

The Oklahoma City bomb explosion, April 1995, killed 168 people. Hundreds more were injured. The Red Cross provided food, shelter, and crisis counseling.

What a ministry of compassion!

Number One City!

Despite the possibility of a major earthquake along the west coast of British Columbia, Victoria was selected in 1996 by the *Condé Nast Traveler* "as the best city in the world for environment and ambience." The 87.8 percent rating puts Victoria ahead of San Francisco, Santa Fe, Paris, Florence, and Salzburg.

Evil

Living with Evil

The small town of Dunblane, Scotland, will never be the same. At about 9:25 A.M. on March 13, 1996, Thomas Hamilton, known by some as "Mr. Creepy," walked into the Dunblane primary school's kindergarten class and opened fire. Sixteen children and their teacher were killed; twelve more were wounded.

Beyond theological and philosophical explanations, the problem of evil persists. However manifested, it remains mysterious and heartbreaking. The old question of justice resurfaces again and again. Why must the innocent suffer?

Ron Taylor, headmaster of the school where the massacre occurred, summarized the tragedy in these words: "Evil visited us yesterday, and we don't know why. We don't understand it and never will."

Toward an Understanding of Evil

The late, distinguished Unitarian clergyman, John Haynes Holmes (1879–1964), offered this interpretation of wickedness, suffering, and inequity: "Evil," he said, "is here in the world, not because God wants it or uses it here, but because he knows not how at the moment to remove it. . . . Evil, therefore, is a fact not to be explained away, but to be accepted; and accepted not to be endured, but to be conquered."

A List of Evils

According to Mahatma Gandhi, the following are evils:
wealth without work

pleasure without conscience
commerce without morality
science without humanity
worship without sacrifice
politics without principles.

The Gambling Game

The point man in the nationwide battle against the gambling industry is the Reverend Tom Grey. He does not have an office, staff, or regular salary. His activism started when he was pastor of the United Methodist Church in Galena, Illinois, and a riverboat casino was proposed for that Mississippi River town. Although local citizens voted by an 81 percent margin against the casino, the state ignored the voice of the people and granted the gambling industry a license.

That is when Tom Grey organized a coalition whose influence has exceeded all expectations. For example, in Florida the gambling lobby spent $16.5 million in an unsuccessful referendum campaign. In this and other victories for opponents of the gambling game, Grey was the principal strategist. A gambling consultant referred to him as "our most dangerous man in America."

Although the Reverend Grey does not claim to be a crusader, he arouses citizens "against politicians in league with a 'predatory and greedy' gambling industry that makes money off the dreams of the poor and the middle class."

Not His Brother's Keeper

The Unabomber confounded law-enforcement authorities for eighteen years. After twenty-three injured victims, three deaths, countless interviews, twenty thousand telephone calls, and an estimated expenditure of $50 million, the FBI arrested Theodore J. Kaczynski on April 3, 1996, as a prime suspect in the case. The recluse was apprehended in his one-room, ten-by-twelve-foot backwoods cabin, some five miles from Lincoln, Montana. According to some sources, the hermit's hideaway was crammed with books, bomb-making materials, and other incriminating evidence.

Kaczynski graduated from Harvard at age twenty and received his Ph.D. from the University of Michigan in mathematics. After teaching for two years at the University of California at Berkeley, he virtually withdrew from society.

Ironically, after years of FBI investigation, it was a tip from the suspect's family that led investigators to an arrest. While preparing to sell her home in suburban Chicago, Mrs. Kaczynski found letters from her son, Ted. Some of the words and thoughts were similar to those used in the Unabomber's manifesto, published in *The New York Times* and *The Washington Post* in September 1995. The implicating evidence was given to proper authorities.

Imagine the anguish endured, the courage and integrity demon-strated by Theodore Kaczynski's mother—Wanda—and brother—David—who turned the evidence over to the FBI!

Skinned Alive!

When a twelve-year-old boy in Palatka, Florida, went out to feed his dog, "Dawg," a beagle mix, on Sunday, February 19, 1995, he was horrified. Much of the dog's hide was hanging down over his rump. He had been skinned alive!

Dr. Gary Shelton, of Interlachen, reattached the skin using over 125 stitches.

Compassion money poured in from across the country; some for medical bills, some for the apprehension and conviction of the assailant.

Dawg, renamed "Prince," is expected to make a full recovery.

The Death of Satan

In our postmodern, American society, fewer and fewer people use the name "Satan." Taking their cue from the silent pulpit, only 26 percent of American Roman Catholics say they have been tempted by Satan and 31 percent of nonevangelical Protestants insist there is no such thing as the devil (*Newsweek,* November 13, 1995).

Yet Andrew Delbanco, a professor of American literature at Columbia University and author of *The Death of Satan,* laments the loss of the sense of radical evil that the devil represents. Although twentieth-century atrocities occur—the Nazi Holocaust, Hiroshima and Nagasaki, Stalin's death camps, the "killing fields," mass graves in Rwanda, "ethnic cleansing" in Bosnia—Delbanco argues that "we have no language for connecting our inner lives with the horrors that pass before our eyes."

Because evil by any other name is still evil, he criticizes the social sciences for trying to explain it away. "The idea of evil," Delbanco writes, is something "on which the health of society depends. We have an obligation to name evil and oppose it, in ourselves as well as in others."

The Absence of Conscience

Evil is more than the absence of good; evil is also the absence of conscience.

Matthew Fox, theologian and teacher of "creation spirituality," made this point while explaining the modern separation between science and religion.

"The key was the breakdown of the medieval cosmology in the fifteenth century and then the religious wars of the sixteenth century, which scared the hell out of scientists. And then in 1600 the church burned Giordano Bruno, a scientist and Dominican, at the stake.

"In the seventeenth century, they arranged a truce. Scientists said, 'We'll take the universe and you Christians can have the soul.' So the soul became more and more introspective and punier, unconnected to the universe. And science went out to find the power of the universe—atomic energy—without a conscience. Scientists sold themselves to warmongers, politicians, and nation-state ideology, and the church became more and more trivial and silly" (from an interview in *The Sun,* April 1995).

Good and Evil Irreconcilable

While commenting on the cyclical nature of history since World War II, Elie Wiesel, Holocaust survivor and 1986 Nobel Peace prize recipient, said, "After the war we were all very optimistic, thinking that racism, anti-Semitism, bigotry, fanaticism would never happen again. And here we are, 50 years later, and racism is still here, war is still here in many areas of the world, and fanaticism is on the rise. So wherever we turn, we realize that good and evil are still irreconcilable."

Monster or Normal?

During a *60 Minutes* interview with Holocaust survivor Yehiel Dinur, who testified at the 1960 trial of Adolf Eichmann, Mike Wallace asked Dinur why he cried and then collapsed to the floor at the trial. Dinur explained that his reaction was not what he had anticipated. Although Eichmann personified evil, the encounter made Dinur realize that sin and evil are the natural human condition.

"I was afraid about myself," Dinur concluded. "I saw that I am capable to do this . . . exactly like he."

Then Mike Wallace faced the camera and asked whether Eichmann was a monster or "something even more terrifying—was he normal?"

Faith and Doubt

Faith

Faith is not a magic wand. It is a consuming trust in God's justice, love, and mercy. Faith is more than the acceptance of a body of beliefs, though doctrines are important. Faith is growing in the knowledge and love of Jesus Christ. It is staking one's life on God's promises.

Sustaining Faith

Ezekiel was a youth in Jerusalem when it was captured and virtually destroyed by the Babylonians. Many of his kinsmen were taken away into exile. As a young man, Ezekiel lived the life of a slave under his captors.

Despite unfavorable circumstances, something happened to the young prophet that stamped his name in history. Ezekiel became one of the creators of the new Judaism. This is the way he described the transforming experience: "And when [the Lord God] spoke to me, a spirit entered into me and set me on my feet" (Ezekiel 2:2).

Believe in Something

After 128 days at sea, the founders of Jamestown—the first per-manent English settlement in the New World—arrived at Cape Henry, Virginia, on April 26, 1607, at four o'clock in the morning. On this windswept shore, the grateful settlers raised a "large wooden cross" and thanked God for their safe arrival. Jamestown was selected as their settlement site on May 14.

These were dark and daring days. The disease-infested swamps, together with skirmishes with Native Americans, claimed many lives. Food was scarce. Several hundred colonists came to Virginia in the first six years of her founding, and at one point only sixty persons survived.

On June 7, 1610, it was decided to abandon the settlement. The colonists sailed down the James River once again to challenge the Atlantic. However, the next morning, Sir Thomas Gates, lieutenant governor of the colony, received word that Lord De la Warr had arrived at Point Comfort with settlers and supplies. It is said that Lieutenant Governor Gates returned to the empty fort and, falling on his knees, thanked God the colony had been saved.

While visiting Jamestown, our family boarded authentic repro- ductions of the three ships that made the crossing. The smallest vessel, the *Discovery*, displaced about twenty tons of water and measured 50 feet 2 1/4 inches from stem to stern. We were shocked to find it did not have full headroom and the rough "below" was partitioned for four bunks. Yet the *Discovery* brought over twelve passengers and a crew of nine.

An inadvertent remark made by a tourist in our party lingers in my mind: "You certainly would have to believe in something, wouldn't you, to come across in this thing?"

"Yes," I replied, "you surely would. And they did."

Are You Sure?

When Dr. Wilbur Cosby Bell, distinguished professor at Virginia Theological Seminary, learned of his approaching death, he said, "Tell the boys that I've grown surer of God every year of my life, and I've never been so sure as I am right now."

Why Wait?

Back in the days of preaching missions, I shared a pulpit with the noted Presbyterian minister Peter Marshall. He preached on the story of the Jewish leader Nicodemus who came to Jesus by night to interrogate him about the kingdom of God. After projecting several vivid images of the powerful Pharisee, his concerns and his fears that possibly led him to approach the Master under the cover of darkness, Marshall asked, "Has it ever occurred to you that Nicodemus could not wait until morning?"

Living the Prophecy

Evander Holyfield began boxing when he was eight years old. During those early days, his coach told him that if he continued to follow instructions and work hard, one day he would become the world champion. Over the years he became an Olympic boxer, light heavyweight champion, and eventually heavyweight champion of the world.

When the famous fighter was asked about his former coach's prediction, Holyfield replied, "I believe him!"

From the Mouths of Babes

While putting our four-year-old daughter to bed one night, she leaned across the pillow and whispered in my ear, "Daddy, I don't understand life."

Shocked by her disclosure, I nonetheless replied, "I don't under-stand life either but the best part is working it out together."

Instantly she responded, "The 'funest' part is doing it with God."

Beyond Discouragement

The late William O. Douglas once rode a freight train from Yakima, Washington, to New York City to study law at Columbia University. He arrived grimy, weary, and hungry. His clothes were a mess. His suitcase was held together by a rope. He had six cents in his pocket.

Despite unbelievable disappointments and sacrifice, seventeen years later he was appointed to the U.S. Supreme Court where he served for thirty-six years.

You Are the Light!

Jesus declared, "You are the light of the world" (Matthew 5:14).

The late Harry Emerson Fosdick said, "A saint is a person through whom the light shines."

Yes, We Do!

In *The Robe*, Lloyd C. Douglas has Marcellus, who had determined to become a disciple of Jesus, write his lover, Diana, in Rome, about his conversion. She replied, "It is a beautiful story, let it remain so. We don't have to do anything about it, do we?"

Yes, we do!

Family

Children, Not Flowers

A devoted father was teaching his young son how to operate a gasoline-powered lawn mower. The safety-conscious dad walked by his son's side, reiterating procedures and precautions. Suddenly, the mother called to her husband from the back door. He stopped, turned, and answered her. Meanwhile, the mower got away from the boy, cutting a swath two feet wide through a beautiful flower bed. As the father was chewing out his son, the mother called again. This time she said, "Remember John, we are raising children, not flowers."

Family Pride

The ability to adjust to the passing scene is what Charles Chaplin conveyed in his autobiography. This remarkable entertainer said his mother eloped at the age of eighteen with a middle-aged man and lived in Africa. Later, she returned to London and married a struggling artist, his father, who died at the age of thirty-seven from too much whiskey.

Chaplin's spirited mother knew poverty and disappointment, lost her singing voice, and was forced to move from one miserable apartment to another. Even so, he wrote: "Mother always stood outside her environment and kept an alert eye for the way we talked, correcting our grammar and making us feel that we were distinguished."

Superparent

In the lexicon of baseball, the name Cal Ripken Jr. is in italics. This phenomenal player is a superathlete and holder of numerous major league records—including the one for most consecutive games played. He is also a superparent. Regardless of the time of his arrival home—either late-night or early-morning—from the park or road trip, he gets up and eats breakfast with his family: his wife, Kelly; daughter, Rachel Marie; and son, Ryan. Afterward, he drives Rachel to school.

Family Faithfulness

A sad but inspiring story that emerged from the Vietnam War was about the stamina and cohesiveness of the Elmo Zumwalt family.

Admiral Elmo Zumwalt Jr., a graduate of Annapolis, quickly progressed from rank to rank. He was appointed chief of naval operations at age forty-nine, the youngest person ever to hold that position.

Lieutenant Elmo Zumwalt III embraced his father's credo: "Duty, honor, intelligence, and compassion." Much against the admiral's wishes, the young man elected to serve in Vietnam. He neither sought nor received special treatment from the Navy. In fact, his assignment was an extremely dangerous one: patroling the rivers in small craft. During this time the powerful chemical defoliant, Agent Orange, was used along the riverbanks.

In 1983, Lieutenant Zumwalt learned that he had developed cancer. It was traceable to Agent Orange; ironically, his father had given the order to use it.

Their book, *My Father, My Son*, details the unbelievable account of the family's courage and commitment to one another. There was no blame; each man did what he thought he had to do. The son's painful days finally ended. However, before his death he wrote his father a beautiful letter. Here is the last paragraph:

"How I loved you. How I would have loved to have contin-ued to fight the battles by your side. You always made a difference. You made my last battle, the journey to death, more gentle, more humane.

"I love you,
Elmo"

Dream Catchers

While visiting the Taos Indians near Taos, New Mexico, I was greatly impressed with their culture. They resided in this pictur-esque valley before Columbus "discovered" America, and were settled in their unique adobe multihousing buildings when the first Spanish explorers came through northern New Mexico in 1540. The fifty families that now inhabit the pueblo live very much like their ancestors did centuries ago, while members who live beyond the village walls occupy conventional homes on tribal land.

Native American parents take great pride in their children and exhibit contagious love. The children are usually strong, healthy, and beautiful. They are schooled in every aspect of their culture and tradition. Imagine a nine-year-old girl running a craft shop and pointing with pride to items she has made! Consider the maturity and charm of a ten-year-old boy helping his mother prepare and collect payment for fried bread! For Native American children, every day is a practice in living.

The daughter of the ninety-two-year-old spiritual leader of the community summarized the Taos philosophy of child rearing with these words: "Yes, we love our children and never leave them alone until they are about fifteen." Then she concluded, "We always hang a dream catcher (handcrafted web) over their beds."

Pushing Pays Off

Mike Piazza, of the Los Angeles Dodgers, is one of the finest catchers in baseball. In 1993, he was Rookie of the Year in the National League. But Mike did not achieve stardom overnight.

His father, Vincent Piazza, a successful businessman, always wanted his son to be a baseball player. Recognizing the youngster's talent, Mr. Piazza provided the proper atmosphere, equipment, motivation, and daily discipline necessary to develop Mike's poten-tial. He also provided him the opportunity to see major league players in person, including the then Dodger manager, Tommy Lasorda.

Although Mike rebelled at times, practice continued. There was little time for permissiveness in the Piazza family. On television, I heard the now well-known catcher say, "I love my father all the more for staying on me."

Teaching Responsibility

In his autobiography, *It Doesn't Take a Hero,* H. Norman Schwarzkopf recalls his childhood in Lawrenceville, New Jersey. A formative event occurred in August of 1942. Young Norman was with his father and mother in the backyard about dusk when he was informed that his "pop" was going off to war the next day. After affectionate admonitions, senior Schwarzkopf made his son "man of the house."

His father, a West Pointer and destined to become a general, left the informal conference, went into the house, and returned with his Army saber. "I'm placing this sword in your keeping until I come back," he said. "Now son, I'm depending on you. The responsibility is yours."

Responsibility for his mother and two sisters at age seven!

Continuing Parental Influence

John Franco, ace relief pitcher for the New York Mets, lost his parents before he became a star. However, their character and exam-ple continue to motivate him. He has two small rubbing stones in his locker at the ballpark. He carries the stones—one for each parent—with him when he visits their graves in the cemetery. Sometimes on the pitching mound, when the game is on the line, Franco will talk to his father, asking for help.

Living Sacrifice

Thirty years ago John W. Allen Jr. was a shining star on the European opera circuit. He was a contemporary of Luciano Pavarotti at the Juiliard School of Music in New York City. However, Mr. Allen's operatic career was interrupted by his mother's illness. He returned to Jacksonville, Florida, to assist with her care, which required round-the-clock support for fourteen years—much too long for an opera singer to stay in voice.

Mr. Allen died May 23, 1994, at the age of seventy-three. A colleague at a Wal-Mart store in Jacksonville, where Allen worked as a greeter, said, "He had a great attitude. He had to give his opera up, but he didn't let it get him down."

Following the admonition of Paul, John Allen offered himself "as a living sacrifice" (Romans 12:1).

"Hi, Mom!"

A five-year-old boy was fed up with his mother. The angry child ran up to his room, found a suitcase, packed it, and came stomping down the stairs, sputtering threats and saying how wonderful it would be to get away from home. The gentle mother told her son good-bye and closed the front door.

From a window she watched her distressed boy trudging down the street with the old suitcase bumping his leg. Now and then, the youngster would stop and look back. At last, he turned in at a neighbor's house and walked up the steps and rang the doorbell. As if she had been cued for her role in the drama, the gracious housewife invited him in and gave him cookies and fruit juice. Meanwhile, the boy's mother telephoned the neighbor to explain what had transpired.

Toward evening, the lad thanked the neighbor for a pleasant visit and went bouncing home with his suitcase as if nothing had happened. Slamming the front door behind him, he exclaimed, "Hi, Mom!"

After dinner and their nightly ritual, the tired son went to bed. Curious to see what her son had taken on his trip, the mother opened the suitcase and found his favorite cowboy hat and toy pistol, some bubblegum, a toothbrush, and his packet of church envelopes.

God

Looking for God

In *A Twentieth Century Testimony*, Malcolm Muggeridge says, that "the true purpose of our existence in this world, which is, quite simply, to look for God, and in looking, to find Him, and, having found Him, to love Him, thereby establishing a harmonious relation-ship with His purposes for His creation."

God in the Cockpit

An Air Force captain at Wheelus Air Base in Tripoli came striding into the Protestant Men's banquet very late. We were all but finished with the meal. He was still in his flying gear. His face bore the marks of weariness and strain. He was president of the Protestant Men of the Chapel. Rapping for attention, he thanked the men for coming and apologized for being late.

Then, in a voice laden with emotion, he said, "Men, it has been a hard day. Flying out of Turkey I had difficulty with the radio, and finally lost it altogether. Then, when I approached our field, the landing gear would not come down. I circled and I circled and I circled, but the gear would not come down. As I contemplated what I should do, something told me to circle once more. I did, and the landing gear came clear. . . . God was in the cockpit with me to-night."

The Face of God

Jacob looked up and there was Esau, coming with his four hundred men; so he divided the children among Leah, Rachel,

and the two maidservants. He put the maidservants and t_____
children in front, Leah and her children next, and Rachel and
Joseph in the rear. He himself went on ahead and bowed
down to the ground seven times as he approached his
brother.

But Esau ran to meet Jacob and embraced him; he threw his
arms around his neck and kissed him. And they wept. Then
Esau looked up and saw the women and children. "Who are
these with you?" he asked.

Jacob answered, "They are the children God has graciously
given your servant."

Then the maidservants and their children approached and
bowed down. Next, Leah and her children came and bowed
down. Last of all came Joseph and Rachel, and they too bowed
down.

Esau asked, "What do you mean by all these droves I met?"

"To find favor in your eyes, my Lord," he said.

But Esau said, "I already have plenty, my brother. Keep what
you have for yourself."

"No, please!" said Jacob. "If I have found favor in your eyes,
accept this gift from me. *For to see your face is like seeing the face
of God.*" (Genesis 33:1-10 NIV, italics added)

Can anyone see God in your face?

America Believes in God

Although cultural pundits frequently characterize America as a
post-Christian, postmodern nation, belief in God has remained a
strong constant, according to the results of Gallup surveys throughout the 1990s. Virtually everyone in America—96 percent in a 1994
survey—expressed belief in God or a universal spirit.

When asked to describe how they image God, 83 percent in a 1991
Gallup survey viewed God as a deity, while 12 percent portrayed
God as a spirit or life force. Remarkably, only 3 percent articulated
an agnostic position (they either said they did not know or did not

feel that humans could know about God). Even fewer—2 percent—claimed that there was no God in any form.

Among those respondents who professed a belief in God, 80 percent described their relationship with God as personal and an equal percentage said that they expected to be called before God on Judgment Day.

The Lord Was at the Hospital

A visitor came to my hospital room. After exchanging pleasantries with this attractive, obviously bright woman, we began discussing books—a conversation that was prompted by my reading materials. In due time, I remarked that I was writing a book and needed assistance. The kind person replied, "I would love to help you, but I am committed. . . . I'll keep you in mind."

A month later, an individual called to say that she had heard from my hospital visitor that I was working on a writing project and needed some help. She was interested.

An interview was arranged. During the conference it became clear that the applicant possessed the right skills and computer equip-ment.

God works in marvelous ways.

Playing God Doesn't Work

In a thirty-two-year ministry at Glide Memorial United Methodist Church, the Reverend Cecil Williams has helped build the church into the most comprehensive nonprofit provider of human services in San Francisco. With a $4.3 million annual budget in 1995, this 5,500 member congregation supports 35 outreach programs. The newest project is the $9 million Cecil Williams Glide Community House, a nine-story residential facility for homeless persons and families.

But Williams resisted having the building named after him. "I'm not an empire builder," he explained. "You then become a god for people, and I don't want that. I've tried to play God before and it doesn't work."

Beautiful Before God

The book of Acts is a thesaurus of Christian faith and action. It is filled with the spirit of adventure and togetherness. Many stalwart souls stride across its pages as the church emerges.

In Acts, we are reminded that there arose one in Egypt who had not known Joseph, and he dealt craftily with the people. It was a dangerous and discouraging period. "At this time Moses was born, and he was beautiful before God" (7:20).

The life of Moses, this brilliant lawmaker, judge, and giant of righteousness, reminds us that God is present in every crisis, and we are blessed.

The Presence of God's Absence

As we gathered in the seminary chapel for the opening worship service of a Saturday workshop, it quickly became apparent that we were missing a key person. The participants were present, but the worship leader was nowhere to be found. He was a no-show.

In this postmodern, post-Christian world, the absentee worship leader stands as a metaphor for the world's experience of God. Too often we experience the presence of God's absence more profoundly than the actual presence of God.

But where do we go to encounter the holy? Although God's venue is all of creation, the church is the locus of God's redemptive presence in the world. In and through its brokenness, the church embodies the mystery and majesty of God in the world.

God Provides

As I approached the gate for my flight to a church convention, I was surprised to see our retired pastor in the waiting area. After a brief conversation, we realized that we were seatmates on the plane. We boarded and had an enjoyable flight catching up on families and interests.

After landing, we negotiated the terminal, located our luggage, and shared a taxi to a downtown hotel.

As we departed outside the hotel, I asked him if he had anyone to assist him during the convention. "Oh yes," he replied, "two people are already here who will help. And they will return with me on the same flight."

My friend is in the beginning stages of Alzheimer's disease and should not be traveling alone.

As I walked away, shaking my head, I remembered a sermon he had preached affirming the providence of God.

Thank God I was on that flight. Thank God that God provides!

Are You Related?

It was a bitterly cold day in a western city. A small boy stood shivering on a steel grate in the sidewalk. His clothes were thin and tattered. A woman, appropriately dressed for the weather, stopped and engaged the youngster in conversation. He was indeed a child of the street. The compassionate stranger took him to a clothing store and outfitted him from head to foot, including cap, scarf, and gloves.

The lad was filled with joy and gratitude. He could not thank her enough.

As they said good-bye and walked in opposite directions, the elated boy turned back to ask, "Are you God's mother?"

The gentle woman answered, "Oh no! I'm just a child of God."

Whereupon the smiling lad remarked, "I knew you were related."

Grace

Undeserved Grace

In an instant, Gerald Sittser's life changed forever. A car slammed into his family vehicle, killing his mother, his wife, and his four-year-old daughter. He, like countless others, asked the proverbial question "Why me?"

Yet over time, Sittser began to question the assumption that he had a right to a life that is completely fair. Although he did not deserve their deaths, he also knew that he did not deserve their presence in his life either.

"On the face of it," he wrote in an article in *Christian Century* (January 17, 1996), "living in a perfectly fair world appeals to me. But deeper reflection makes me wonder. In such a world I might never experience tragedy; but neither would I experience grace. . . . The problem of expecting to live in a perfectly fair world is that there is no grace in that world, for grace is grace *only when it is undeserved.*"

I'll Always Be Your Eyes

Because she had been blind for thirteen years and dependent upon her fifteen-year-old son to be her eyes, Sally Colin lived the life of a recluse in Fort Smith, Arkansas. But on Sunday, March 19, 1995, all that changed. Christopher, her son, was hit by a car and suffered massive head injuries. On Monday, doctors declared him dead.

When his mother agreed to donate his organs, a nurse wondered whether Ms. Colin could receive one of her son's corneas. The hospital physicians determined that her degenerative eye disease—keratoconus—could indeed be corrected by a transplant.

After his memorial service, Ms. Colin checked into the hospital and had one of her son's corneas transplanted into her
right eye. When bandages were removed on Friday, March 24,
she could see!

With tears streaming down her cheeks, she remarked, "He kept
his word. He promised, 'Momma, I'll never leave you and I'll always
be your eyes.' "

Two Bowls of Bread and Milk

John Henry Jowett, one of the world's great preachers, was included in *The Royalty of the Pulpit*. He came from Scotland to the
famed Fifth Avenue Presbyterian Church in New York City. Eagerly
anticipating his arrival, the church planned an elaborate welcoming
party, and a suite had been reserved at the Gotham Hotel.

Dr. and Mrs. Jowett sailed to America on the *Mauretania*, but the
ship was delayed by rough seas. Management of the hotel ordered
one of their favorite chefs to stay on duty, irrespective of the hour,
to prepare whatever the Jowetts desired to eat when they arrived.
The menu would be called in from the ship.

The *Mauretania* docked about midnight. The order to the hotel
chef read: "We would like two bowls of bread and milk."

Catching Grace

In *A Pretty Good Person*, Lewis B. Smedes relates grace to the
ordinary when he writes: "The moment of grace comes to *us* in the
dynamics of any situation we walk into. It is an opportunity that God
sews into the fabric of a routine situation. It is a chance to do
something creative, something helpful, something healing, something that makes one unmarked spot in the world better off for our
having been there. We catch it if we are people of discernment."

Shoes, Anybody?

It is said that when Mahatma Gandhi boarded a train one day, a sandal slipped off his foot and landed beneath the train. The distin- guished Indian leader did not have time to retrieve it. Quickly Gandhi removed the other sandal and threw it back down the track in the direction of the other sandal. When asked for an explanation, the teacher replied, "The poor man who finds the shoe lying on the track will now have a pair he can use."

Embrace Lazarus!

Jesus told the parable of a rich man, incorrectly associated with the name "Dives" by tradition (Latin for "rich man"), and a poor man known as Lazarus (Hebrew for "one whom God helps") to illustrate that however one lives in the here and now determines how one lives in the hereafter (Luke 16:19-31).

Each day the poor beggar was carried to the gates of the big house looking for help. Hungry dogs would lick his ulcerated body. Occa- sionally, a servant would provide some scraps from the master's table.

Eventually, both Dives and Lazarus died. Although Dives was tormented, the pitiful Lazarus was promoted to eternal glory.

As a young man, it was the reading of this parable that convicted Albert Schweitzer. He concluded that Africa was a beggar lying at the doorsteps of Europe. Someone had to see it; someone had to do something about it. He did. He gave his life to his beloved hospital in Lambaréné, French Equatorial Africa. One of the world's most gifted and brilliant men found and embraced Lazarus.

Good Samaritans

During the 1995 Christmas season, a flat tire forced the driver of a sleek limousine to pull onto the shoulder of a busy New Jersey highway. The chauffeur stood by the stranded car hoping someone would see their predicament and stop to help.

At last, a passing motorist offered assistance. The stranger was pleasant and knowledgeable. Upon completing the dirty job of changing the tire, the good Samaritan was thanked profusely by the chauffeur.

Then a darkened window rolled down in the limo and the occupant asked what he could do to repay the favor.

"Just send my wife a big bouquet of flowers." With this cordial comment, the volunteer handed the passenger a card with his wife's name and their address.

Two weeks later a gorgeous bouquet of orchids arrived at the designated address with a card, signed by a famous billionaire and his wife, that read simply: "We paid off your home mortgage."

Touched by Grace

I entered the chancel in sheer dread. Nothing had prepared me for this moment—neither seminary nor life. My thirty-year-old twin brother was dead and I was to give the funeral prayer.

As I slowly scanned the congregation, spotting my wife and other relatives, I tried to avoid direct eye contact, preferring to stay focused, trying desperately to stay composed. But even as our father spoke, eloquently and tearfully, of our mutual loss, I could feel the tenuous grip on my self-control slipping away.

It was time for my prayer. I did not move.

The presiding pastor tapped me on the shoulder and motioned me to step forward.

Slowly I rose and walked to the pulpit. As I grasped its edge, my body trembled. And for what seemed like an eternity, I stood transfixed, sobbing uncontrollably; my grief pouring out of every fiber of my body. I could not speak, let alone utter a prayer.

Suddenly, I felt the reassurance of a hand on my shoulder. And like an afternoon thunderstorm on a hot, sultry summer day, the tears disappeared as quickly as they had formed.

I neither turned to acknowledge the hand nor spoke to offer gratitude. I had been touched by grace, so I prayed.

Growing in Maturity

John Wesley was an amazing man. He was not only the outstand-ing preacher of the eighteenth century in England, but he was also one of Christ's most devoted servants. He wrote scores of books and pamphlets. He traveled on horseback to countless preaching ap-pointments. He frequently preached three times a day. At age eighty-three he wrote: "I am a wonder to myself. I am never tired, either with preaching or writing or travel."

A Grieving Moment of Grace

In a column for *The Christian Ministry* (September/October 1995), Victoria A. Rebeck tells about the time she stood by a friend in a Cook County, Illinois, criminal courtroom. Her friend was accused of hitting and killing two people with his car while driving under the influence of alcohol.

After the proceedings, in which her friend pled guilty, a woman approached the defendant's mother and offered these words of comfort. "Excuse me," she interrupted. "I'm the mother of one of the people who died. I just want you to know that I know you must be in great pain, and that I feel for you. I know he didn't mean to do it. I just wanted you to know that."

Rebeck concludes her column with these words: "Amid the vio-lence and sorrow came a courageous, gentle word of grace, empathy and hope. . . . People like this grieving mother are building the realm of God in the urban rubble."

Guilt and Forgiveness

O, For a Second Chance!

Albert Camus, French existentialist and novelist, told the story of a lawyer who heard the screams of a drowning woman from the waters beneath a bridge as he walked home. He refused to risk his life to save her. The tyranny of that awful moment haunted him day and night. At last, the remorseful man cried out, "Throw yourself into the water again so that I may a second time have the chance of saving both of us."

A Revealing Dive

Greg Louganis was the greatest diver in the world; perhaps in the history of the event. He was an Olympic champion, physical poetry in graceful motion.

In his book *Breaking the Surface*, Louganis recalls his difficult childhood. His parents were unmarried. His father was a Samoan; his mother's family came from northern Europe. Soon after his birth, the unwanted child was given up for adoption. The boy's new father was an alcoholic who neglected and abused him. Because his skin was dark, kids at school called him names. He got into drugs, and attempted suicide. As if all of this were not enough to discourage anyone, Greg had dyslexia. Yet, he emerged from this heap of problems as a splendid athlete.

In a diving accident in the Seoul Olympics, Louganis sustained a cut that required four stitches. But after this, he resumed competition and went on to win a gold medal.

However, he was frightened. Knowing he was HIV positive, he worried that his blood would contaminate the pool or the physician who had sewn him up without wearing gloves. There was contro-versy, embarrassment, and sorrow.

A revealing dive!

To Do and Not to Do

One evening as my wife and I were preparing to enjoy quiet time and reading, the doorbell rang. Upon answering the door, I found standing there two beautiful little girls—our neighbors—ages six and nine. With considerable poise the older one handed me a small package saying, "This is your belated valentine!"

"Oh, thank you," I said, "and won't you come in?"

I called my wife and she joined us in the living room. At their suggestion we opened the dainty parcel. It was a box of delicate chocolates. I offered some to the children. "No," they said, "we gave up candy for Lent."

"Mrs. Jones did, too," I replied. "So I guess I will have the box to myself."

Observing their bewildered faces as I ate a chocolate, I went to the dining room for some mixed nuts. Passing them to the girls, the elder declined saying, "I consider them the same as candy." Then I offered the younger one some nuts. Quickly she removed her glove and carefully selected the one she wanted. Within a few minutes the ritual was repeated. After four helpings I asked, "My dear, did you give up nuts for Lent?"

"Yes," she replied, "but I still eat them!"

This innocent yet exceedingly bright child unknowingly brought into dramatic focus a perennial problem of the human race: to generate sufficient power to do what one has committed to do and to refrain from doing what one has determined not to do.

This is the message of Paul's dilemma as he writes with disarming honesty in the seventh chapter of Romans. In dealing introspectively with the enigma of humanity, he observes, "My own behaviour baffles me. For I find myself doing what I really loathe but not doing what I really want to do" (7:15 JBP).

A Boy's Remorse

In his memoirs, H. Norman Schwarzkopf shares his feelings about a time when, as a boy, he killed a bird. While playing with his bow and arrow one day, he saw a robin in the backyard. Little Norman let the arrow fly. It went directly through the bird. The robin struggled and died while the hunter stood helpless.

Young Schwarzkopf rushed into the house, found an appropriate box, lined it with soft cloth, and placed the bird in it for private services. He offered prayers and vowed he would "never, ever, ever again shoot a bird or anything else, if I could be forgiven for having committed this terrible crime."

A Constricting Conscience

Ken Burns is a successful documentary filmmaker. Although he is frequently accused of interpreting history too subjectively, his three miniseries, *Brooklyn Bridge, The Civil War,* and *Baseball,* are entertaining, as well as instructive.

When Burns and his wife, Amy, completed *The Civil War,* the documentarian felt compelled to reward himself for the achievement. So, he went out and bought a fire-engine red Miata. He drove the sports car home. However, his Calvinist-conditioned conscience would not permit him to enjoy it. He did not have any money and royalties had not been received. Overcome with guilt, he left the Miata parked for one year until income justified his purchase.

Burns's behavior reminded me of the late Bishop Edwin Holt Hughes who said, "I could not preach if my socks were not paid for."

A Prodigal Son

During his rebellious teens, Franklin Graham, son of the noted evangelist Billy Graham, resented any "comparisons" with his father. His indignation expressed itself in drinking and carousing. He was expelled from school.

Today, in his midforties, the "prodigal" has returned home. Franklin Graham is now first vice-chairman of his father's crusade organization.

Our Old Shoes

Eugene W. Brice, former pastor of University Christian Church in Fort Worth, Texas, related a story he once heard.

This is "about a traveler who was touring West Germany a few years after the end of World War II. In one of the towns he was visiting, he was invited to spend the night with a certain family. The family consisted of a father and mother and a 12-year-old boy.

"The father began to tell the traveler something about the family and especially about the circumstances surrounding the adoption of his youngster whom they had rescued during the war years. The father said, 'Our boy was just a poor orphan when we first saw him. He was in rags and very dirty, but his shoes were the worst of all. The upper parts were in tatters, and the shoes had huge holes in them. When we took him in, we gave him new clothes and threw his old ones away. We decided, however, to keep those battered shoes as a reminder of how bad off he had been when he first came here. I keep them on a shelf, and when the boy complains or becomes unruly, I merely walk slowly to the shelf, haul the shoes down, and remind him of how much we have done for him.'

"The traveler saw that the boy looked hurt and ashamed and, in fact, a bit unwanted as this story was told. The traveler didn't say anything since he didn't want to offend his host, but he thought to himself, 'What a blessing it is that God doesn't continually drag out *our old shoes!*' "

Forgiveness Was My Issue

In 1984, four months after undergoing surgery to remove a cancerous lung, Greg Anderson was informed that the cancer had spread from his lung through the lymph system. His surgeon gave him "about thirty days to live."

Desperate and dying, he called organizations around the country, speaking to individuals who had lived through a similar situation. The one, constant message he received was forgiveness. Gradually Anderson came to realize that "forgiveness *was* my issue."

Yes, he possessed a "critical" attitude, but there was more. Three months before his cancer diagnosis, he and a new controller at work began a series of escalating attacks and recriminations on each other. Within thirty days of Anderson's diagnosis, his adversary was diagnosed with prostate cancer. Anderson finally admitted that there was a "link between my toxic behavior and the onset of my illness."

After compiling a list of people to forgive and silently forgiving these people from his sickbed for four days, Anderson knew that he must visit his adversary from work. With heart pounding and adrenaline rushing, he visited the man in his home and managed to utter, "I have come to say I am sorry. I deeply regret the hurt I have caused you."

Struggling to sit up in his own sickbed, his adversary replied, "Greg, I am the one who needs to say I'm sorry. I'm old enough to be your father. Yet I treated you like the outcast son. Please forgive me."

While they embraced and cried, the former adversary muttered a prayer, "Dear God, forgive us all."

Greg Anderson, wellness crusader and successful author, identifies this one week devoted to the sincere work of forgiveness as the "absolute turning point" in his physical healing (*The 22 Non-Negotiable Laws of Wellness*, 1995).

The Fourth Temptation

In his novel, *The Chain*, Paul Wellman shares a scintillating story attributed to African Americans. According to the legend, after Jesus emerged victorious from the wilderness temptations, his disciples deserted and denied him, and enemies and friends alike conspired in his crucifixion. Then the devil returned and whispered in his ear, "They ain't worth it, Lord." In response the Master was heard to say, "Father, forgive them; for they do not know what they are doing" (Luke 23:34).

Christ Commands It

The late Edgar DeWitt Jones of Detroit shares this experience in his book, *A Man Stood Up to Preach*:

After preaching on the topic of forgiveness, he received a letter from a woman in the congregation whose husband had been killed. The letter contained this question: "How could you expect me to forgive those despicable murderers who took the life of my dear husband?"

Dr. Jones responded: "No, dear friend. I don't expect you to forgive those murderers of your husband, for I am a frail human being like yourself. But Christ expects it of you and expects it of me. No matter what happens, we must try to love our enemies and to pray for those who despitefully use us. . . . Christ so taught us and so lived."

Health and Health Care

Expanding Horizons

Robert Louis Stevenson was a remarkable man. His demeanor and faith were enviable. Although he endured poor health in the latter years of his life, he nevertheless said, "I refuse to let a row of medicine bottles be the circumference of my horizon."

Couch Potatoes

Couch potatoes beware! Warning labels will now appear on the products, tags, and packaging of forty sporting goods manufacturers. The label will read: "The surgeon general has determined that lack of physical activity is detrimental to your health."

Why the fuss? The government estimates that 60 percent of Americans lead dangerously sedentary lives. "There's an epidemic of inactivity," says Tom McMillen, cochair of the President's Council on Physical Fitness and Sports.

Coincidentally or providentially, on February 6, 1996, the day after the surgeon general's campaign was announced, former National Hockey League coach Tom McVie, who was between jobs, was quoted in the newspaper as saying, "I make the Maytag repairman look like a workaholic."

Control

In the baseball minor leagues, he had a "major league" control problem. He threw so hard that he once knocked out his own catcher; he was so wild that one of his errant pitches broke the arm of a spectator in the stands.

Through work and discipline, however, he became a master of control. Before he retired from the major leagues in 1993 at age 46, Nolan Ryan held over 50 records, including most strikeouts—5,714—and seasons played—27.

His recipe for success and longevity: stay in shape. During the season he would exercise three to five hours a day. After he pitched his seventh no-hitter on May 1, 1991, he rode a stationary bike for thirty minutes.

As the "perfect poster boy" for the health-conscious baby boomer generation, Nolan Ryan's message is simple: "You have to exercise some degree of control. If you can't control your body, you can't control your mind. Make an appointment with yourself to exercise and keep it."

AIDS Patients Need Aid

From Capitol Hill to the county seat, almost everyone agrees we need health care reform. But the fine points elicit strong reactions.

Jesse Helms, a U.S. senator from North Carolina, provides a case in point. On July 5, 1995, Helms proposed that all government money for AIDS research should be cut because the disease is transmitted via "deliberate, disgusting, revolting conduct" by people "engaging in unnatural acts."

Regrettably, Helms has misplaced certain facts. At the time of his announcement there were seventy-seven children under the age of thirteen in North Carolina who had AIDS, most of whom were born with the virus. Since 1981, 5,541 babies in the United States have been born with the AIDS virus. In addition, 7,223 AIDS patients in America were infected through transfusions and transplants.

Justification on the basis of righteousness not only denies reality, it also denies the moral use of money to combat the AIDS virus. But more important, AIDS is not a moral issue; it is a health issue. Because people are suffering and dying, AIDS patients need aid, too.

121

Ignorance and AIDS

"I honestly believed I had a better chance of winning the lottery than contracting (AIDS). . . . I'm here to tell you I thought that I was bulletproof, and I'm not."

With these words, Tommy Morrison, former World Boxing Organization heavyweight boxing champion with a 45-3-1 professional record, confirmed at a press conference on February 15, 1996, that a second round of tests found him HIV positive. One week earlier a mandatory blood test revealed the AIDS virus just before he was scheduled to fight Arthur Weathers in Las Vegas.

Although medical experts insist that the odds of transferring the virus in the ring are remote, Morrison did not rule it out as the source of his infection. However, he did admit to a promiscuous lifestyle as well as ignorance about the way AIDS is transmitted.

"I ask that you no longer see me as a role model," the twenty-seven-year-old boxer said, "but see me as an individual who had an opportunity to be a role model and blew it. Blew it with irresponsible, irrational, immature decisions . . . that one day will cost me my life."

A Deliverer

Dr. Jonas Salk, son of a garment industry worker, was born October 28, 1914, and died June 23, 1995. This medical pioneer became a household name after developing a vaccine to prevent polio. *Life* magazine reported that polio "was the AIDS of the 50s. And then . . . one man delivered us."

Like many leaders, he was controversial, but his contributions to humankind were incalculable. Dr. Salk once said, "There have to be people who are ahead of their time. And that is my fate."

In addition to publishing three books, Jonas Salk was committed to developing a vaccine for the prevention and treatment of AIDS. In 1995, the media quoted Dr. Salk as saying, "My own view is we will overcome. I am a perennial optimist. We certainly have the knowledge. The question is whether we have the wisdom."

Paper or Patients?

A recent study published in the *American Journal of Public Health* confirms the urgent need for health care reform. From 1968 to 1993, the percentage of U.S. medical care workers who mostly "push paper" rose from 18.1 percent to 27.1 percent, while the proportion of doctors and nurses fell from 51.4 percent to 43.7 percent over the same period. The number of health care administrators grew by an enormous 692 percent over the last twenty-five years, although the number of doctors grew by only 77 percent and nurses by 164 percent. The study found that our complex market-based health care system required physicians' offices to add over a half-million full-time employees just to keep pace with the paperwork.

Offering Life

There are thirty-five thousand Americans on the waiting list for organ donations. Although approximately five thousand persons annually offer life-giving organs, eight persons die every day while waiting for a life-saving donation.

What to Give Up?

A cartoon dramatizes a conversation between a young woman and her physician. The patient asks, "What can I do to feel better without giving up what's making me feel awful?"

This is a daily concern. What can we do to feel better without giving up what we like to do?

Profile of a Physician

Sir William Osler (1849–1919), of Canada, was the most famous physician of his time. This Renaissance man brought brilliance, character, and boundless energy to his profession. He not only discovered the presence of platelets in the blood but he also pioneered in hospital reform, nurses' training, and public health. In addition, he participated in the design of the Johns Hopkins University Hospital. Dr. Osler's books, lectures, and practice propelled him to world prominence.

While teaching at McGill University, he admonished his students to treat the poor with dignity and compassion. Little did they know that their distinguished teacher, when practicing medicine, not only treated the indigent with care, but also frequently gave them money.

One of Dr. Osler's famous classroom quotations was from the seventeenth-century physician-philosopher, Sir Thomas Browne: "No one should approach the temple of science with the soul of a moneychanger."

Heaven and Hell

En Route to Heaven

On a stormy afternoon in September 1583 near the Azores, the *Golden Hind*, commanded by Sir Walter Raleigh, came alongside a much smaller vessel, *The Squirrel*, commanded by Sir Humphrey Gilbert. *The Squirrel* was in danger of sinking.

Gilbert sat in the stern of *The Squirrel* with an open book. Sir Walter Raleigh called out to him above the angry sea and invited him to come aboard. Gilbert refused, saying he would not leave his companions. Later, Raleigh heard Gilbert's voice over the waves, "Heaven is as near by sea as by land."

At midnight those aboard the *Golden Hind* saw the lights of the smaller ship suddenly go out. In that moment Gilbert and his crew were swallowed up by the dark, raging sea.

Heaven is as near by sea as by land! A tremendous statement of Christian discernment. It is very close to what Paul meant when he said, "Whether we live or whether we die, we are the Lord's" (Romans 14:8*b* RSV).

"The Heavens Abandoned Us"

Although Israel has signed peace agreements with Egypt, Jordan, and the Palestinians, negotiations with its northern neighbors—Lebanon and Syria—have progressed sporadically and cautiously. On April 11, 1996, however, the peace process was seriously threatened when Israel launched air attacks on southern Lebanon in an effort to prevent the Iranian-backed, Lebanon-based Shiite Muslim militant group Hezbollah from sending rockets across the border. One week later, Israeli shells slammed into a United Nations refugee camp in southern Lebanon, killing more than one hundred people, many of whom were burned alive. Even by Mideast standards, the "carnage in the camp" was ghastly and horrific.

"Look at this," cried hospital custodian Abdulla Mutari, holding the limp hand of a young girl. "This day, the heavens have abandoned us."

On the Way Home

Henry Alfred English, pastor and church leader, was born into a family that gave England five generations of clergymen. He graduated from Trinity College, Cambridge. A splendid writer and preacher, Henry Alfred was Dean of Canterbury from 1857 until his death in 1871. He is buried there. His epitaph reads: "The inn of a traveler on his way to Jerusalem."

Poetry of the Heavens

On April 3, 1996, people living east of the Mississippi River were treated to the first total lunar eclipse since November 1993. A lunar eclipse occurs when the earth, during a full moon, moves between the moon and the sun. Jack Horkheimer, of the Miami Planetarium, calls eclipses "the poetry of the heavens."

A Glimpse of Heaven on Earth

In his book *The Glory of Christian Worship,* G. Edwin Osborn provides a glimpse of heaven on earth in the following true story.

"A village auction (during the Depression) in a small New England town had brought out the usual crowd of interested natives and eager collectors. Among them was a family whose appearance told their poverty. The wife, and mother, particularly pathetic looking, was interested in one article only—an old, but well-preserved sewing machine. When the bidding on it started and the crowd realized the poor couple wanted it, no one bid against the woman's timid murmur of 'two dollars.' Hopefully she looked at the auctioneer whose darting eyes had taken in the situation, and he hastily started his 'going, going, gone!' What a look of happiness came over the woman's tired face as she realized the sewing machine was hers! As they roped it on their ancient car and piled in their five children, the woman was overheard remarking to her husband, 'Wasn't we lucky that nobody else wanted a sewing machine today?'

"And then the writer (of the story) commented: 'The silent conspiracy of the crowd was human nature at its warm-hearted best.' "

The Rumor of Heaven

According to a recent poll of Americans, nearly 80 percent believe in heaven, and among adherents about four in five anticipate spending time in an afterlife. (Not surprising in this "don't worry, be happy" era, damnation has few advocates!)

Mally Cox-Chapman, in *The Case for Heaven: Near-Death Experiences as Evidence of the Afterlife*, refutes the post-Enlightenment reduction of heaven to a "spiritual metaphor" by arguing that near-death experiencers (like herself) have been to the other side and have returned with a map. "Human beings affirm Heaven not just because we want to escape the fact of death, but also because so many of us have experienced the reality of things unseen and confirmed in our own way the rumor of Heaven."

Aim at Heaven

In *The Joyful Christian*, C. S. Lewis said, "It is since Christians have largely ceased to think of the other world that they have become so ineffective in this. Aim at heaven and you will get earth thrown in; aim at earth and you will get neither."

Hell Is Other People

In Jean-Paul Sartre's one-act play *No Exit*, first performed in 1944, three recently dead strangers arrive in hell and serve as one another's torturer. As the drama unfolds, the three make two paradoxical discoveries. On the one hand, they realize that "hell is other people" and therefore resolve to ignore one another; on the other hand, they realize that personal identity is dependent on others and therefore seek one another's company. At the end of the play, the door to their room opens but they are too afraid to exit. Cognizant of their hopeless situation, they break into hysterical laughter. The three become silent as the curtain falls.

Jonestown: Hell on Earth

The Jonestown, Guyana, horror of November 18, 1978, in which 909 persons died in a ritualistic mass suicide, confirms the axiom that religion is irreligious when it becomes deceptive and deceitful. Jim Jones preached a gospel of liberation and love. But his People's Temple, dedicated against the evils of racism, hunger, and injustice, became the grotesque epitome of what it deplored. He reigned over the commune with undisciplined emotion and lust, using violence to enforce conformity. Members were stripped of their passports and possessions and were assigned onerous jobs. Cultists had little freedom.

Jones ordered his followers to call him "Dad." An old associate commented, "Jim stopped calling himself the reincarnation of Jesus and started calling himself God."

Let us remember the words of Jesus: "Beware of false prophets, who come to you in sheep's clothing but inwardly are ravenous wolves. You will know them by their fruits" (Matthew 7:15-16a).

Killing Fields

United States Ambassador to the United Nations Madeleine Albright appeared stunned as she walked carefully around the edge of a dirt field near the town of Zvornik in Bosnian Serb-controlled territory in March of 1996. Beneath her feet lay pieces of bone, scraps of clothing, and decomposed body parts—evidence of a mass grave holding as many as one thousand Muslims massacred by Serb fighters in July of 1995.

"I'm so overwhelmed by the horror of this," she commented, "and that it's possible for people to behave this way toward fellow human beings."

Later in Sarajevo, Albright condemned residents and passersby who looked the other way. Because the site of the mass grave is only a few hundred yards from a highway as well as homes, people must have heard what was happening. "I find it very difficult to deal with the fact that scores of people must have known what was going on," Albright concluded.

Heroes

A Pillar of Fire

Eighteen-year-old Noa Ben-Artzi, granddaughter of the late prime minister of Israel, Yitzhak Rabin, spoke beautiful and bonding words at the November 1995 memorial service for the assassinated leader, "Grandfather, you were a pillar of fire . . . in front of the camp . . . you were our hero."

Everyday Heroes

From my huddle of everyday heroes, I select three.

Ed has been in a wheelchair for forty years, a victim of polio. He was stricken just months before Dr. Jonas Salk developed the highly successful vaccine. Ed is not bitter; he does not blame God or anyone for his condition. He goes to his office in a special van. He is a gracious gentleman—a joy to be around. Ed is the most courageous person I know!

You would never guess that the slender lady in floppy, ill-fitting clothes and a crazy-looking hat was a retired college professor with a Ph.D. But when you get within smiling distance, you realize you are in the presence of a remarkable person: bright, caring, and committed; a practitioner of her faith. Although never married, she is in love with her large family, her church, and the community. Wherever there is need, sorrow, or joy, Dorothy is there with the appropriate response. She is the "Mother Teresa" of Ashland, Virginia.

Carl's father was a coal miner. He did not have an opportunity to attend college, but he and his wife saw to it that all three of their children did! After a hitch in the Navy, Carl spent years working at a frozen food distribution center in our nation's capital. His wife is dead, and he now lives alone. He is active in his church. His children are a source of pride and joy. And why not? The daughter is a college and seminary graduate and pastor of a church. Both of his sons have master's degrees and are certified public accountants. What a family!

"The Advantage of Disadvantage"

In his autobiography, *Up From Slavery*, noted educator Booker T. Washington spoke of "the advantage of disadvantage." He shares the exciting story of his pilgrimage from slavery to education and freedom. Young Washington was allowed to carry his White master's books to the school door, but he was not allowed to enter.

After the Civil War, the young man migrated with his family to Malden, West Virginia, where he worked in the mines and as a house servant. Encouraged in his thirst for knowledge by his new employer, in 1872 he set out on foot from Malden to Hampton, Virginia—approximately five hundred miles—to attend school. He arrived at Hampton Institute with nothing more than a tremendous desire for an education and a willingness to work hard.

Out of his disadvantage came a consuming devotion to his race, and ultimately to the founding of Tuskegee Institute in Macon County, Alabama, in 1881.

Harvard conferred an honorary master's degree on him in 1896, and Dartmouth an LL.D. in 1901.

"Honest Abe"

He was born February 12, 1809, in a Kentucky log cabin. His parents were poor, honest, and devoutly religious. They lived enduring ideals of truth and honesty, and taught them to their son.

As a young man, he worked as a clerk in a general store near Salem, Illinois. One day, he inadvertently overcharged a woman six and one-quarter cents. After closing for the day, this conscientious clerk took the lady her change; a round-trip of several miles on foot.

On another occasion, when there were more customers in the store than usual, the young man gave short weight to a customer. Upon discovering the error, at first opportunity the merchant tied up the four ounces of tea due the shopper and walked a great distance to deliver it.

The man, of course, was Abraham Lincoln, and he carried this same sensitivity into his law practice, politics, and ultimately the presidency of the United States. His character was so impeccable that he truly earned the nickname "Honest Abe."

Persistence Pays Off

The first time Douglas MacArthur applied for admission to West Point, he failed to gain acceptance. Indeed, he was denied entrance a second time. Persistent young MacArthur applied a third time, was accepted, and history has framed his portrait.

High Purpose

In 1961, President John F. Kennedy declared that Americans had the ability and the resources to land a man safely on the moon by the end of the decade, then return him safely to earth. After a number of limited but ever-expanding experiments, Neil Armstrong, Edwin E. "Buzz" Aldrin Jr., and Michael Collins (the crew of the Apollo 11 Mission) answered the president's challenge. The first lunar landing was achieved on July 20, 1969.

At the end of a three-day space journey, the astronauts arrived at a lifeless world and fired their engine to ease them into lunar orbit. As they began their long-anticipated descent, they noticed *Eagle*'s computer was malfunctioning. Mission Control advised them "to keep going." When only one thousand feet above the moon, sur-rounded by boulders the size of small automobiles and with fuel dwindling, the moment of truth had arrived! Could these highly skilled pilots cope with this sudden crisis? Their academic acumen and endless training prepared them for this defining moment. Neil Armstrong took over the semi-manual control and steered *Eagle* to a safe touchdown with only twenty seconds of fuel left!

Inside *Eagle*, Armstrong and Aldrin looked at each other, grinned, and without speaking a word, shook hands—a gesture that spoke volumes! They had beaten the odds. At the beginning of the space program, the projected chance of success for a moon mission was 3 percent; at the time of the Apollo flight, it was 60 percent. But the crew of Armstrong, Aldrin, and Collins scored it at 100 percent.

During the celebrations of our twenty-fifth anniversary of space exploration, Buzz Aldrin appeared on the television show *Larry King Live*. One could still feel the strength of this splendid physical person who earned a Ph.D. from M.I.T. Toward the end of the interview, Larry King asked his guest if he had any counsel or wisdom to pass along to aspirants in any field. "Find high purpose," Aldrin said, "and bring to it commitment and courage."

Redefining Heroes

What's happening to our sports heroes? Like a row of dominoes, one after another tumbles: Pete Rose, Mike Tyson, Tonya Harding, Jennifer Capriati, and O. J. Simpson. Hollywood's finest writers could not equal the Simpson script; the compelling, bizarre drama surrounding the white Ford Bronco streaking along the Los Angeles freeways. News and police helicopters shadowed the fugitive from above, while a phalanx of patrol cars maintained a steady rearguard watch. Clusters of well-wishers cheered Simpson from select vantage points along the way. It was an incredible demonstration of fanaticism, curiosity, and loyalty.

Los Angeles District Attorney Gil Garcetti was not the only one who referred to Mr. Simpson as "an American hero." Yet he is not an American hero. He is a football hero!

Among other things, the Simpson event should motivate us to redefine and rediscover authentic heroes: unsung persons struggling to maintain credibility; individuals actualizing character and faith.

Flawless Mission

On June 2, 1995, Captain Scott O'Grady's Air Force F-16 fighter plane was shot down behind enemy lines in Bosnia, but he parachuted to earth. For six miserable days, he lived on whatever the unrelenting terrain provided. "I was," he said, "a scared little bunny rabbit just trying to hide, trying to survive."

Pilot O'Grady relied on his survival training to avoid capture. His conduct was exemplary.

Following positive identification of O'Grady's distress call, "Basher 52," by Captain T. O. Hanford of the 510 Squadron, communications between those in charge of *U.S.S. Kearsarge* and the bases at Aviano, Italy, and Washington D.C., were intensified. Within hours a carefully planned rescue mission was in place.

Approximately forty warplanes were involved, including two Sea Stallions ($26 million apiece), two AH-1W Sea-Cobra gunships ($12.5 million each), and four AV-8B Sea Harriers ($24 million apiece). High above those planes were AWACs ($250 million apiece) directing traffic. All of this sophisticated, powerful, expensive machinery and some two hundred men were deployed to rescue one man! The United States was a proud nation when success was achieved; its flag flew a little higher.

Declining to accept celebrity status, Captain O'Grady said the real heroes were the Marines who risked their lives to save him.

Make Sure You're Worth It!

A vacationer walking along the beach noticed that a young swimmer was in serious difficulty. Risking his life, the stranger swam through a treacherous riptide to rescue the youngster.

Afterward, the lad said to the courageous person, "Thanks for saving my life."

Looking him in the eye, the man replied, "That's okay, kid, just make sure your life was worth saving."

History

The Light of Truth

The early Roman statesman, Marcus Tullius Cicero, said, "History indeed is the witness of the times, the light of truth."

The Essence of History

The nineteenth-century Scottish essayist and historian, Thomas Carlyle, said, "History is the essence of innumerable biographies."

Too Small for the Part

Edith Hamilton, in her book, *The Great Way*, wrote on the decline of influence, "The Athenian people were led by men too small for the part to which they aspired."

For the Love of History

Don't try to convince Doris Kearns Goodwin, the 1995 Pulitzer Prize winner for her book *No Ordinary Time: Franklin and Eleanor Roosevelt—The Homefront in World War II*, that there is no connection between history and baseball. She began a public lecture with the following anecdote:

"I date my love of history to the time when I was 7 years old and my father brought me home this beautiful red scorebook and taught me how to keep score of the Brooklyn Dodgers games (which were on the radio) while he was at work during

135

the day. When he would come home at the end of the day we would sit on the porch and go over—detail by detail, inning by inning, play by play—everything that happened in the game that day.

"So when you're 7 years old and the most important person in your life thinks you're doing okay as a historian, it's a great impetus to do something similar later in life. He made it even more magical by not telling me that it was described in the newspaper the next day. So I thought that without me he'd never know what happened to the Brooklyn Dodgers."

History As Soap Opera

The distinguished British Christian scholar, Malcolm Muggeridge, speaks of the endless procession of celebrities in *A Twentieth Century Testimony*. They are accounted for and their images preserved in wax in revered places. Kings and queens, presidents and politicians, soldiers and sailors—"their names written on water, or, in what amounts to the same thing in contemporary terms, written on a television screen, all stars in an interminable soap opera called history."

In Spite of Ourselves

When slavery was a distressing and divisive issue in our country, President Abraham Lincoln said in his message to Congress, December 1, 1862, "Fellow citizens, we cannot escape history. We of this Congress and this administration will be remembered in spite of ourselves."

United States of Amnesia

Memories are like items in a garage sale: what is one person's trash is another person's treasure. But when celluloid memories involve the White House, the difference between trash and treasure is usu-ally left to the critics.

For example, debate over the movie *Nixon,* directed by Oliver Stone, began long before the film opened on December 20, 1995. Although Stone defended his work as "a Nixon"—not "*the* Nixon" or even "the definitive Nixon"—that was not a sufficient disclaimer for many authorities on the former president.

Stephen E. Ambrose, a respected Nixon biographer, claimed that "the past is there to be raped, and Hollywood has been doing it." After reading the film script, he declared it riddled with inaccuracies.

Mark C. Carnes, chair of the Barnard College history department and editor of the book, *Past Imperfect: History According to the Movies,* identified an even greater concern. "If Stone's purpose is to get Americans to rethink the past by putting out provocative myths," Carnes said, "one of the problems is that in these United States of Amnesia, many Americans haven't thought about the past the first time."

He then concluded, "Right or wrong, *Nixon* is going to stimulate discussion of our past, and that in itself is a good thing. This republic has never been harmed by too much talk on historical issues."

History As Weapon

The study of history is not just an academic exercise. Rather, history functions for a people much like memory does for an indi-vidual. Deprive a person of memory and that individual becomes disoriented, not knowing where she has been or where she is going. Deprive a nation of history—its collective memory—and that coun-try becomes disabled, not knowing its past or future.

As the constitutive element of a nation's identity and destiny, history is, according to Arthur Schlesinger Jr., "a means of shaping history." Because perceptions of the past influence the present as well as the future, history must be subject to constant and critical analysis. Without dialogue and dissent, history runs the danger of becoming a weapon of domination. The party slogan in George Orwell's *1984* conveys this truth: "Who controls the past controls the future. Who controls the present controls the past."

Who Will Write It?

Sir Winston Churchill is reported to have said that history would be kind to him because he was going to write it!

Understanding Backward

Søren Kierkegaard, nineteenth-century Danish philosopher, remarked that "we live life forward by understanding it backward."

Hope

A Prisoner of Hope

In an interview with *Christianity Today* (October 5, 1992), Desmond Tutu, 1986 Nobel Peace prize laureate and Anglican archbishop of Cape Town, South Africa, was asked if he was hopeful about the future.

"I am always hopeful," he replied. "A Christian is a prisoner of hope. What could have looked more hopeless than Good Friday? . . . There is no situation from which God cannot extract good. Evil, death, oppression, injustice—these can never again have the last word, despite all appearances to the contrary."

We Haven't Been to Bat

In *A Second Helping of Chicken Soup for the Soul*, Jack Canfield shares a story about the time he stopped in at a Little League baseball game on his way home from work. As he sat near the first base line, he asked the boys the score.

"We're behind fourteen to nothing," replied one youngster.

Canfield continued, "You don't look very discouraged."

"Why should we be discouraged? We haven't been up to bat yet."

One Hundred Days of Hope—and More

On April 19, 1995, the bombing of the Alfred P. Murrah Federal Building in Oklahoma City killed 168 people, including 19 children. Only six youngsters survived. Two of those survivors were the children of Jim and Claudia Denny: three-year-old Brandon and two-year-old Rebecca.

When Jim Denny first arrived at the Murrah building, he did not think any children in the day care center on the second floor could have possibly survived the blast. "I didn't think we had any children left," he said. "So from there, it has all been a plus."

Although Rebecca went home after ten days in the hospital, her brother was less fortunate. Brandon was so severely injured that his father recognized him only by a birthmark on his thigh. Debris from the bomb blast embedded in his head with such force that chips of Brandon's skull were crushed into the left side of his brain. He spent forty-four days in intensive care at Presbyterian Hospital in Oklahoma City and fifty-five days at Baylor University Medical Center's Pediatric Center for Restorative Care in Dallas, Texas. After four operations and intense physical therapy, Brandon could sit up and stand, and take a few steps. One hundred days after the bombing, Brandon went home.

Although doctors are reluctant to predict how much improvement he will make or if he will ever be able to talk or walk on his own, his father made his own prognosis: "If he doesn't get better we'll be happy, but he will get better. Where there's life, there's hope."

I Have Hope

After a three-month layoff due to pancreatic cancer, the late Cardinal Joseph Bernardin of Chicago returned to work and was subsequently interviewed by the *Chicago Sun-Times* in September of 1995. In response to a question as to whether he had any fears in light of his confidence that there is a heaven, he replied, "That's why ultimately I have hope. But you can't shed completely your emotions as a human being. There's no contradiction of having fear or being emotionally distraught at times and at the same time being a person of faith. I know we're on the road to something better. But to say that you have no fear, no anxiety, I think that would be somewhat abnormal."

Living Among the Stars

The first Black female American astronaut, Mae Jemison, M.D., was one of only fifteen persons selected from two thousand applicants to enter the space program. When asked what motivated her to train for travel in space, she replied, "The stars!"

From childhood, she was fascinated by the stars and wanted to live closer to them.

Hope Enough

The statistics are sobering at best and downright terrifying at worst. Over forty thousand Americans are killed each year by gun violence. And for every fatality there are three nonfatal shootings. Politicians almost literally trip over themselves as they rush to introduce tougher and tougher crime legislation.

But columnist William Raspberry of *The Washington Post* is not convinced that you can coerce people into decent behavior. "We keep imagining," he writes, "that the problem is that young people aren't frightened enough, so we keep toughening criminal sanctions to the point where our national incarceration rate is the highest in the Western world. The real problem is that our young people aren't hopeful enough."

Pursue Your Dream

Early in the nineteenth century, a young man in London aspired to become an author. Although he was obsessed with writing, his life was hard. His father spent time in jail because of his inability or unwillingness to pay his debts. The lad finished only four years of schooling. He worked at menial jobs and slept in a dreary, rat-infested attic while pursuing his dream. Story after story was rejected. The aspirant became so discouraged and embarrassed that he would sneak out at night to mail manuscripts.

Finally the day arrived when one of his pieces was accepted. Although he was not paid for the story, his confidence soared: An

141

editor had recognized his talent! From this unlikely background emerged one of England's greatest novelists, Charles Dickens.

Appreciating Life

The popular actress Mary Tyler Moore is admired not only for her professional accomplishments, but also for the way she has coped with a series of personal tragedies. Her sister died in 1978. A year later she lost her only son, Richard, at age twenty-four. Then, her brother succumbed to kidney cancer. This was followed by the death of her mother.

As if these traumatic experiences were not enough to defeat anyone, Mary Tyler Moore has battled diabetes since she was in her twenties.

This courageous survivor says, "The pain is just as intense as it is for someone who gives up and gives in."

Her suffering has made her more sensitive and responsive; more grateful for life. "I appreciate," she continues, "much more the now. I don't take tomorrow for granted, because it simply may not be there."

Hope Is Dangerous

After spending two weeks in the "hole" (solitary confinement) for playing Mozart over the prison public-address system, Andy Dufresne (Tim Robbins), in the movie *The Shawshank Redemption*, returns to the dining hall for his first meal with the other inmates. While describing the beauty of music to his buddies at the table, he launches into a soliloquy on the self.

"Don't forget . . . that there are places in the world not made of stone. Something inside that they can't get to, they can't touch, that's yours."

"What are you talking about?" his best friend Red (Morgan Free-man) asks in bewilderment.

"Hope," replies Andy.

"Hope is a dangerous thing," Red instructs everyone. "It can drive a man insane."

Be Hope

Glide Memorial United Methodist Church is the most comprehensive nonprofit provider of human services in San Francisco. With a $4.3 million annual budget in 1995, this 5,500 member congregation supports 35 outreach programs that serve 3,500 meals a day, educate 226 children, train 1,132 adults in computer technology, see 525 crisis clients weekly, offer job skills workshops to 220 participants, and provide women's health services to 1,500 a month.

How is it possible to sustain this magnitude of ministry without succumbing to burnout? Jan Mirikitani, Glide's executive director, explains, "I really believe the person in line for lunch, who is maybe unpleasant, maybe doesn't smell so good, might be the one to knock on my door and tell me something new, something I didn't know. If you think you can save people, you'll burn out here. What you can do is be there to be the glimmer, the hope."

Humor

Pastoral Call

A pastor went to call on one of the old saints of the church. Her health was deteriorating. She lived frugally and alone. The pastor found her in a shabby reclining chair near the window with a tray of peanuts nearby.

The pastor sat facing her. They reminisced. All the while he was munching on her peanuts. The affectionate and pleasant visit concluded with prayer.

As the pastor stood to leave he realized that he had consumed most of her peanuts and apologized.

Leaning forward and cupping a hand around her ear she asked, "What you say, pastor?"

"I've eaten most of your peanuts."

Whereupon the dear soul replied, "It's all right. Now that I ain't got no teeth no more, all I can do is lick the chocolate off."

Pick Up the Check

Dr. Merton S. Rice was a splendid preacher, gifted writer, popular lecturer, and contagious Christian. He was generous to a fault. It is said that his wife would give him a daily allowance because he would give away whatever money he had in his pocket.

Dr. Edgar DeWitt Jones told me this story concerning his colleague and friend, Merton Rice. Following an overnight train ride, as the pastor walked through the station, he was approached by a panhandler whom Dr. Rice invited for breakfast. The stranger accepted and ordered a huge meal. When it was time to pay the bill, Dr. Rice said, "I'm sorry, but I don't seem to have any money."

"That's okay," replied the stranger, "I'll pay the check."

According to the story, at this point, the famed preacher introduced himself, and among other things said, "I serve one of the largest congregations in the city—Metropolitan Methodist. We'll take a cab out to the church and I'll repay you."

"No," replied the panhandler, "You beat me out of breakfast, but I ain't going to pay for your cab!"

Color of Hair

A neighbor asked a little boy the color of his baby sister's hair. Silence. Then he blurted, "Vanilla!"

Tight

A friend declared that his neighbor was so tight "that he left his wife home when he went on his honeymoon."

Sideways

A large man quipped, "As a young lad in school I was so thin that if I sat sideways in my seat the teacher would mark me absent."

Bible Humor

Question: Who was the most successful doctor in the Bible?
Answer: Job. He had the most patience.
Question: What evidence does the Bible give to show that Adam and Eve were rather noisy?
Answer: They raised Cain.
Question: Who was the best financier in the Bible?
Answer: Noah. He floated stock while the world was in liquidation.
Question: How long did Cain hate his brother?
Answer: As long as he was Abel.

Question: When was medicine first mentioned in the Bible?
Answer: When God gave Moses two tablets.

Student Bloopers

A friend passed along the following "certifiably genuine student bloopers" collected by teachers throughout the United States—from eighth grade through college level.

"The Bible is full of interesting caricatures. In the first book of the Bible, Guinesses, Adam and Eve were created from an apple tree. One of their children, Cain, asked 'Am I my brother's son?' God asked Abraham to sacrifice Isaac on Mount Montezuma. Jacob, son of Isaac, stole his brother's birthmark. Jacob was a patriarch who brought up his twelve sons to be patriarchs, but they did not take to it. One of Jacob's sons, Joseph, gave refuse to the Israelites."

"Pharaoh forced the Hebrew slaves to make bread without straw. Moses led them to the Red Sea, where they made unleavened bread, which is bread made without any ingredients. Afterward, Moses went up on Mount Cyanide to get the ten commandments. David was a Hebrew king skilled at playing the liar. He fought with the Philatelists, a race of people who lived in biblical times. Solomon, one of David's sons, had five hundred wives and five hundred porcupines."

"The Renaissance was an age in which more individuals felt the value of their human being. Martin Luther was nailed to the church door at Wittenberg for selling papal indulgences. He died a horrible death, being excommunicated by a bull. It was the painter Donatello's interest in the female nude that made him the father of the Renaissance. It was an age of great inventions and discoveries. Gutenberg invented the Bible. Sir Walter Raleigh is a historical figure because he invented cigarettes. Another important invention was the circulation of blood. Sir Frances Drake circumcised the world with a one-hundred-foot clipper."

Ecumenical Difference

While living in St. Louis during my primary school years, one of the highlights of the summer was receiving an invitation from our neighbors to join them for a weekend trip to their cottage on a lake in the Ozarks. They were Catholic and we were Protestant, and each excursion was a mini-workshop in ecumenism.

On this particular occasion, Laura, their daughter my age, and I were walking around the lake on the access road. It was hot and humid, and we soon regretted not wearing our bathing suits.

Finally Laura urged, "Let's go swimming."

"But our parents won't let us swim without an adult," I insisted. "And furthermore, I don't want to lose any future invitations to the lake."

"Don't worry," she assured. "We can take our clothes off so they won't get wet and our parents will never know the difference."

After an extended conversation, I consented. We agreed to get undressed behind two separate trees, and then count to ten and run for the water without looking.

As the countdown concluded and we dashed to the shoreline, I could not help but employ my peripheral vision. I was astounded. "Gosh, I didn't know there was that much difference between a Protestant and a Catholic!"

Thin No More

The steeple of First Church dominates the skyline. In fact, the medical helicopter based at the city hospital uses the steeple as a reference point when flying in bad weather. The problem is that the steeple constantly needs painting.

Several years ago the church hired a company of professional painters to paint the steeple. The painters had to use a crane as well as scaffolding to reach the top.

About halfway through the project the foreman realized that he was not going to have enough paint to complete the job, so he thinned the paint and the crew kept working.

With one-quarter of the steeple still unpainted, he noticed that he was still running low, so he again thinned the paint. Before they reached the top of the steeple, he had to thin the paint one more time.

Just as they finished the job and were ready to descend, a huge rain cloud moved over the church and unleashed a downpour, washing all the new paint away. The foreman was distraught.

Then a voice cried out from heaven, "Repaint! Repaint! Go and thin no more!"

God's Scales

A man says to the Lord, "Is it true that in your scale of reckoning a thousand years is like a minute?"

The Lord assures him that it is.

"And is it true that in your weights and measures, a thousand dollars is like a penny?"

Again the Lord assures him that he is right.

The man then says, "Lord, I am a poor man. Give me a penny."

The Lord says, "In a minute" (Richard Deats, *How to Keep Laughing*).

Inspiration

Keep Going!

A fidgety nine-year-old boy sat by his mother at the concert. She brought him to the marquee event in hopes that he would be so inspired by the performance of the great Polish pianist, composer, and statesman Ignacy Paderewski that he would take his piano lessons more seriously.

During the intermission, the lad dashed onto the stage, plumped himself down on the piano bench, and began to play "Chopsticks."

Hearing the piercing notes of an amateur, Paderewski hurried back to his beloved piano to see a youngster at the keyboard. Standing directly behind the lad, he bent forward, placed his arms around the intruder, and played an appropriate accompaniment. All the while the masterful musician was whispering in the child's ear, "Don't quit, don't quit, keep going!"

Not as dramatically, but just as assuredly, the master of our lives, the Lord Jesus Christ, stands by us in our ups and downs with his everlasting arms around us, admonishing us not to quit, to keep going. "I am with you always, to the end of the age" (Matthew 28:20).

A Win for the Old Master

After missing the cut in three of the four previous golf tournaments, no one expected Ben Crenshaw to contend for, let alone win, the coveted green jacket at the 1995 Masters. To complicate matters, on Wednesday, the final tune-up day, Crenshaw left Augusta, Georgia, for Austin, Texas, to serve as a pallbearer at the funeral of his old master teacher and mentor, Harvey Penick, who had put a golf club in Ben's hands when he was only seven.

As the final putt settled into the bottom of the cup, and the unlikely Crenshaw won, he neither raised his arms in triumph nor pumped his fists into the air. Rather, he buried his head in his chest and cried.

When later asked about the emotionally draining week, Crenshaw replied, "I had a fifteenth club in my bag this week. That was Harvey Penick."

Curb Cuts

Children on bicycles, parents pushing baby strollers, and people in wheelchairs use them daily. But most of us do not even know what they are called, let alone who is responsible for them. Those tiny ramps connecting sidewalk and street are called "curb cuts," and thanks to Ed Roberts we all enjoy the convenience.

But for Roberts they were a necessity. After polio left him a quadriplegic at age fourteen—unable to move below the neck except for one finger, and dependent upon an iron lung to breathe—he refused to let his disability stop him. Thanks to a motorized wheelchair with a portable respirator on the back, his dreams became reality.

In 1962, he matriculated at the University of California at Berkeley, slept at night in an iron lung at Cowell Hospital, and endured newspaper headlines like "Helpless Cripple Attends UC Classes." Inspired by Roberts, other severely disabled men and women also enrolled, and soon they comprised the "rolling quads." Ramps replaced the erstwhile physical barriers, a twenty-four-hour emergency wheelchair repair service was started, and personal care attendants were hired. The "demedicalized" approach to keeping people out of institutions was born and now there are three hundred independent living centers modeled after Berkeley across America.

After graduating from Berkeley, Roberts taught political science at his alma mater, ran California's Department of Rehabilitation, married and fathered a son, started an Oakland-based disability think tank, served as president of the World Institute on Disability, and lobbied successfully for the 1990 Americans With

Disabilities Act that requires businesses and governments to make accommodations.

In March of 1995, after forty-two years on a respirator, Ed Roberts died of a heart attack. Virtually every street corner in America testifies to his courage and tenacity with curb cuts.

My Creed

A friend provided the following testimony: "Life is a great gift and I hope to feel at home in God's world; by seeing Him in songs of birds, the perfume of flowers, the colors of the sunset and the goodness of human hearts; by trying to recognize the good intentions of other people and by regarding their time and their conveniences equal to my own; by rejoicing in the happiness that comes to them, as well as that which comes to me; by trusting that whatever happens has meaning and is for the best; that death is not a curse, but a blessing; through all the expressions of life to grow a little more to the stature of one made in the image of God" (Louise Folsom, April 1956).

Character Over Cash

Ryne Sandberg, one of the best second basemen to play the game of baseball, announced his sudden retirement on June 13, 1994. A ten-time All-Star for the Chicago Cubs and the recipient of nine Gold Glove awards, he was in the second year of a four-year, $28 million contract. In a very emotional press conference, he confessed that he had lost "the edge." The thirty-four-year-old legend went on to say, "I didn't have what I felt I needed to go on the field everyday, give my very best and live up to the standards I set for myself."

Sandberg, though a .290 career hitter, was in a 1-for-28 batting slump when he shocked the sporting world with the news that he was hanging up his spikes.

How refreshing, however, in this money-driven world, to encounter a man who is bigger than money, who can walk away from millions with dignity and honor.

To everyone's surprise, Ryne Sandberg returned to the Cubs for the 1996 and 1997 seasons.

A Contrast in Comebacks

Michael Jordan's decision to give up baseball (he batted .202 in minor league play) and return to professional basketball was a marquee event. Rumors of his return electrified the sports world: Writers, announcers, fans, and media had a field day! When the announcement of his return to the Chicago Bulls was confirmed, tickets to his second coming, March 19, 1995, were quickly gobbled up.

When the Bulls took the floor, Jordan was wearing number 45, his high school number, and not the retired 23. This superstar, one of the greatest to play the game, had a mediocre game by past standards: nineteen points, six rebounds, six assists, three turnovers; seven of eighteen from the field. In an interview after the game, the marvelous, but rusty, athlete voiced disappointment. Then he added, "The fans treated me like a god; I'm just a human being."

About the same time, another superstar was quietly struggling to make her comeback. While stepping down from a train, Rachel Barten, a brilliant, twenty-year-old violinist, snagged a strap from her violin case and was dragged a considerable distance by the train before being rescued. Both legs were severely injured. She endured ten operations. With neither marquee announcement nor media hype, she is back! From her wheelchair, this courageous woman is working with gifted young violinists to help them fine-tune their talents.

A contrast in comebacks!

My Symphony

"To live content with small means; to seek elegance rather than luxury, and refinement rather than fashion; to be worthy, not respectable, and wealthy, not rich; to study hard, think quietly, talk frankly; to listen to stars and birds, to babes and sages, with open heart; to bear all cheerfully, do all bravely, await occasion, hurry never; in a word, to let the spiritual, unbidden and unconscious grow up through the common: this is to be my symphony" (William Henry Channing).

Homespun Chicken Soup

When the common cold has you beat, there's no better cure than homemade chicken soup for the body.

When life's common problems have you beat, there's no better cure than homespun *Chicken Soup for the Soul.*

This popular book of 101 stories "to open the heart and rekindle the spirit" has been on *The New York Times* best-seller list for over a year. But the story behind the book is as inspirational as the book itself.

Mark Victor Hansen, a motivational speaker, and Jack Canfield, a friend, envisioned a book of "heartwarming" stories. Canfield meditated an hour a day until a catchy title popped into his head. Then they secured an agent and shopped New York for a publisher.

But more than thirty publishers rejected the book as "too Pollyan-naish." A small Florida firm, Health Communications, took a chance. The rest, as they say, is history.

"It's never fun to be rejected, but when someone says 'No,' we say, 'What next?' " explained Canfield.

In addition to being a top seller, the book also won the coveted ABBY Award for 1995 from the American Booksellers Association as the book members most enjoyed selling.

Readers and booksellers agree: There's no better cure than home-spun chicken soup.

A Test for Life

Four handwritten notebooks by Walt Whitman, which had disap-peared during a move to Ohio for wartime safekeeping in 1942, were recently returned to the Library of Congress. Among one notebook's entries was recorded this "Test of a Poem": "How far it can elevate,

153

enlarge, purify, deepen and make happy the attributes of the body and soul of a man."

What a perfect test for life!

The Legend Continues to Inspire

Knute Rockne was football coach at Notre Dame from 1918 to 1930. His phenomenal record reads: 105 victories, twelve losses, five ties. He possessed the ability to read, develop, and inspire players to perform beyond their natural abilities and expectations. In the Rockne era, football was not a game of brute strength. He taught ingenuity, intelligent teamwork, and execution. The famous "Four Horsemen" of the 1920s averaged only about 160 pounds.

The beloved coach was also known for his fairness, discipline, and loyalty.

In the spring of 1931 Rockne was killed in a plane crash over Kansas. He was en route to California. The nation was in shock. Notre Dame memoralized him in several meaningful ways, including naming the football stadium after him.

In *The Book of Virtues*, William J. Bennett concluded a chapter on loyalty with these words: "Before departing for California, Rock had left a pair of tan, high-topped shoes to be half-soled. No one ever called for those shoes. And nobody in football has ever come close to filling them."

Take Risks

Dr. Ruth Simmons, president of Smith College, is the first African American woman to lead a nationally ranked American college. How does the great-great-granddaughter of slaves and the youngest of twelve children born to Texas sharecroppers ascend to the top of the academic ladder? In one word—risk.

"If you are the kind of person who listens to conservative advice," Simmons advises, "you may do okay in life, but you probably won't ever be a fantastic leader. You have to take risks, and you also have to go against conventional wisdom, because conventional wisdom doesn't make for startling advances in society."

Jesus Christ

Jesus Cannot Be Ignored

Inscribed on a plaque at the Yokefellow Institute in Richmond, Indiana, is this quotation by Elton Trueblood: "Jesus Christ can be accepted; he can be rejected; he cannot reasonably be ignored."

"A Good Word For Jesus Christ"

In the book, *Beside the Bonnie Brier Bush,* there is a chapter entitled "His Mother's Sermon." It is the story of a Scottish lad who gladdened the heart of his saintly mother when he committed himself to the Christian ministry. Although she did not live to hear him preach, she admonished him, when entering the pulpit, to always say "a good word for Jesus Christ."

The young man did well in the university and seminary. At last he had "his own church." His first sermon was only a week away. He worked scrupulously on the message; it was theologically correct and erudite. Toward the end of the week he read his masterpiece to his aunt with whom he lived. She listened patiently and proudly. When asked for her comments, she congratulated him on the beautiful language, but reminded him that the congregation was composed of poor, hardworking, humble souls, who needed comfort and encouragement. She concluded, while gently pressing his hand, "Oh laddie, be sure you say a good word for Jesus Christ."

The Scandal of Particularity

Once upon a time there was a man in Kentucky who got married. He had long been enamored with the idea of marriage, so when he met "the woman of his dreams," he immediately proposed to her. Things went well at first. He told his friends that his new wife was "all I ever hoped for in a woman." She was beautiful, intelligent, and witty. His friends observed that here was "a marriage made in heaven."

Unfortunately, this initial bliss was not to last. Gradually, in day-to-day living, he began to notice certain imperfections in his new wife. She was beautiful, but not always. Sometimes, say, before nine in the morning, she was downright unattractive. She could look stunning for great parties and social occasions, but marriage meant that he had to look at her before she put on her makeup in the morning, and he couldn't help thinking of that more than her beauty.

Slowly, but surely, he found himself growing cool to this woman. Marriage had proved to be different than he had thought. It had been fun to be with her on a Saturday night, to dance with her into the wee hours of the morning. But marriage wasn't like that at all.

Marriage was cold cereal for breakfast, and someone sleeping beside you with large curlers in her hair. It was disagreements over finances, visits from her Texas relatives, and that chicken lamp that she had bought for the living room. That was marriage! Now, don't get me wrong. He still believed in love more than ever. He still longed for the perfect partner. He continued to cling to the idea of marriage.

The idea was great; it was the particular experience of marriage that bothered him!

The man in our story quickly learned the difference between abstraction and particularity.

The man who marries "the woman of his dreams" or the woman who marries "Mister Right"—each will eventually discover that the particular experience of this person is quite different from the ideal.

The story of Jesus is a unique story because it is about a particular person. And it is the particularity of the story that makes it so striking, as well as so scandalous. As we read the Gospels, we can almost taste the dust along the roads, smell the shepherds, and hear the crowds as they gather around Jesus. We read about mustard seeds and lost coins, wretched lepers and prodigal sons. We read about the crucified messiah. This is the scandal of particularity.

In Miniature

When Leo Tolstoy heard of Abraham Lincoln's death, the great novelist remarked, "He was a Christ in miniature."

Should not this be the intention of every believer?

The Lord Was at the Bank

Arriving home from a surgical stay at the hospital, I called my banker to thank him for his concern and support. After a few pleasantries, and knowing that my wife was in a nursing home, Jim asked, "Is there anything I can help you with?"

"No," I replied, "unless you know where we can find some good, part-time help."

"As a matter of fact," he added, "we have a lady who has been a caregiver to a ninety-year-old couple for several years. They are now deceased and her contract expires this Friday. I'll give you her name and number."

I called the woman and explained our situation. Without asking about schedule or compensation, she said, "I'll help you . . . we can talk details later." She started the following Monday.

This is more than a case of unbelievable timing. This is more than just coincidence. This is a case of the Lord at work at the bank.

A Poem: The Connection

> Jesus understood
> The loving reach of God
> The longing reach of men
> In his life, in his death
> He joined their hands together.
> (Anonymous)

Jesus Walked

A father informed his son before he departed for his first year of college that if he did well and lived up to his father's standards, he would buy him a car that summer.

At the end of the first semester his son came home not just with good grades but also with long hair and a beard. The father was distraught. He reminded his son of their agreement, but he also assured his son that if he kept the beard and long hair he would never get the car.

After their talk, the father was confident that his son would shave and get a haircut.

When summer arrived and the son returned home for the second time, the beard and long hair were even more conspicuous.

Incensed, the father asked him why he had not shaved.

The son replied, "Dad, while I was in college I learned about a man whom you greatly respect and admire, even love . . . his name was Jesus. And he had long hair and a beard."

"Yes, he did," responded the father, "and he *walked* everywhere he went."

Lost Voice to Jesus

When my wife had laryngitis, our three-year-old daughter was distressed about Mommy's voice, or lack of voice. My wife tried to comfort our child by saying that Mommy had just temporarily lost her voice and it would come back.

As only a child can do, our daughter inquired, "Where did your voice go?"

When her mother replied that it had not really gone anywhere, that explanation proved unsatisfactory.

"But you said you had lost it," insisted our daughter.

How do you explain a figure of speech to a small child?

My wife tried another approach. "It's still inside me, but there are some germs that are keeping it from coming out."

Not any more convinced by this explication, our daughter provided her own interpretation. "Your voice has gone to Jesus because he loves you and he'll take care of it and make it better."

Looking for Jesus

Christmas should be a centering moment. It should turn us around and send us away with renewed spirits because we have found Jesus.

The Federico Fellini film, *La Dolce Vita*, opens with a helicopter slowly flying through the sky bearing beneath it in a strange contraption a life-size statue of a man dressed in a robe, his arms outstretched. The chopper flies over workers, beaches, and swimming pools. A man shouts, "Hey, it's Jesus!" Some run, some weep.

The helicopter makes its way to St. Peter's Square. Cameras focus on the bearded face of Christ. On the screen the face is drawn closer and closer, just a face in the sky with outstretched arms! Then there is silence, searching silence, a centering moment.

Perhaps this is the way Christian faith operates. There are moments of tremendous import and personal appeal, moments when we see the face in the sky, his spirit in others—and we are never again the same.

"Go and search diligently for the child" (Matthew 2:8).

Perennial Thanksgiving

Thanksgiving is a reply to God. Although the day is uniquely associated with the heroic efforts of the Pilgrims and it is a distinctly American holiday, deeper than the colorful pageantry of the harvest, thanksgiving is a perennial condition of the heart. Thus it affords opportunity to inventory ourselves, to enumerate and register our blessings.

Paul expressed the gratitude of Christians in this wonderful sentence: "Rejoice always, pray without ceasing, give thanks in all circumstances; for this is the will of God in Christ Jesus for you" (1 Thessalonians 5:16-18).

Lord's Supper and Baptism

Gates of Heaven

Because Christ is the host at the Lord's Supper, the table is bigger than any one person or any one church. No one has a right to judge a participant and thereby exclude someone from partaking. One believer has declared, "The Lord's Table is as wide as the gates of heaven!"

Companions at the Table

At the table of our Lord we become what we eat. By sharing the bread of Christ, we become the "body of Christ." By partaking of the one eucharistic loaf, Christians become companions with Christ and one another. The Latin derivation of "companion," *companis* (*com* = with and *panis* = bread), literally means "breaking bread together" or "people who break bread together."

"The bread that we break, is it not a sharing in the body of Christ? Because there is one bread, we who are many are one body, for we all partake of the one bread" (1 Corinthians 10:16*b*-17).

Lean on the Church

At a seminary luncheon for field education supervisors, a pastor told a story about a widow who came to worship the Sunday after her husband's funeral. As the people came forward to receive communion, one of the celebrants noticed that the woman did not have enough strength to break off a piece of bread and dip it in the chalice. The pastor approached her, leaned forward, and literally held her, forehead to forehead. There they stood, supporting each other with the broken body and spilled blood of Christ between them.

This is a "flesh and blood" portrait of what the community of faith is called to be. In these troubled times, lean on the church and let the grace of God support you.

The Inclusiveness of Christ's Church

In *People of the Chalice* Colbert S. Cartwright relates an experience from his pastorate in racially torn Little Rock, Arkansas. One Sunday a Black family visited the all-White church for worship. There were no visible repercussions until the time for communion. As one deacon realized that he was assigned to serve the pew where the Black family sat, "he placed his trays back on the table, turned, walked up the aisle and out the door."

"In an instant," Cartwright recounts, "another member of the congregation stepped forward to take the deacon's place and the service continued. That was a test of the congregation's catholicity. To have done otherwise would have violated the inclusiveness of Christ's church."

Hi Jesus!

A United Methodist bishop tells about the time his five-year-old granddaughter stepped forward to receive communion. When asked why she went to the Lord's Table, she replied, "To say hi to Jesus!"

The Ethiopian Eunuch

Because the New Testament provides few narratives of early church initiatory practices, the infrequent examples are very influential in shaping the baptismal rite. The most detailed account is

Philip's baptism of the Ethiopian eunuch, found in Acts 8:35-38. (Verse 37 is absent in some texts and is, therefore, set in brackets.) The pericope begins with a form of catechesis or instruction, moves to a profession of faith by the eunuch, and concludes with them going down "into" *(eis)* the water where the eunuch is baptized.

> Then Philip began to speak, and starting with this scripture, he proclaimed to him the good news about Jesus. As they were going along the road, they came to some water; and the eunuch said, "Look, here is water! What is to prevent me from being baptized?" [And Philip said, "If you believe with all your heart, you may." And he replied, "I believe that Jesus Christ is the Son of God."] He commanded the chariot to stop, and both of them, Philip and the eunuch, went down into the water, and Philip baptized him.

"Reborn, Good as New, All Over Again"

On September 11, 1995, eighteen-year-old Michelle Carew, youngest daughter of Rod Carew, one of baseball's greatest hitters, entered the hospital after collapsing while doing homework on her personal computer. She was diagnosed with acute nonlymphocytic leukemia. Only a bone marrow transplant would save her life. However, Michelle's genetic background—Rod is Black with West Indian and Panamanian roots, while Marilynn, her mother, is White and of Russian-Jewish descent—made a donor match, according to doctors, as unlikely as "finding a needle in a haystack."

Out of desperation, the Carews agreed to a new procedure—an umbilical cord blood transplant. On March 22, 1996, the family gathered around Michelle's hospital bed to watch the new blood cells trickle from an IV tube into her arm. "I had the exact same sensation then as when I saw her in the delivery room for the first time," said Rod Carew. "As I watched those new blood cells going into her, I kept thinking, Maybe I'm watching my daughter being reborn. Maybe today's the day she'll be reborn, good as new, all over again."

Michelle Carew died on April 17, 1996.

My Baptism

During the annual revival at our country church, I accepted Christ as Lord and Savior and was baptized at the age of twelve.

Our white-frame church building, nestled in the woods, offered few amenities; certainly not an indoor baptistery. Because our denomination practices immersion, we used a nearby creek.

At the appointed hour, on a warm Sunday afternoon, the congregation gathered at the creek to worship and enact the ancient rite of Christian initiation. Untrained voices praised the Lord in song. Our saintly pastor read Scripture and prayed. Then he walked into the water about waist deep, stuck a marker, and the solemn ceremony began.

When I entered the water, our pastor met me and whispered procedural instructions. Clasping my left wrist with his left hand and raising his right hand skyward, he said with great dignity, "Upon your profession of faith in Christ, I baptize you—George Curtis Jones—in the name of the Father, the Son, and the Holy Spirit. Amen." Then I was quietly immersed.

Afterward, while walking through a cornfield to a neighbor's barn to change clothes, I was uniquely aware of God's presence in my life. The spirit of the Lord was upon me. Although I had been submerged in discolored creek water, I arose clean and committed.

Put It Back Together

After the April 19, 1995, terror bombing of the Alfred P. Murrah Federal Building in Oklahoma City, in which 168 people were killed and more than 400 injured, five-year-old Peder Davis had this to say to the people responsible for the attack, "You put it back together. . . . You redo those people."

The Lord's Supper offers an eschatological glimpse of our sinful world put back together by God. At the table, God's vision for the healing of the world breaks into the present.

In Jerusalem

Our delegation celebrated Holy Communion in Jerusalem near "Gordon's Calvary." The international congregation stood beneath an azure sky in reflective gratitude. Following Scripture, hymns, and homily, worshipers came forward in single file to receive the Lord's Supper. Some stood before a large rock, used as a table for the sacraments, while others knelt on a flat stone. It was a spirit-filled experience.

A decade later, following worship at Union Avenue Christian Church in St. Louis, during the fellowship hour, a stranger sought me out and said, "You don't remember me, but I remember you . . . you served me communion in Jerusalem."

We were all served communion in Jerusalem.

Love

The Hardest to Learn

William Penn remarked, "Love is the hardest lesson of Christianity, but for that reason, it should be the most we care to learn."

Words of Love

At the funeral of Prime Minister Yitzhak Rabin of Israel on November 6, 1995, the personal pain of the family momentarily eclipsed the national tragedy when his granddaughter, seventeen-year-old Noa Ben-Artzi, spoke: "People greater than I have already eulogized you, but none of them was fortunate like myself to feel the caress of your warm, soft hands and the warm embrace that was just for us."

I Love You, Not the Car!

This story was originally told by Paul Harvey. A woman was driving her new automobile when she barely scratched another vehicle. Damage was minimal. However, the sympathetic man in the marked car expressed the necessity of exchanging pertinent information. The embarrassed woman was extremely nervous. As she rummaged through her handbag for legal documentation, a note fell out. It was from her husband: "It's you I love, not the car!"

Where Love Meets

David L. McKenna, retired president of Asbury Theological Seminary, told the following story in a sermon:

"Jewish people, it is said, have a story to answer every question that a child might ask. My favorite is the story that is told in answer to the child's question, 'Why did God choose to build his Temple where he did?'

"Two brothers in Jerusalem shared ownership of a mill for grinding grain. One brother was a bachelor, the other was married with three children. At the end of each day, they took the grain they had milled and divided it equally into separate sacks.

"One night the bachelor brother thought, 'This is not right. I am alone and don't need much but my brother has a wife and family. He deserves the larger share.' So, sneaking back to the mill each night, he took part of his share and poured it into his brother's sack.

"The married brother also thought one night, 'This is not right. When I am old, I will have children to support me, but my brother will be all alone. He deserves the larger share.' So, sneaking back to the mill each night, he took part of his share and poured it into his brother's sack. They thought it a miracle to find their sacks refilled each morning.

"One night, however, the brothers left home at the same time to sneak back to the mill, and by coincidence met on the streets with their sacks in hand. Instantly, they knew what was happening and fell into each other's arms weeping. God looked down upon the scene and said, 'Here is where love meets. Here I will build my Temple.' "

From Toughness to Tenderness

Behind the tough talk and demanding exterior of Knute Rockne, football's greatest coach, lived a caring and compassionate man. During his coaching career at Notre Dame, he learned that the mother of one of his players had a terminal illness. Eventually she died with cancer. When her safe-deposit box was opened, letters of encouragement and comfort from Mr. Rockne were found. He had written to her over an extended period of time.

Lost and Found in Love

An unforgettable experience of my life was being a houseguest for a week in the home of the former prime minister of Rhodesia, Garfield Todd, in 1961. This man of marvelous bearing, mental superiority, and spiritual sensitivity served as a Christian missionary for more than twenty years. Then he went into politics, believing that he could accomplish more for native Africans in this role. He was so successful that the White people did not send him back to office.

Among the many episodes shared with me, this phenomenal man recalled the most frightening experience of his life—that of being lost in the jungle and walking alone all night. It was just after World War II and fencing wire was scarce. He had heard of used wire for sale at a distant ranch and went to examine it. He arrived late in the afternoon, found the wire fence and started following it, examining its condition and estimating the cost of removing it, prior to submitting a bid.

The time was later than he realized and almost suddenly he was enveloped in darkness. In following the circuitous path of the fence, he lost his sense of direction. Although he walked and walked, he had only moved deeper and deeper into the jungle. To survive, he realized that he had to follow the fence and keep walking, for he could hear animals pursuing him. He also reasoned that at some point the fence would probably reach a clearing and there perhaps he could gain his bearings. Furthermore, if he could find a road in the clearing, he would be rescued by his wife who he knew would be circling the jungle in her car.

After the most horrendous night imaginable, at about dawn he stumbled into a clearing, then to a road. Shortly thereafter he saw lights from a car and his wife Grace appeared. Garfield Todd, exhausted, half-frozen, clothes in tatters, body bleeding, dropped at her feet. There was tender rejoicing.

Love had persisted all night. While love was trying to find its way out of darkness; love was also diligently searching for the one in darkness. Both were lost, and found, in love!

Love and Longevity

In an age of casual commitments, Evelyn and Arlie Thornton are a delightful exception. On July 25, 1995, they celebrated their seven-tieth wedding anniversary—a real testimony to enduring love and modern medicine.

When asked about their remarkable feat of love and longevity, Mr. Thornton readily admitted that he has been a terrible test for his wife all these years. "She's going to heaven for sure," he said.

Yet Mrs. Thornton did not have an unkind word to say about her husband. In fact, when asked what made Arlie so attractive as a young man, she replied with an embarrassing laugh, "He had a car and the rest (of the boys) didn't."

For the record, he was eighteen, she was fifteen, and the automo-bile was a 1923 Model T Ford touring car.

Lingering Love

In *Parade Magazine* (July 2, 1995), managing editor Larry Smith shares a visit he had with Gregorio Fuentes, ninety-six, in Cojimar, Cuba. The old fisherman had been Ernest Hemingway's friend and boat captain for thirty years. He recalled the day, when motoring along Cuba's north coast, they encountered an old man and a boy in a skiff about two miles from shore. The two had hooked a mighty marlin, and Hemingway offered assistance. It was refused. Regard-less, they gave the struggling fishermen some Cokes and candy bars.

Hemingway positioned his boat, the *Pilar*, a distance away and observed for three hours the battle with the great fish. This experi-ence inspired Hemingway to write *The Old Man and the Sea.*

The *Pilar*, now the property of Fuentes, is tied up near the author's house at Finca Vigia, east of Havana. The old captain has never considered selling the thirty-eight-foot boat, and he has never used it since Hemingway's death.

Gregorio so reveres the memory of the renowned novelist that he punches visitors who accuse Hemingway of being "a drunkard and womanizer." When Larry Smith asked Gregorio Fuentes why he decks people who speak disparagingly of Hemingway, he said, "Because he had a good heart. I loved him like a brother."

"A Supreme Virtue"

The late Conrad N. Hilton referred to himself as "an innkeeper." Recipients of his philanthropy knew him as a good Samaritan.

Born in an adobe house in San Antonio, Conrad Hilton, one of seven children, learned many skills while working in the family store, and eventually became an international business leader and statesman.

This excerpt from his will, published in the *Mayo Magazine* (Fall/Winter 1995), speaks volumes: "There is a natural law, a divine law, that obliges you and me to relieve the suffering, the distressed and the destitute. Charity is a supreme virtue, and the greatest channel through which the mercy of God is passed on to mankind."

Fall in Love Again

After 1,940 days as a Middle East hostage, British journalist John McCarthy, 34, was freed in August 1991 by the Islamic Jihad. In a subsequent BBC interview, he was reported to have said, "It is wonderful to fall in love again with the woman you already love."

Money

Money Mad

In *The Rockefeller Billions,* author Jules Abels quotes Mark Hanna's description of the oil magnate, John D. Rockefeller: "Mad about money, though sane in everything else."

The Scariest Things

When Michael Jordan retired from professional basketball in September 1993, B. J. Armstrong, Jordan's closest friend on the Chicago Bulls, said he worried for Jordan because he would now have "the two scariest things in life: a lot of money and a lot of free time" (quoted by Phil Jackson in *Sacred Hoops*).

Full Circle

According to *U.S. News & World Report* (August 14, 1995), back in 1954 when the growing Walt Disney Company was searching for money to build Disneyland, ABC was approached to make a $500,000 investment. Now, the former solicitor owns the former solicited.

A Trillion Dollars

Most of us understand the size of a million dollars. We probably know someone who has a million, or we may have that amount ourselves. A million dollars is $1,000 times one thousand.

There are also billionaires in America, like Warren Buffet and Bill Gates. A billion dollars translates into a thousand million.

But it is difficult to conceptualize a trillion dollars. Americans 65 and older are said to be worth, collectively, between 8.5 and 12 trillion dollars. If you decided to give away $8.5 trillion at the rate of $1 million a day, it would take 23,287 years to dispose of it.

Blizzards and Budgets

In January of 1996, while politicians debated how to balance the federal budget, a struggle that resulted in twice shutting down much of the government, Mother Nature further complicated the debate by dumping 24 inches of snow on the nation's capital.

The blizzard of 1996 paralyzed much of the eastern seaboard: Philadelphia received 30.7 inches of snow, New York City had 20.6 inches, and Boston endured 18.2 inches.

It was an expensive storm. Loss of wages and sales, as well as cost of the cleanup were projected to be in the billions of dollars. At least one hundred deaths were attributed to the blizzard.

Budgets seldom have adequate contingencies. Therefore, when the unexpected occurs, it is devastating.

Referring to the snow-in, John Sturdivant of the American Federation of Government Employees quipped, "It's kind of God's revenge on the craziness of Washington."

Never?

In George Burns's book, *Wisdom of the 90s*, the star shares insights learned from show business. He writes, "I've learned never to give away what you can charge for."

Disney Culture

The 1995 acquisition of ABC by the Walt Disney Company for $19 billion shocked the business community and raised some serious concerns. Will Disney have a monopoly on entertainment? Will the illusions of the Magic Kingdom consume personal creativity and production? Will the merger give children even more leverage on their parents' spending habits?

With all deference to the accomplishments and contributions of this global company, one may ask whether its "mainstream mythology" will complicate the work of those who are trying to teach individuals how to cope with real people and with real problems in the real world.

The Britisher Who Broke the Bank

Nicholas William Leeson, financial trader for historic Barings Investment Bank of London, allegedly brought down the 232-year-old institution by himself. With the assistance of highly sophisticated, complicated marketing skills and the ambiguity of dealing in what are known as "derivatives," this twenty-eight-year-old Englishman gambled large sums of money on the ups and downs of the Osaka Stock Market in Japan.

Remember, this was the bank that financed British armies during the Napoleonic Wars of 1796–1815. This was also the bank that underwrote the Louisiana Purchase for the United States. And this was the bank of British royalty. But Barings is now barren! Its losses are currently estimated at $1.5 billion.

The power of a single person!

More Than Money

Toward the end of *The Art of the Deal,* Donald Trump says, "I've spent the first twenty years of my working life building, accumulating, and accomplishing things that many said could not be done. The biggest challenge I see over the next twenty years is to figure out some creative ways to give back some of what I've gotten.

"I don't just mean money, although that's part of it . . . I've never been terribly interested in why people give, because their motivation is rarely what it seems to be, and it's almost never pure altruism. To me . . . doing and giving time is far more valuable than just giving money."

Money Should Be Used

In his autobiography, *As I See It*, J. Paul Getty said he tried to follow the credo of his father, George F. Getty Sr.: "Money should be used, put to work in business enterprises that produced goods and services, provided gainful employment for others and contrib-uted to the progress and welfare of society."

Peace

Give Peace a Chance

On May 14, 1948, the state of Israel was established. The very next day it went to war with its Arab neighbors. Four wars and forty-five years later, on September 13, 1993, two bitter and long-standing enemies, Israeli Prime Minister Yitzhak Rabin and PLO Chairman Yasir Arafat, signed a peace accord on the White House lawn and initiated the journey toward nonviolent coexistence.

However, peace comes slowly and painfully to this volatile region. Terrorist attacks by both Islamic and Jewish fundamentalists continue to disrupt the peace process. And then there was the unthinkable: Prime Minister Rabin, the soldier of shalom, was assassinated by an Israeli fanatic on November 4, 1995, while leaving a peace rally in Tel Aviv.

Through it all, the passion for peace persists. "I am not sure if this peace is good or not," commented Nachom Gilboa, an Israeli veteran of all four wars. "But I do know one thing. We tried to win in so many wars and in the end we're at the same place that we started. We have to give this peace a chance. We have no choice."

No More *Bullets*

The word "bullet" has long been associated with speed and power. Superman continues to streak across the cinematic screen "faster than a speeding bullet" and athletic teams proudly wear the name "bullets." But times are changing.

Abe Pollin, owner of the Washington Bullets of the National Basketball Association, returned from the funeral of Yitzhak Rabin, prime minister of Israel, in early November of 1995 and announced, "My friend was shot in the back by bullets. The name *Bullets* for a sports team is no longer appropriate. . . . The Bible says that if you save one life, you save the world. Hopefully, we will save many more than that."

On May 15, 1997, the team name was officially changed to the Washington Wizards.

"A Peep into Hell"

At 8:15 the morning of August 6, 1945, bombardier Tom Ferebee squeezed the trigger that released a fifteen kiloton atomic bomb from the *Enola Gay*, a B-29, over Hiroshima, Japan. The plane accelerated to avoid the heat and smoke from the blast. At the moment they did not know that seventy thousand to one hundred thousand people had been killed; thousands were wounded and left homeless.

From the viewpoint of the tail gunner, Sergeant "Bob" Carson observed, "It's like bubbling molasses down there . . . it's like a peep into hell."

Reaction to the use of "the bomb" was, and continues to be, mixed. The popular view was that it saved lives; it shortened the war.

The Christian Century called the bombing of Hiroshima and Nagasaki, "America's atomic atrocity."

President Harry Truman was in the Atlantic, returning from the Potsdam Conference aboard the U.S.S. *Augusta*, when he received word of the detonation of the bomb. Mr. Truman said, "Captain Graham, this is the greatest thing in history."

Referring to the fiery hell unleashed on Hiroshima, David Lawrence, editor of *U.S. News & World Report* wrote, "Surely we cannot be proud of what we have done. . . ."

James Agee of *Time* said the war "shrank to minor significance" in view of the atomic bomb, which to him was "the second worst thing to happen to the human race. The worst was creation."

Dr. Albert Einstein said it succinctly, "The atomic bomb has changed everything except the nature of man."

Remember the Forgotten War?

On the heels of World War II, weary America was called upon once again to send troops to a distant place. This time to the barren peninsula of Korea. It was referred to as a "police action" under the auspices of the United Nations. It was a costly conflict that lasted thirty-seven months and claimed the lives of some fifty-four thousand Americans.

Joseph L. Calloway of *U.S. News & World Report* (August 7, 1995) made the following statement about the Korean War: "The war that wasn't a war eventually ended in a peace that wasn't a peace—a cease-fire on July 27, 1953." Approximately thirty-seven thousand American soldiers continue to stand vigil over that shaky and dangerous truce.

After forty-five years of anguish, ambiguity, and inaction, Americans came together to honor veterans of the Korean conflict and to unveil a fitting memorial to them in our nation's capital the last week of July 1995. The $18 million memorial was financed by donations.

General William C. Westmoreland, who commanded an airborne brigade in Korea, said it simply: "This is beautiful."

And it is!

Swivel Head

On March 5, 1946, Winston Churchill delivered the now famous "Iron Curtain" speech at Westminster College in Fulton, Missouri.

Basking in the euphoria of postwar peace, America was unreceptive. Columnist Walter Lippmann denounced the speech as an "almost catastrophic blunder." President Harry Truman, who introduced the former British prime minister at Fulton, not only denied that he had seen the speech in advance but also invited Joseph Stalin to Fulton for a response. Stalin declined.

Another example of Churchill's political foresight occurred during an exchange between him and Truman while en route to Fulton by train. Truman called Churchill's attention to the presidential seal on the wall of the train car by explaining that at the end of World War II he had ordered the eagle's head turned to face the olive branch it clutched in one claw and away from the arrows in the other. It is reported that Churchill replied that the eagle's head should be on a swivel.

Peace Among Religions

According to Swiss Catholic theologian Hans Küng, peace among religions is the first step toward peace between nations. Although religion can be used for political purposes, religion can also play a significant part in reducing tensions and avoiding wars. Citing the role of both the South African Council of Churches and the Catholic Church of the Philippines to effect nonviolent radical change, Dr. Küng asserted that "today's priority is to create a new global ethic." A new world order can only be built, he said, "on the basis of a new global ethic, encompassing cultures and religions, and bringing together states and leaders."

On the eve of Passover and Easter in April 1996, twelve patriarchs and church leaders in Jerusalem took a decisive first step toward reconciling religious differences by appealing for an end to violence in the Middle East. All Jewish, Muslim, and Christian people, the religious leaders urged, "should no longer see in the other an enemy but a brother and a sister with whom to build the new society and the new era in the region."

Swords and Silos

Isaiah envisioned the new age of peace as a time when "they shall beat their swords into plowshares" (2:4). Yet swords are now more commonly associated with the movies and the past. From Dr. Strangelove to the Berrigan brothers, missiles are our modern symbol of warfare. So when Vista de la Montana United Methodist Church decided to build their sanctuary on top of what was once an intercontinental ballistic missile (ICBM) silo, church members called it a "symbol of peace on a former symbol of destruction."

When the SALT II treaty was signed with the former Soviet Union in 1979, it required the United States to eliminate the Titan II ICBM system. The location of the church, fifteen miles north of Tucson, Arizona, was one of eighteen abandoned missile locations. Before selling the land at a "good price," the U.S. Air Force destroyed the multistory concrete silos that housed the missiles, filled the cavities with rubble, and smoothed the surface.

Although silos are not exactly plowshares, they can be transformed into a foundation for a positive future.

Frustrated Family

Before leaving Vietnam, General H. Norman Schwarzkopf received a letter from a couple in Iowa whose son, Michael Mullen, had been killed by "friendly fire" while under the general's command.

The Mullens came to see Schwarzkopf while he was in the States. They expressed antigovernment, antiwar feelings. The noted commander reviewed with them the conditions under which Michael had been killed. On the night of February 18, 1970, his unit, C Company, had asked artillery for fire in case the Vietcong were close.

Later it was discovered that the lieutenant at the firing center had miscalculated the trajectories—he had not allowed for hilltop vegetation. The round of fire did not clear the canopy, but hit a tree and exploded. Many were sprayed with shrapnel. Two soldiers were killed; Michael was one of them.

The conference concluded more cordially than it had begun. Mr. Mullen shook hands with the general.

In a subsequent letter to General Schwarzkopf, the Mullens enclosed a half-page advertisement they had placed in *The Des Moines Register*: "A silent message to the mothers and fathers of Iowa. We have been dying for nine, long, miserable years in Vietnam in an undeclared war. . . . How many more lives do you wish to sacrifice because of your silence?"

The ad was paid for with Michael's $2,000 Army death gratuity.

Himself He Could Not Save

The prime minister of Israel, Yitzhak Rabin, was gunned down by a law student, Yigal Amir, on November 4, 1995, at the conclusion of a peace rally in Tel Aviv.

An estimated one hundred thousand people had celebrated peace with the prime minister in Kings of Israel Square. After singing the "Song of Peace," Rabin placed the paper with the lyrics in his coat pocket. The assassin's bullet left the words drenched in blood, and the young nation in shock and grief.

Mr. Rabin, a tough soldier and general, survivor of three wars, became a powerful advocate of peace. In 1994, he shared the Nobel Peace prize with Yasir Arafat.

Peacemakers have never been popular. They seem to arouse suspicion, hatred, and violence. They have always been targets for malcontents.

In his death, Yitzhak Rabin joins a short list of illustrious warriors for freedom and martyrs for peace: Abraham Lincoln, Mahatma Gandhi, John F. Kennedy, Martin Luther King Jr., and Anwar Sadat. These giants could no more save themselves than a Jew who died two thousand years ago at Calvary.

Partnership in Space

On June 29, 1995, 245 miles above the Pacific, the American space shuttle *Atlantis* docked with the Russian space station *Mir*. Commander Robert "Hoot" Gibson had flown such a perfect route that *Atlantis* was only seconds off projected time of arrival and four-tenths of a degree out of alignment. Commander Vladimir Deihurov of *Mir* wore blue, Commander Gibson wore red. They greeted each other with a vigorous handshake.

The two space vehicles were connected for five days during which time the six astronauts and four cosmonauts ate together and worked together on predetermined projects. The camaraderie was beautiful! It was victory day for space technology.

The connected spacecraft were an awesome sight. Together, the 100-ton *Atlantis* and the 123-ton *Mir* reached the height of a 15-story building.

Even more exciting than the visual image is the possibility of an extended period of peaceful and productive relations with Russia. It bodes well for the future.

If the inhabitants of Planet Earth could collectively replicate the sense of courage and commitment demonstrated by the astronauts and cosmonauts on their daring and historic flight, then a new world order would emerge, full of trust and hope.

People

Connected

Speaking to the graduating class of Wellesley College in 1995, Madeleine Korbel Albright, at the time U.S. Ambassador to the United Nations and later U.S. Secretary of State, said, "The greatest lesson of this century is that, what happens to people anywhere should matter to people everywhere."

Be Yourself

When Irving Berlin and George Gershwin first met, Berlin was already famous and Gershwin was a struggling composer, working for $35 a week. Recognizing Gershwin's talent, Berlin offered the aspiring young man a job as his musical secretary at approximately three times what he was making writing songs.

What a temptation!

Surprisingly, Berlin admonished his young friend not to accept the proposition. "If you do," he continued, "you may develop into a second-rate Berlin. But if you insist on being yourself, someday you will become a first-rate Gershwin."

Gershwin accepted Berlin's prophetic counsel. He remained Gershwin. And America and the world adore his music.

The Renaissance Man

Whether starring in the NFL, acting as a bodyguard for Robert Kennedy, or campaigning for Jimmy Carter, Rosey Grier has a gift for being at the right place at the right time.

For example, when Bobby Kennedy was fatally wounded in the Ambassador Hotel in Los Angeles on June 5, 1968, Grier helped subdue Sirhan Sirhan, put the assailant's gun in his own pocket, and then protected the alleged assassin from the angry crowd.

This gentle giant fraternized with the Kennedys, visited our troops in Vietnam, sang in Carnegie Hall, worked with kids in the ghetto, wrote a novel, appeared in the film *The Thing With Two Heads*, was a regular on the television show *Kojak*, and took up needlepoint.

After a string of successful involvements, he lived through a divorce and a decade when he "cried every day."

During his down days, a friend introduced him to the Bible. He became an enthusiastic believer. Family reconciliation was achieved. In 1983 he was ordained to the ministry. Now he reads the Bible daily and prays with the obscure and the famous, including O. J. Simpson and his defense team.

Richard Hoffer said it best in his *Sports Illustrated* article (March 20, 1995), "Whenever history takes a turn, there's Rosey Grier standing on the corner, directing traffic."

This renaissance man resonates compassion and hope.

Keeping Focused

Jacqueline Kennedy Onassis died May 19, 1994. She was sixty-four. Although frequently portrayed as a "calculating," "snooty," "greedy," and "difficult" person, this charming, regal lady handled life's triumphs and tragedies with enviable grace and dignity. Despite being married to fame and fortune, she nevertheless earned worldwide respect, admiration, and affection. Her style was emulated and her gallantry extolled.

Twelve years younger than her husband, John Kennedy, Jackie was thirty-one when she became First Lady. However, she left her deft touch on the White House and her discerning legacy on Washington and the world.

Essentially a private person—she went twenty-five years without granting an interview—her subtle elegance and contagious persuasion usually resulted in attaining desired objectives.

When asked to name her chief accomplishment, she replied, "I think it is that after going through a rather difficult time, I consider myself comparatively sane. I am proud of that."

And well she should be.

Instead of resigning to sorrow, wallowing in wealth and idleness, this punctilious perfectionist focused on her children and cultural pursuits. After the death of Aristotle Onassis, Jackie returned to work. She was a senior editor at Doubleday.

How Is Your Acting?

Marlon Brando is one of the most acclaimed actors in the world. He is also one of the most controversial and contradictory masters of his craft; a man of pathos as well as antithesis. He claims to believe in a classless society but he appears elitist; he speaks with disdain of his profession but he enjoys its compensation. Money seems to drive him. If Hollywood paid me "as much to sweep the floor as it did to act, I'd sweep the floor," he confesses.

Brando is a very private person, and seldom grants interviews. He allowed Larry King to visit with him because of a contract with the publisher of his autobiography, *Songs My Mother Taught Me*, that stipulated that he had to appear on television to promote his book.

His psyche was greatly shaped by early experiences. Brando grew up in Omaha, Nebraska, and Libertyville, Illinois. His parents were alcoholics. He did menial tasks, including cleaning out horse barns. His unhappy childhood made him feel rejected and worthless. As if this were not enough discouragement, at age nineteen, not yet a senior, he was expelled from military school.

Subsequently, he joined his sister Jocelyn in New York City, where she was pursuing an acting career. Brando enrolled in the Dramatic Workshop and the New School for Social Research. There he encountered Stella Adler, who recognized his extraordinary gifts and took him under her wing. She claims to have taught him little, except to assist him in "discovering possibilities of thinking, feeling, experiencing, and as I opened those doors, he walked right through."

From the Broadway show *A Streetcar Named Desire*, in 1947, to winning his first Oscar for *On the Waterfront* in 1954, Brando was

"Hollywood's most bankable star." His thirty-fifth film, *Don Juan DeMarco,* was released in January of 1995.

After fortunes waned, marriages failed, and his son was accused of murder, this once Greek god was reduced to a tragic and angry man.

Even so, there is much to learn from this complex individual. In addition to his superior acting he is actively involved in global environmental issues, an avid ham radio operator, and a zealous advocate of Native American rights. In fact, he declined his second Oscar because he felt Hollywood had mistreated the Native Americans.

Marlon Brando demonstrates a rare modesty; he does not know where his Oscar is (unless his secretary has it); he does not read reviews of his work; and he has never read even one of the many books written about him.

At age seventy this dynamic, enigmatic person is less rebellious and more at peace with himself.

"Acting," he says, "is the most important thing in the world because everyone does it."

One Cool Cat

Nowadays, when it is hot enough to fry an egg on the sidewalk, most people are inside enjoying the comforts of air-conditioning. But that was not the case in the summer of 1902 for the Sackett-Wilhems Lithographing and Publishing Co. of Brooklyn, New York. It was so hot and humid that summer that printing paper was absorbing too much moisture and expanding, causing colors to blur, at best, and not even to register at worst.

The company hired a twenty-five-year-old engineer fresh out of Cornell University to solve the problem. Using a sophisticated version of a fan blowing over a block of ice, Willis Haviland Carrier designed a machine that blew air over artificially cooled pipes. He called it "The Apparatus for Treating Air." We now call it "air-conditioning." (The term "air-conditioning" was first used to describe another cooling system designed by Stuart Cramer in 1906.)

Carrier was president of his company from 1915 to 1930, and board chair until 1948. He died in 1950, just two years before his company developed the first mass-produced central air-condition-ing unit for homes. Today, Carrier Corporation is the world's largest manufacturer and marketer of heating and air-conditioning equip-ment with a 20 percent share of the market.

Steady Anchor

Lynn Russell, CNN anchorwoman, is anything but a cosmetic manikin. She is not only wholesome looking, but she resonates the characteristics of a fine athlete—which she is! She holds a black belt in Choi Kwang Do, a Korean martial art. Her smile is genuine and natural; her voice is full and measured. She possesses what the industry calls "pop-up quality."

In addition to her professional skills and presence, Lynn Russell is committed to community involvement. Her participation ranges from directing traffic to screening visitors at the county jail in Atlanta to being a private investigator. Risky jobs? Yes. But she replies, "Who wants to be safe all the time? If you're afraid of everything, you won't accomplish anything."

When asked if she had any acting experience, she replied, "Only my first marriage and that was more tragedy than comedy."

The star of Turner Broadcasting's "Headline News" is also an exceptionally disciplined person. She works out several times a week; she does not eat "anything with a face"; and she meditates twice a day.

Being the only child of John Russell, an Army officer, and Carmela Pasqualina Evangelista, she received an abundance of affection. Referring to her strict Italian mother, Russell quipped, "She's been so devoted to me, it's like I'm her life's work."

Disposable People

When I was privileged to feed one of our granddaughters for the first time, the proud mother handed me the child and I asked, "Are these puncture-proof pants? They look different."

Smiling, she replied, "These are disposable diapers; they are perfectly safe."

Then she handed me a rather strange looking cylinder. "What is this?" I asked.

"It is her bottle. It, too, is disposable."

Quickly I added, "Let's keep the baby!"

Is not this symbolic of our dilemma? We live in a throwaway world: from garbage disposals to disposable razors; from paper dresses to paper products.

In this kind of world what a temptation it is to deal with people as if they, too, are disposable!

A Monumental Contrast

For the last four decades, relatives and admirers of Franklin Delano Roosevelt, the thirty-second president of the United States, have pursued their dream of creating a monument to his memory in Washington, D.C. Although a memorial commission was authorized by Congress in 1955, a series of design and funding problems delayed the start of construction until October 1994.

Although the monument was dedicated on May 2, 1997, controversy continues. The National Organization on Disability and some historians voiced concern that none of the memorial's three sculptures and bas-reliefs of Roosevelt depict him in a wheelchair or with the braces that he was forced to use because of polio. Although Roosevelt functions as the quintessential role model for the fifty million disabled Americans, the memorial committee decided to veil his disability just as the press did throughout his four terms in office.

By contrast, during the past forty years Ed Roberts has refused to veil his disability. After polio left him a quadriplegic and dependent on a respirator as well as a wheelchair, he tenaciously pursued his dream of a college education and a career. He completed his degree at the University of California at Berkeley, taught political science at his alma mater, ran California's Department of Rehabilitation, married and fathered a son, started an Oakland-based disability "think tank," served as president of the World Institute on Disability, and lobbied successfully for the 1990 Americans with Disabilities Act that requires businesses and governments to make accommodations for people with disabilities. One of those adaptations is a "curb cut," the tiny ramp that connects sidewalk and street so that wheelchairs have access. When Ed Roberts died of a heart attack in March of 1995, virtually every street corner in America bore that monument to his courage.

The Deaf Miss America

When twenty-one-year-old Heather Whitestone of Alabama won the sixty-eighth annual Miss America Pageant on September 17, 1994, she did not hear the announcement. She lost most of her hearing when she was eighteen months old, after a reaction to a diphtheria-tetanus shot. Whitestone is the first Miss America with such a disability.

The Birmingham native was the only contestant to win two preliminary competitions, in the swimsuit and talent categories. Whitestone enchanted the judges with her two and one-half-minute ballet routine performed to "Via Dolorosa." Although she cannot hear the music, she counts the beats in her head and synchronizes her dance to reflect the changes in pitch.

Anyone who knows Heather Whitestone is not surprised by her determination and success. It took her six years to learn how to pronounce her last name!

Politics

Politically Correct

Being politically correct is more popular than ever. One is coun-
seled to use the correct words, symbols, and images. Everything is
so politicized that it is difficult to discern substance from charade.
This helps explain why so many Americans are "turned off" by their
leaders in Washington. And yet, democracy is a process, a spirited
challenge, a forum—not a framed legal mosaic under glass.

E. J. Dionne Jr. concludes his book *Why Americans Hate Politics*
with this provocative sentence: "A nation that hates politics will not
long survive as a democracy."

The Voice of Conscience

In 1972 Barbara Jordan defied race, gender, and region when she
became the first Black, southern woman to be elected to the United
States Congress. With a deep, sonorous voice that many equated
with the voice of God, this first-term representative from Texas was
selected to sit on the House judiciary panel that heard impeachment
proceedings against President Richard Nixon.

With judicious insight that emanated from an unwavering reverence for the Constitution, Jordan charmed and captivated the American public throughout the televised hearings. Then, in August 1974,
at the close of the proceedings, she condensed the hearings into a
single sentence when she insisted, "I am not going to sit here as an
idle spectator to the diminution, the subversion, the destruction of
the Constitution."

On January 17, 1996, Barbara Jordan died of pneumonia. At her
funeral in Houston, Texas, President Bill Clinton eulogized her with
these words: "Through the sheer force of the truth, she spoke. With

the poetry of her words and the power of her voice, Barbara always stirred our national conscience."

"Man of the Year"

Time chose Newt Gingrich as its 1995 Man of the Year. Whether you characterize him as ruthless, brilliant, or obnoxious, you must admit that the Speaker of the House shifted the political center of gravity in Washington.

Speaker Gingrich has stalked destiny from childhood. At age ten he went to Harrisburg, Pennsylvania, to lobby state officials to build a zoo. He had done his homework; he knew the price of animals.

Seniors at Baker High School, near Columbus, Georgia, voted him the "most intellectual" and also the "most eccentric" member of their class.

The Speaker says, "My strength and my weakness is that I see normally impersonal events vividly and personally."

As a youth, Gingrich aspired to become a great politician or a zookeeper. Someone has observed, "As Speaker of the House, he got both his wishes."

Courage to Say, No!

Many Americans were disappointed when General Colin Powell announced he would not enter the 1996 presidential race. Because this distinguished soldier and citizen resonated grace, integrity, and leadership, a Powell campaign promised, for many, to unite America by transcending social and racial divisions. But he chose not to run.

General Powell's reasons for not running were "personal, not political." He could not find "the passion to put himself and his wife and children through the ordeal of a campaign."

From Prisoner to President

Nelson Mandela, first president of a multiracial, democratic South Africa, became a man at the age of sixteen. According to the customs of the Xhosa people, each male enters manhood only after partici- pating in a tribal circumcision ceremony. Mandela's ceremony not only initiated him into adulthood, it also introduced him to the realities of Black life in South Africa. Chief Meligqili concluded his traditional remarks (as quoted in Mandela's autobiography, *Long Walk to Freedom*) with these unexpected words: "There sit our sons, young, healthy, and handsome, the flower of the Xhosa tribe, the pride of our nation. We have just circumcised them in a ritual that promises them manhood, but I am here to tell you that it is an empty, illusory promise, a promise that can never be fulfilled. For we Xhosas, and all black South Africans, are a conquered people. We are slaves in our own country. We are tenants on our own soil. We have no strength, no power, no control over our own destiny in the land of our birth. . . . These gifts today are naught, for we cannot give them the greatest gift of all, which is freedom and independence."

Although Mandela and most Black South Africans, at the time, perceived White people as benefactors and not as oppressors, the chief's words planted an unconscious seed in young Mandela that gradually grew to fruition. Trained as a lawyer, Nelson Mandela became president of the African National Congress and head of South Africa's anti-apartheid movement. In the 1950s, he helped orchestrate the escalating political warfare between the revolution- ary movement and the apartheid government. His resistance ended with the Rivonia Trial of 1964, when he and his collaborators were sentenced to life imprisonment.

After serving twenty-seven years in prison, he was released on February 11, 1990, by then President F. W. de Klerk. Four years later, the country's first national, nonracial, one-person, one-vote election was held. And on May 10, 1994, Nelson Mandela was inaugurated president of South Africa. He told the assembled guests and the watching world:

Today, all of us do, by our presence here . . . confer glory and hope to newborn liberty. Out of the experience of an extraordinary human disaster that lasted too long, must be born a society of which all humanity will be proud. . . .

Never, never, and never again shall it be that this beautiful land will again experience the oppression of one by another. . . . The sun shall never set on so glorious a human achievement.

Let freedom reign. God bless Africa!

Nelson Mandela's long walk from prisoner to president had culminated in freedom for all South Africans.

The Significance of One Vote

The question of how best to select persons for military service has triggered vigorous debates. For years, civilian draft boards had the power of selection. The constitutionality and fairness of the procedure were, however, arguable. In fact, the Congress of the United States debated the issue in October of 1941. The vote to retain the draft system carried by one vote. Pearl Harbor occurred two months later!

In February 1995, Myrlie Evers-Williams, widow of the civil rights martyr, Medgar Evers, defeated incumbent Dr. William F. Gibson by a single vote to head the National Association for the Advancement of Colored People.

On March 2, 1995, the proposed balanced budget amendment to the Constitution of the United States, sponsored by Republicans and carried easily in the House of Representatives, was defeated in the Senate by the margin of one vote.

Harbinger of Hope

Politics, especially at the national level, is so financially and personally expensive that many splendid candidates refuse to run for public office. The 1996 Republican presidential primaries provided an exception in Steve Forbes.

Except for the family name identified with *Forbes* magazine, he was politically unknown. Although he was rebuked for negative advertising in the Iowa primary, Forbes emerged as a thoughtful and committed candidate. This Princeton graduate, reported to be one of the best-informed persons in the country, challenged America to rethink its tax code, its health care system, and its trade and foreign policies. This pro-growth advocate made a positive contribution to the political process.

This harbinger of hope spent an estimated $30 million of his own money to communicate his message. Expressed in terms of delegates, each was won at a cost of $400,000 in campaign expenditures.

A Profile of Character

Former Chief Justice Warren E. Burger died June 25, 1995. He served our country with dignity, deep convictions, and courage. His commanding presence, white hair, and baritone voice set him apart in any crowd. Some described him as pompous and petty; others thought he was generous and kind.

Although Mr. Burger was chief justice for seventeen years, he never forgot the rough road he had traveled to reach the high bench. He never lost the common touch. How could he forget selling insurance by day and going to the University of Minnesota by night for an undergraduate degree? He also earned a law degree at night from St. Paul College of Law.

Whether breaking up a street fight in London, attending a fellowship prayer breakfast in Washington, reforming the Court, writing more than two hundred opinions, heading the Bicentennial Commission of the U.S. Constitution, or visiting an ill colleague, Judge Burger resonated genuineness.

He will forever be remembered as the judge who wrote the 1974 opinion that forced President Richard Nixon, who had nominated Burger to the Supreme Court in 1969, to surrender tape recordings relevant to the Watergate scandal.

Chief Justice Burger had "the right stuff": character!

Spirituality and Politics

When Sharon Kirtdoll founded the Women's Center in Steubenville, Ohio, in 1977, it was the primary advocate for the town's

African American community. Through the years, the services pro-vided by the center have expanded to include health and housing issues, youth and older adult concerns, and crisis intervention.

Although more and more of Kirtdoll's time is devoted to fund-raising, her basic commitment to social change has not wavered: "I don't believe you can really be a Christian and not care about people. Politics should enhance the lives of other people. And if you *really* care about people, your political ambition should be to change the structures to enhance the lives of others. Sometimes I think, 'Why can't I just walk away and forget about it?' It's something in me, a spiritual conviction that makes me political."

The Light of Democracy

After forty-eight years of conflict between Palestinians and Is-raelis, the ballot proved mightier than the sword. On January 20, 1996, more than 80 percent of one million registered voters cast ballots in the West Bank and Gaza Strip. Yasir Arafat, longtime PLO leader, was elected—with 88 percent of the vote—as head of the Palestinian Authority's Council, the highest position in the new self-governing Palestine.

An exuberant Palestinian remarked, "People without democracy live in darkness. Now we will move forward into the new world."

Potpourri

Mental Writing

Although Terry Waite appeared to be idle while in solitary con-finement as a hostage in the Middle East, he was busy writing his autobiography in his head. With amazing skill and powers of recall, he ultimately produced a profound book: *Taken on Trust.*

After surviving 1,763 days of captivity, he was provided living and writing accommodations in Trinity Hall, at Cambridge Univer-sity. In the book's foreword he writes, "During my long years of solitary confinement in Beirut when I had no pen or paper, no books and no news of the outside world, I 'wrote' in my imagination. . . . On my release I took a pen and started to write."

Commendable Graduate

Myrtle Estella Shannon, ninety-one, received her bachelor of arts degree from Roosevelt University in Chicago, Illinois, in January 1996, after nearly fifty years of perseverance.

This woman, a history major, demonstrates not only dedication to high purpose, but also civic commitment.

"Now," she says, "I can keep up with things going on in the world."

Clicking with People

Alfred Eisenstaedt was one of the great photojournalists of the twentieth century. He died on Martha's Vineyard in August 1995, at the age of ninety-six. Born in Prussia, he worked as a button salesman and took pictures when he could. Eisenstaedt had photographed

Haile Selassie, Hitler, and Mussolini before immigrating to the United States in 1935.

Shortly thereafter, he became one of the original photographers for *Life* magazine. Alfred Eisenstaedt is said to have carried out two thousand assignments and left a trove of one million pictures over his sixty-eight-year career.

It was appropriate that this small man—he was five feet four inches tall, yet saw everything—should capture the end of World War II with the image of a sailor, dressed in blue, "locking lips" with a woman dressed in white on V-J Day, in New York City's Times Square on August 15, 1945.

Eisenstaedt was not only a perceptive, prolific photographer, he was also a polite one. His motto: "It's more important to click with people than to click with the shutter."

Paid the Price

Stephen Covey, author of the national bestseller *The 7 Habits of Highly Effective People*, was being interviewed on the radio. But instead of asking the standard questions, the interviewer confessed that he was "too busy and seemed unable to balance his life with any degree of success."

After listening thoughtfully to his interviewer's explanation, Covey responded by asking this provocative question: "Have you paid the price of deciding what kind of person you want to be?"

Like a boat on a river, we too often drift where the cultural currents take us, seldom deciding our own life direction.

Yet real change requires that we pay the price of deciding what kind of life we want to live.

Covey concluded his response with this declaration: "It's not too late. It's never too late."

Under Oath

During his coaching years at Notre Dame, Frank Leahy had a lineman named Frank Szymanski. The young man was once called as a witness in a civil suit at South Bend.

The judge asked Szymanski if he played football for Notre Dame.
He politely replied, "Yes, Your Honor."
The judge continued his questioning. "What position?"
"Center, Your Honor."
"How good a center?"
The usually modest lad finally blurted out, "I'm the best center Notre Dame has ever had."

Afterward, Coach Leahy, who had attended the hearing, asked Szymanski why he had been so boastful.

"I hated to do it coach, but I was under oath!"

Quebec's Secession

Our family frequently discusses current events at the dinner table. On Monday night, October 30, 1995, the conversation included Quebec's unsuccessful effort to secede from Canada.

As my wife and I talked about the possible implications, our son, who has Canadian cousins, asked, "If Quebec leaves Canada, where will it go?"

Burglar with a Heart

After three bypass operations, Erma's seventy-year-old heart does not tolerate stress. Excitement is against doctor's orders.

But one night around ten, while she was watching television, her cat came tearing into the living room and kept staring with huge eyes toward the kitchen. Thinking it was a rat, Erma got up to investigate. As she made her way down the hall, a man in a white T-shirt grabbed her from behind and put his hand over her mouth.

"I'm not going to hurt you," he told her. "I just want money."

"He had on a pair of latex gloves," Erma recounted, "and I'm kind of claustrophobic, so I started struggling. It caused me to have chest pains, and I kind of buckled."

She immediately asked for her nitroglycerin pills and, to her surprise, the burglar started looking for them in her nightstand drawer. Although he located several vials, he could not find the nitroglycerin.

As her breathing got worse, the burglar, still unable to find the pills, went into the living room and dialed 911.

"Trace this call. A woman's dying!" he told the operator, and he left the phone off the hook. Then he returned to Erma, told her of the call, and left the house empty-handed.

After she was treated with oxygen, she told her story to the disbelieving police who dubbed the man the "burglar with a heart."

Commitment

The renowned physician Sir William Osler was a household name around the turn of the century in English-speaking countries. Whatever the circumstance, this extraordinary person was always thinking about medicine.

One day, as Osler strode down a street in Montreal, he encountered an alcoholic panhandler. He gave the man his overcoat in exchange for the promise that the individual would bequeath him his liver for research.

Tabernacles of the Holy Spirit

In an interview with *Christianity Today* (October 5, 1992), Desmond Tutu, 1986 Nobel Peace prize laureate and Anglican archbishop of Cape Town, South Africa, was asked how the Christian faith has led him to fight against apartheid.

Using trinitarian language, Archbishop Tutu defended the struggle against oppression and injustice by declaring that the intrinsic value of every person derives from being created in the image of God and from being redeemed by the Christ. Then he concluded, "As if that were not enough, God says, 'I will sanctify you by the gift of my Holy Spirit.' So human beings are of worth not only because they have been created in the image of God and are offered redemption

197

by the precious blood of our Savior, but also because they may become tabernacles of the Holy Spirit."

Pay Day

There is a Spanish proverb that says: "Take what you want; take it, and pay for it."

Prayer

Praying For You

When Transylvania University celebrated its 175th anniversary in 1954, President Dwight D. Eisenhower was the featured guest. Just prior to this historic celebration, the president of Transylvania, Dr. Frank Rose, learned that his mother had died. Dr. Rose carried on with courage and grace.

When President Eisenhower arrived, he asked to be shown the chapel. After the program, Dr. Rose accompanied the president to his plane. They shook hands and said good-bye. Just before reaching his plane, President Eisenhower turned and walked back to Frank Rose and said, "I have been praying for you today."

Prayer Is Love

Augustine once said, "Whole prayer is nothing but love."

Discerning the Difference

Although Reinhold Niebuhr did not copyright his famous "Serenity Prayer" until Hallmark Cards used it in its 1962 graduation line, it was written at least by the time of World War II and distributed by the USO to hundreds of thousands of servicemen. After the war, Alcoholics Anonymous adopted it as an official prayer. The following form is how Niebuhr published it in a 1951 column:

> "God, give us the serenity to accept what cannot be changed;
> Give us the courage to change what should be changed;
> Give us the wisdom to distinguish one from the other."

A Definition

Douglas Steere said, "Prayer, in its deepest levels, becomes a simple, loving response to the creative love of God."

A Saint Among Us

Mae Yoho Ward was a beloved leader of the Christian Church (Disciples of Christ). After years of distinguished missionary service, she became an efficient and compassionate administrator. She was a deeply spiritual person and an excellent preacher.

Following her death in 1983, her son, Don Ward, edited his mother's prayer journal, *The Seeking Heart*. From it, we learn that this saintly soul had written twenty-five hundred letters to God. They are conversational in style, exposing her doubts as well as embracing her faith. Listen to this conversation:

"Dear God,
"The sun shines on the grass, so very green. It sparkles with dew-diamonds. Thank You that my house guests were so happy. I wanted the work at the Building and now that I have it, I wonder. I wanted work, but not responsibility. Be with me. I want to put my head back and close my eyes and let You guide my thoughts, but I know my inertia leads me, not to meditation, but to sleepiness. Shame!

"How shall I fill this day wisely? Time rushes at me and I put up my hands saying, 'Wait, wait, I am not ready for the Bible study, not ready for the retreat, not ready for teaching the class, not ready to start a garden. Wait, please wait. I must read a great deal. I must write letters. I must make phone calls. I must be quiet and ponder.' But Time, you will not wait.

"So, today, I am . . .
a bundle of fears about the future
a bundle of nerves wanting a tranquilizer
a lump of clay longing to be molded
a spirit housed in a deteriorating body
a fisherman trying to catch tiny darting ideas in a net of many

opportunities
    a car caught in a snowdrift of laziness, spinning my wheels
and getting noplace
    burdened by the programs I must write
    a squirrel scampering here and there in search of truth
    a cat falling asleep when I mean to pray
    a runner in the Marathon of Life, not eager to stay running
until I reach the finish line
    a human being, trying to be a Christian.
    "How confused I am about life, and You, and Your presence
and Your guidance. I feel You are near, and then I wonder if
that is my imagination. Am I just 'whistling in the dark'? I read
and sing about taking no thought for the morrow, and then
worry about getting the steps fixed!"

Prayer Works

From the home to the hospital, Christians ask about the relation
of prayer and health. Because there is no simple or single biblical
theology of prayer, people of faith want to know whether prayer
works.

While research into the relation between prayer and health has
not always met rigorous standards and though some studies indicate
a negative correlation, Michael McCullough, a counselor with Fuller
Psychological and Family Services in Pasadena, California, claims
that health benefits are real. After reviewing the literature dealing
with studies on prayer and health, he concludes that prayer rich in
mystical and religious experience is for the most part positively
correlated with "subjective well-being."

"We do not need empirical evidence that 'prayer works,' " he
writes. "Two millennia of church history convince us of that. However . . . research may demonstrate to the skeptic that biblical spirituality yields outcomes such as sense of purpose, sense of
communion with the divine, and contact with spiritual power; that
prayer can lead, in many cases, to better adaptation to life stressors;
that God answers prayer."

Working in Order to Witness

On his approach to my hospital bed, the badge on the coat lapel of this somberly dressed and sincere looking stranger told me he was with the chaplain's office. During our conversation he indicated that his church affiliation was far removed from mainline Protestantism. Although he operated a small office-cleaning business to support his wife and three children, he volunteered one day a week at his church and each Wednesday at the Mayo Clinic. As I held his heavy, muscular hand in prayer, I felt I was in touch with the tentmaker, Paul.

He Delivered

Captain Scott O'Grady, the Air Force pilot who ejected from his F-16 fighter plane on June 2, 1995, when his aircraft was hit as he flew a mission over Bosnia, attributed his survival to God's love for him and his love for God.

On the ground, as he endeavored to avoid being captured, he prayed frequently. "I prayed to God and asked him for a lot of things . . . he delivered. . . . When I prayed for rain, he gave me rain."

One time O'Grady prayed, "Lord, let me at least have someone know I'm alive and maybe come rescue me." That night a fellow pilot, Captain T. O. Hanford, picked up the distress call, "Basher 52."

This signaled the beginning of the end of his six-day ordeal.

Body and Soul

A friend, a retired Native American physician, has a number of health problems. He never complains; he is always cheerful and enthusiastic. In one of our visits, he shared some of his reading materials with me as he affectionately opened his Bible. Then he added, "I take medication eight times a day; I use these periods for meditation and prayer."

He simultaneously cares for body and soul.

Amen

One of the saints of the church lay dying. She had begun her journey home. She was motionless. The nurse said she was inarticu-late and incoherent. Gently I took hold of her hand and offered a prayer. To my surprise, and to the utter amazement of the nurse, when I said "amen," she whispered, "amen." In a few hours she was gone.

In quiet dignity, this dear soul not only confirmed her faith, but she also affirmed the confident words of Robert Browning:

> Grow old along with me!
> The best is yet to be,
> The last of life, for which the first was made.
> Our times are in his hand.

Race Relations

Don't Punish Me

In *Amazing Grace*, Jonathan Kozol introduces us to the residents of the South Bronx, the poorest congressional district in America. The people who live in this isolated, filth-infested community—35 percent of whom are children—are subjected to violence, disease, and discrimination. Murder, rape, and robbery are common. Drug dealers, prostitutes, and hungry people roam the streets.

Kozol observes that the American ghetto "is not a social accident, but is created and sustained by greed, neglect, racism, and expedi-ence."

Standing one night with Mrs. Washington, who was listening to her kneeling children pray, Jonathan Kozol heard these sobering words: "God bless Mommy, God bless Nanny. God, don't punish me because I'm black."

The Burden of Race

In his autobiography, *Days of Grace*, Arthur Ashe chronicles his life from his tennis triumphs and social activism to his ordeal in the face of death from AIDS. Yet AIDS was not his greatest burden.

At the conclusion of an interview with a reporter for *People* magazine, the journalist asked, "Mr. Ashe, I guess [AIDS] must be the heaviest burden you have ever had to bear, isn't it?"

After a momentary pause, Ashe replied, "No, it isn't. It's a burden, all right. But AIDS isn't the heaviest burden I have had to bear."

The reporter queried, "Is there something worse? Your heart attack?"

"You're not going to believe this," Ashe responded, "but being black is the greatest burden I've had to bear. . . . Having to live as a minority in America. Even now it continues to feel like an extra weight tied around me."

The Lady Who Refused to Move

After a hard day of stitching and ironing shirts, Rosa Parks rode home on a green and white public bus in Montgomery, Alabama. It was Thursday, December 1, 1955. As more White people entered the bus, the four African American passengers were told to move to the back. The three Black men obeyed the bus driver's order. Rosa Parks kept her seat. She was subsequently arrested, fingerprinted, and jailed.

Mrs. Parks's decision to challenge discrimination in Montgomery galvanized the Black community and inaugurated the bus boycott.

Southern segregation received a powerful economic and spiritual blow; a blow that contributed to the dawning of a new era in American race relations.

Rosa Parks, and millions of African Americans with her, was fed up with being pushed around.

The Divisive Verdict

After 253 days of trial, 126 witnesses, numerous playbacks of 911 tapes, and 45,000 pages of testimony, the most costly and controversial trial in American history was finally over. Although sequestered 266 days, the jury deliberated for less than a day before reaching its decision. The verdict was announced October 3, 1995, before a television audience of 150 million people: "We . . . find the defendant, Orenthal James Simpson, not guilty of the crime of murder . . . upon Nicole Brown Simpson, a human being."

Reaction to the quickly determined verdict ran from jubilation to anger, from racial tension to criticism of the judge's handling of the case and the attorneys' conduct.

There were more losers than winners in the Simpson case: the prosecution lost its focus; the defense team lost its composure; the Los Angeles Police Department lost its credibility; many Americans lost confidence in the judicial system; and race relations lost years of bridge building.

Two White Racists

After the O. J. Simpson acquittal on October 3, 1995, and the Million Man March led by Louis Farrakhan, Minister of the Nation of Islam, on October 16, 1995, America was obsessed with race relations. People wanted to know how Blacks and Whites could see things so differently. Orlando Patterson provided one explanation in his essay "The Paradox of Integration" (*The New Republic*, November 6, 1995).

In his article, Patterson argued that the number of Whites who hold racist beliefs, as measured by unfavorable attitudes toward miscegenation, integrated housing, and job equality, has declined from a majority in the 1950s to a quarter of the population today. Yet progress is relative. He concluded with this observation: "But, even with only a quarter of all whites holding racist beliefs, it remains the case that for every black person there are two white racists."

The March!

The Million Man March on Washington held on October 16, 1995, was a phenomenal accomplishment. Although the controversial leader of the Nation of Islam, Louis Farrakhan, claimed divine selection for the call to mobilize, the march was not about Farrakhan. He was neither the message nor the bearer of the message. At most, this inflammatory leader was the convener.

The remarkable drama confirmed what many already knew: We have moved from racial segregation to racial isolation. The march also revealed proud, hard-working, middle-class African Americans demonstrating self-reliance, dignity, and solidarity. There were no arrests, no trash to collect after the celebration.

It was a liberating experience for many of the men; freeing them from fear, unifying them in a consensus to be better husbands, fathers, and citizens. The march was more of a spiritual awakening than a political demonstration. Transforming the admonitions and ideals of a one-day rally into local accomplishments will be the ultimate test of the significance of the Washington celebration.

As one participant phrased it, "We left as one million black men. We returned home as one million black brothers."

From Suspicion to Friendship

Racial unrest gripped America in the 1960s. There were those who fought to preserve the two-tiered social and economic structures, and there were those who fought to dismantle them. Marches, riots, and killings resulted.

The world of professional athletics was not exempt from racial animosity. Although locked into tradition, there were those inside the system trying to bring about change; new ways of evaluating players and their performances.

A powerful example of this embarrassing yet emancipating strug-gle existed in the elite battery of the St. Louis Cardinals baseball team: Pitcher Bob Gibson and catcher Tim McCarver. They typified the ongoing dichotomy in the country.

McCarver, the son of a Memphis policeman, was steeped in southern White tradition, while Gibson, the proud survivor of a harsh Omaha ghetto, epitomized the struggle for Black dignity. Each in his own way was driven to succeed. They could not alter the fact that they were teammates, but could they become friends?

McCarver, six years younger than Gibson, was frequently intimi-dated by the strong Black man who was forever trying to discover and expose the prejudices of his receiver. Gibson resented the fact that he was given a $4,000 bonus to sign a Cardinal contract while McCarver was given $75,000.

One day, as McCarver was leaving the locker room before a game, he encountered a Black man who wanted to see Gibson. Whereupon McCarver called to Gibson saying, "There's a colored guy waiting for you."

"Oh," replied Gibson, "what color is he?"

Gradually McCarver realized that Gibson was pushing him to become a "complete" person.

Although each kept the other on probation, the distance between them narrowed. They began to socialize.

The confirmation of their mutual respect came in the first game of the 1968 World Series with Detroit. Fast working, hard throwing Gibson was at his best. He struck out seventeen batters and established a new record. Afterward, McCarver said, "It was not just a baseball game, it was a work of art."

Gibson and McCarver are permanently linked now, not just in baseball history but also in camaraderie. They have moved from suspicion to friendship.

The Color of the Law

After graduating from college, I postponed graduate school and returned to Macon, Georgia, where I lived with my parents. For the next two years I taught and coached in the public school system.

One day, after football practice, I drove one of the players home. As we entered a predominantly Black part of town, I saw from the corner of my eye a figure run in front of the car. Instinctively, I swerved to avoid a direct hit. Only after I applied the brakes and came to a stop did I fully realize what had happened. In an instant, a literal blink of an eye, I had hit a six-year-old Black girl.

After I hit the child, her mother came running out of the store, screaming and crying, "Oh, my baby, what's happened to my baby?"

I felt horrible. This was the first time I had ever been involved in an accident, let alone a collision with a person. I was devastated. I parked the car and waited for the police.

After the accident report was completed, I drove home, where I literally collapsed in the kitchen and cried. I had hit another person, and although the person was not dead, I did not know the severity of her injuries.

My parents were empathetic. After I recounted the accident, they suggested that I call the hospital and find out the girl's condition. Because I had a copy of the police report, I knew her name. I received wonderful news. She was okay and had already been released.

But the incident was not over. The next day I returned to the scene of the accident with the police report in hand. I thought something was wrong. The police officer had written on the report that the speed limit was 30 mph. I was going about 33. And sure enough, the speed limit sign, not far from the accident scene, indicated a 35 mph zone.

I'll never forget a friend's response when I informed him of the discrepancy. "The police officer was Black and he wanted to make it look bad for you. You can't trust 'em."

I was shocked. If the officer deliberately noted the wrong speed limit on the report and if he did it because of race, what about all those times when White officers arrested Black people?

What color is the law?

In Christ: No East or West, North or South

Central Methodist Church in Ghana was crowded. The service was long and impressive. I was among the few—if not the only—Caucasians in the large congregation. I was very appreciative of the last portion of the litany, which was in English! Was it just for me?

Following worship, the pastors and officers of the church were very cordial and gracious. One man took me to his home for tea. In fact, this splendid soul visited my hotel at least once each of the three days I was in Ghana. He was also most helpful in my work. His support was exceptional, and I asked why he was so attentive.

"Well," he said, "we have a son studying medicine in London. He would not be there were it not for White friends. The only possible way I can repay them is to be kind to others, especially Whites."

Share the Burden

Arriving in South Africa, Terry Waite, envoy of the Archbishop of Canterbury, was met at the airport by then Bishop Desmond Tutu. Following a greeting, the courteous African grabbed the two bags and started off with them. Whereupon Waite said, "Come on Bishop, I can manage them myself."

Flashing a mischievous smile, Tutu replied, "But it's the black man's burden, Terry."

They laughed.

Each man walked away with one suitcase.

Serendipity

Serendipity

The word "serendipity" was coined by the English author and statesman, Horace Walpole, and first used in a letter to his friend Horace Mann, the educator, in 1754. Walpole was fascinated by the fairy tale, "The Three Princes of Serendip." In the story, the princes were forever discovering pleasant things by accident and sagacity. Mr. Walpole could not find an adequate English word to describe such experiences, hence the invention of the term "serendipity."

We have all had the experience. It occurs when you vacuum out the automobile and find the lost key; when you put on a suit that has not been worn for some time and find change in the pockets; or, when you return to your parked car at an expired meter to find a ticket on the windshield. Instead of citing the violation, it reads: "Welcome to our town! Thank you for observing our laws. And come back again."

Glass

It is said that when Phoenician sailors landed on the northern shores of Africa, they were unable to find enough stones to support their cooking pots. Whereupon, they took lumps of saltpeter from the ship to secure their kettles. Heat from the fire melted the saltpeter. It dripped to the ground. When the liquid mixed with the sand and cooled, a clear, hard substance was formed: glass.

Penicillin

In 1928, Dr. Alexander Fleming, a bacteriologist at St. Mary's Hospital in London, discovered penicillin by accident. While discarding some culture plates he noticed one that had been exposed to the air had become contaminated with a fungus. The mold—*penicillium notatum*—produced a bacteria-killing agent that Dr. Fleming called "penicillin."

In December of 1945, Dr. Fleming shared the Nobel Prize in medicine.

Saccharin

A chemist failed to wash his hands before eating lunch. While munching on a meat sandwich he wondered why it tasted sweet. Back in his laboratory, he discovered a substance on his hands that was later to be known as the artificial sweetener saccharin.

A Plowman's Surprise

Jesus said, "The kingdom of heaven is like treasure hidden in a field, which someone found and hid; then in his joy he goes and sells all that he has and buys that field" (Matthew 13:44).

Those of us who have followed a mule behind a plow all day can identity with this story. One can imagine that a poor tenant farmer began his day routinely: He fed the oxen early, then yoked them to a wooden plow for another hard day of tilling the rocky Palestinian ground. The discouraged man creeping along in a narrow furrow was doubtless thinking of his family, their needs, and his inability to meet them. Suddenly his plow struck something. He pulled back the plow, dropped to his knees, and began digging with his hands around the object. To his amazement it was a box. Furthermore, it contained gold!

Had it been stolen, or had someone hidden it in the field? These possibilities ran through his mind as he left the oxen and hurried home to share the good news with his wife. They agreed to sell their limited belongings and buy the little parcel of ground where the plowman had carefully hidden the treasure.

Seeds of Serendipity

In *A Second Helping of Chicken Soup for the Soul,* Jack Canfield and Mark Victor Hansen tell this story:

A woman driving a red Honda approached the Bay Bridge toll booth near San Francisco. She informed the attendant that she was paying for herself and the next six cars immediately behind her, handed over seven commuter tickets, and drove away.

Imagine the surprise of each subsequent driver, money in hand, ready to pay, only to be told by the operator, "Some lady up ahead already paid your fare. Have a nice day."

This anonymous soul was inspired by the words: "Practice random kindness and senseless acts of beauty."

From Convertible to Stardom

When Charlton Heston was a guest on *Larry King Live,* the conversation naturally focused on the motion picture industry. Eventually the versatile actor was asked what propelled him to stardom.

Life, Heston suggested, hinges on serendipities. Then the gallant six-foot-three inch performer shared this experience: One day as he was leaving a studio parking lot in his convertible, with the top down, he passed the legendary director and producer Cecil B. DeMille. Heston waved and drove on.

Later Charlton Heston learned that DeMille had asked his secretary who was driving the car. Then DeMille instructed her to sign Heston for a major role.

America

Christopher Columbus, searching for a direct route to Asia, stumbled onto the Americas.

Phonograph

Thomas Alva Edison invented a phonograph while looking to create an electric light.

Electricity

When Benjamin Franklin saw a spark while playing with a kite during a storm, he had no idea he was starting an industry.

Sexuality, Marriage, and Divorce

Americans and Sex

A team of researchers based at the University of Chicago released in 1994 the most comprehensive and scientific survey of American sex patterns since the highly controversial Kinsey Report over forty years ago.

According to *Time* (October 17, 1994), the study was based on face-to-face interviews with approximately thirty-five hundred Americans, ranging in age from eighteen to fifty-nine. Here are some of their findings:

Fifty-four percent of men think of sex every day; 19 percent of women do.

Married couples have more sexual intercourse.

Over a lifetime, a male may have as many as six sex partners; a female may have two.

Seventy-five percent of the men and 85 percent of the women surveyed have been faithful to their spouse.

Sexual Misconduct

While writing to the Romans, Paul addressed the subject of sexual misconduct: "Their women exchanged natural intercourse for un-natural, and in the same way also the men, giving up natural intercourse with women, were consumed with passion for one another. Men committed shameless acts with men and received in their own persons the due penalty for their error" (1:26b-27).

An Average Guy

According to the March 1996 issue of *Men's Health*, the average adult male in America:

is 5 feet 9 inches tall and weighs 172 pounds
loses his virginity at 17, marries at 26, and has sex with 5 to 10 partners during his lifetime
watches television about 28 hours a week
consumes 11 beers in a week and buys frozen pizza 4 times a month
sleeps 7 1/2 hours a night
saves less than $3,000 for retirement each year
makes a $29,533 annual salary.

Sexual Differences Between the Sexes

According to the 1994 University of Chicago survey *Sex in America* (reported in *Christian Century*, June 21-28, 1995), which interviewed 3,432 adults between the ages of eighteen and fifty-nine, a number of substantial differences in sexual behavior do exist between men and women. For example, more men than women have purchased pornographic material in the last year; 41 percent of men and 16 percent of women. And 16 percent of men have visited a prostitute.

A significant difference exists in attitudes toward first sexual encounters. Over 90 percent of the men but only 70 percent of the women "wanted" to have intercourse that first time. Only 8 percent of men just went along with it, compared to three times the number of women, 24 percent. Twice as many men (51 percent) as women (25 percent) did it out of curiosity. But the numbers reverse when affection is the motivator. Four percent of the women reported being forced into their first sexual relation.

Although the survey does not use the word "rape," it did inventory "forced sex." According to researcher Ed Laumann, this subject locates "not just a gender gap but a gender chasm." Although only 3 percent of the men said they had ever forced a partner to do something she did not want to do, 22 percent of the women reported being "forced." Even more startling, 46 percent of the "coercers" were people the women loved, 22 percent were people they knew well, 19 percent were acquaintances, 9 percent were spouses, and 4 percent were strangers.

Until Death Do Us Part

The affection of Chief Justice John Marshall for his wife, Mary Ambler, who became a semi-invalid early in their marriage, approaches poetic perfection. His love for her grew with her declining years. Despite heavy responsibilities and momentous debates, he was exceedingly attentive and did everything possible to bring her comfort and joy.

This giant statesman, with rustic manner and romantic feelings, delighted in sharing with "Polly" news and insights from the outside world.

Mrs. Marshall was an Episcopalian; he was Unitarian. Even so, the justice would frequently come home after worship and read to his wife from the *Book of Common Prayer*, including the Gospel, collect, and prayers for the day—a ritual, we are told, he continued after Mary Ambler's death.

Postponing "I Do"

According to a 1996 Census Bureau report, Americans are postponing marriage in record fashion. The median age of a first-time bride is now 24.5 years, while for the groom it is 26.7. These are the highest median ages since records were first kept in 1890, when the ages were 22.0 and 26.1 respectively.

Demographers cite three basic reasons for postponing marriage. First, the absence of well-paying entry level jobs for high school graduates in particular and stagnant wages in general discourage young people from marrying early. Second, young women have many alternatives to motherhood. And third, the stigma associated with "living together" has virtually disappeared from our society.

Finish on the Same Beat

The late Erma Bombeck said, "A serious illness is marriage's unspoken fear. The chances of a couple staying healthy together and dying at the same time are Las Vegas odds. Life is a dance you want to finish on the same beat."

Anger and Divorce

From 1960 to 1995, the divorce rate in America has doubled. One in two marriages now fail, as well as 60 percent of remarriages.

Neil Clark Warren, psychologist and marital counselor, believes that "75% of all divorces involve marriages in which at least one partner is emotionally unhealthy . . . [and] marriages can't cure individual emotional problems."

In his book *The Triumphant Marriage: 100 Extremely Successful Couples Reveal Their Secrets,* Warren identifies the "emotional cripplers of marriage." He writes, "More marriages break up because two people don't know how to handle their anger toward one another than any other reason."

Untying the Knot

A 1995 report from the Population Council, a New York–based demography institute, confirms an alarming global untying of the marriage knot. Between 1970 and 1990, the divorce rate has doubled in industrialized countries. In developing nations, approximately a fourth of the marriages of forty-year-old women have ended in divorce. In 1970, 42.3 percent of marriages in the United States ended in divorce; in the 1990s the rate has climbed to 54.8 percent. A major consequence is that more and more women, in both rich and poor nations, are shouldering a greater share of economic responsibility for their children. Compounding the issue is the growing problem of "deadbeat dads." In Japan, 75 percent of divorced fathers are behind in child-support payments while in America 40 percent of fathers are delinquent.

Royal Failure

Following years of scandal and acrimony, Prince Charles and Princess Diana announced in the winter of 1996 their intention to divorce. Each confessed to charges of infidelity.

Their magnificent wedding on July 29, 1981, in historic St. Paul's Cathedral, was celebrated around the world as the marriage of the century. The termination of their union is now called the divorce of the century.

Prince Charles and Princess Diana were not the first members of this royal family to experience marital problems. Cruelty and indiscretion preceded them. Henry VIII had six wives: two marriages were annulled, two wives were beheaded. Alice Keppell is reported to have been the favorite mistress of Edward VII. Edward VIII abdicated the throne for the love of Wallis Simpson.

The regrettable behavior of Charles and Diana not only raised questions about the future of the royal family, but it confirmed the observation that members of the monarchy also have feet of clay. They are as vulnerable to temptation and sin as are commoners.

Sin

Our Sins

When Augustine really came to himself, he prayed, "Lord, save me from that evil man, myself."

James Spence, noted Methodist preacher of years ago, said much the same thing in a different prayer, "Lord, save me from that good man, James Spence."

The danger for most of us is not our obvious sins, but the subtle ones; the complacency that causes us to say, "God, I thank you that I am not like other people" (Luke 18:11a).

Wash Away Sins

At an October 1995 congressional prayer breakfast, Nebraska Senator Bob Kerrey recalled the words of Sam Houston, the founder of Texas who waited until he was sixty to join a church. In a letter to a friend, Houston warned, "They told me that by joining I would wash away all my sins. If that be the case, I pity those poor souls living downstream."

The Shadow Knows

Toilet tissue strewn across the bathroom floor. The window shade crumpled upon the carpet. A Magic Marker starburst on the kitchen wall. All evidence that our three-year-old daughter is alive and well.

When her mother and I inquired if she was responsible for the above incidents, she denied any knowledge of them.

But when we asked if she knew who was responsible, she con‑
fessed, "My shadow did it."

B.C. or A.D.?

In their book *Aristotle Onassis, The London Sunday Times* writing
team of Nicholas Fraser, Philip Jacobson, Mark Ottaway, and Lewis
Chester quotes a friend of the Greek tycoon as saying, "He wanted
history to start with him. You have a definite impression of B.C. and
A.D. in Ari's life."

Court Disaster

In Plato's *Republic* there is a story of a ship's crew who decided
their captain was mad because he took observations from the stars.
The sailors reasoned that a ship sails on the sea and that winds,
currents, and tides are the important points of identification. So they
locked up their captain in the hold of the vessel and sailed on to
shipwreck.

When our points of reference are limited to the self and the
immediate world, we court disaster.

Increase Sin

A National Public Radio program on John Norquist, Democratic
mayor of Milwaukee, included a visit to the mayor's office by a
seventh-grade public school class. When one student asked the
mayor why he entered politics, Norquist replied, "Because my father
was a minister, I had to increase the amount of sin in the world."

Careful, You May Be Sued!

We live in a culture of litigation. According to many, whatever
happens is caused by another party. While the cigarette smoker is

dying with lung cancer, either the individual or a family member sues the tobacco manufacturer. If stock in a given company fluctuates too dramatically, the broker and the company are liable. Although the patient may survive a very risky operation, if the procedure does not produce desired results the surgeon and hospital are sued.

Victims of their own negligence also participate in ludicrous lawsuits. A case that attracted national attention occurred in Connecticut in May 1995. John Lupoli, a nine-year-old pitcher, was warming up between innings at a Little League baseball game. A wild pitch eluded the catcher and hit an inattentive spectator. The person filed suit, claiming the lad was careless in throwing "the baseball at a hard and dangerous speed." The youth was sued for $15,000. After months of bickering, a judge dismissed the case.

Check Credentials!

Jacksonville was shocked. A front-page story in the January 19, 1996, *Florida Times-Union* reported that Jesse Burns, president of the 130-year-old Edward Waters College, had resigned under pressure.

Investigation of the president intensified when college officials discovered that Mr. Burns "had lied about his academic degrees to get hired in 1993." According to the article, he faked his resume; he had neither a master's degree from Stetson University nor a doctorate from the University of South Florida.

This tragic revelation brings to mind the admonition of Moses: "Be sure your sin will find you out" (Numbers 32:23*b*).

Jesus said, "For nothing is hidden that will not be disclosed, nor is anything secret that will not become known and come to light" (Luke 8:17).

Heart Problems

Despite phenomenal progress in the detection and treatment of heart disease, it continues to be one of the leading causes of death in America. Depending on the nature of the disorder, patients now have a number of options. Among the modern procedures are heart catheterization, angioplasty, bypass surgery, and drug therapy. Still additional procedures are emerging.

There is, however, another kind of heart disorder that is quite beyond the reach of modern science and technology; it is hardness of heart: an insensitive, sinful heart. Centuries ago the prophet Ezekiel perceived this spiritual disorder and said to his people, "Get yourselves a new heart and a new spirit! Why will you die, O house of Israel? For I have no pleasure in the death of anyone, says the Lord GOD. Turn, then, and live" (Ezekiel 18:31-32).

There is no substitute for spiritual therapy. To receive a new heart and a new spirit, turn to God in confession and commitment.

Sports

Do the Right Thing

At a 1996 press conference, the University of Oklahoma athletic director introduced the new football coach, Gary Gibbs. Gibbs inherited a program crippled by serious allegations. The new coach's first objective is to restore pride and integrity. During the question and answer session, Coach Gibbs remarked, "All we've got to do is the right thing."

Humble Olympic Heroine

Bonnie Blair is the fastest female speed skater in the world. She has five gold medals to prove it. *Sports Illustrated* named her sportswoman of the year in 1994 (December 10, 1994).

Her coach, Nick Thometz, says two things distinguish Blair as a champion: "her work habits and lifestyle." Blair concurs: "Competing, not just winning, is everything." This has been her philosophy and practice throughout her fantastic career.

Yet she remains the same person she was before her success. Unlike so many sports celebrities, she does not chase money. Naming a street after her in her hometown of Champaign, Illinois, did not change her demeanor.

Skating five hundred meters in under thirty-nine seconds is the equivalent of breaking track's four-minute-mile barrier. Twenty-seven days after the 1994 Winter Olympics in Lillehammer, Norway, Blair was participating in an invitational five-hundred-meter race in Calgary, the venue where she had won her first Olympic gold medal in 1988. She skated to a new world record: 38.99 seconds. Bonnie Blair had shattered the magical barrier, a goal she had quietly pursued. At last she had claimed her dream. But only fifty people saw the race!

I Want to Be Me

In September of 1995, Notre Dame football coach Lou Holtz had an emergency operation to correct a neck condition that could have left him paralyzed. The experience made him reevaluate his life and priorities.

"There's a lot of pressure at Notre Dame, a lot of pressure you put on yourself and people are always comparing you with other people and that's never good," he commented. "I can't be anybody else but Lou Holtz and maybe I haven't done that as well as I should in recent times."

Legend Enshrined

Kareem Abdul-Jabbar was inducted into basketball's Hall of Fame in Springfield, Massachusetts, in May of 1995. The seven-foot-two-inch gentle giant played twenty years in the National Basketball Association.

Consider these accomplishments: He scored a record 44,149 points; played in more games than any other player (1,797); and blocked 3,189 shots, also an NBA record.

Kareem Abdul-Jabbar stands tall and alone in the game of basket-ball.

Unnecessary Roughness

Football is a rough game both on and off the field—especially on the professional level. On his sixty-sixth birthday (January 4, 1996), Don Shula, the winningest coach in the history of the National Football League, resigned as mentor of the Miami Dol-phins. He was under considerable pressure. Beginning the 1995 season with high expectations, the team posted a disappointing 9 to 7 record and lost in the first round of the playoffs. After twenty-six years of coaching, Shula tallied 347 victories, five Su-per Bowl appearances, two Super Bowl championships, and the distinction of coaching the only NFL team to go undefeated in a season. Yet the Miami fans demanded change. They wanted to know, "What have you done for us lately?"

Another coaching legend, Tom Landry, of the Dallas Cowboys, was also replaced under less than gracious circumstances. What a coincidence that Jimmy Johnson should follow both these extraordinary coaches—first in Dallas and now in Miami.

There is a penalty in football for unnecessary roughness. At times, one could wish that the assessment could also be levied against impatient, indignant, and insensitive fans.

Baseball's Icon

On Wednesday night, September 6, 1995, Cal Ripken Jr. broke Lou Gehrig's "unbreakable" record by playing in his 2,131st consecutive baseball game. That's thirteen-and-a-half years without missing a game! Since Ripken's streak started, 3,695 players have been on the disabled list.

This powerful man—he is six feet four inches tall and weighs 225 pounds—is one of the largest to play the pivotal position of shortstop. He is all but flawless in the field. From 1989 to 1994, he made only fifty-eight errors! He had more home runs than any shortstop (321) when he eclipsed Gehrig's record.

When the new number was posted, fans in Baltimore's Camden Yards erupted into twenty-two minutes and fifteen seconds of merrymaking. It was spontaneous and beautiful! Acknowledging the tremendous display of affection, Ripken circled the park, touching as many hands as possible. Among the hundreds of placards, the one that caught my eye read: "class, ability, humility."

During the postgame celebration, Ripken said, "Tonight, I stand here overwhelmed, as my name is linked with the great and courageous Lou Gehrig. I believe in my heart our true link is a common love of the game of baseball, a passion for our team, and a desire to compete on the very highest level."

Another Way

Memories of high school football, for players, usually include slogans and halftime speeches.

Slogans adorned our locker-room wall: "You can't make the club in the tub," "Show me a good loser and I'll show you a loser," "Football is not only the greatest of games, it's a way of life." The most memorable halftime speech exhorted us to "think of the opponents across the line as 'commies' " because Coach B carried "lead in his belly" from World War II. The logic still eludes me!

Although football coaches regularly employ military imagery, Pacific Lutheran Coach Frosty Westering is an exception. As a former Marine squad leader, Westering knows the military. Furthermore, his coaches were, in his words, "military, kick-in-the-rear type guys." "We won a lot of games," reflects Westering, "but there was no fun. Practices were like hell week. I said to myself, there's got to be another way."

Gradually, Westering developed an alternative football philosophy. Pacific Lutheran teams spend the first three days of summer two-a-day practices doing "team building." Players' jerseys have only one name on the back—LUTE. Swearing and trash talking are not tolerated. Hugs greet players who have committed a turnover. Postgame sessions focus on the positive.

Westering's unorthodox coaching method has purpose. "We believe the best thing is to affirm and encourage our players, even when they make mistakes," he comments. "If they aren't down on themselves, the next hit, the next pass could make the difference."

Westering's unorthodox coaching philosophy produces results. His twenty-three-year college coaching career record of 236-73-6 (at the start of the 1995 season) makes him the winningest active coach in NAIA football and twelfth on the all-time coaching list.

Getting Out of the Bleachers

In the 1935 Ivy League championship football game between Dartmouth and Princeton, a unique incident occurred. During a crucial series of downs, when it appeared Princeton would score, an enthusiastic fan rushed onto the field and actually participated in one play.

Controversy surrounds the story, but this much has been verified: There was a twelfth man on the field for a brief moment, and he came from the sideline to assist in the goal line stand.

Officials claimed it was snowing so hard that they had difficulty spotting the extra man.

Giving Something Back

In July 1995, the All-Star baseball celebrations in Dallas were briefly interrupted when Mickey Mantle held a press conference. He looked gaunt and weak following a liver transplant; by his own admission a condition exacerbated by excessive drinking over the years. The near-fatal liver disease and surgery had taken their toll. He lost forty pounds while in the hospital. However, for the most part, he was upbeat and cheerful. His adoring fans never forgot him. He received twenty thousand pieces of mail during his ordeal.

The Hall of Famer talked neither about his lifetime batting average (.298) nor his home run total (536)—but about life. He said, "You talk about a role model, this is a role model: Don't be like me. . . . God gave me the ability to play baseball and I wasted it. I'm going to spend the rest of my life trying to make up. I want to start giving something back."

Mantle died of cancer on Sunday, August 13, 1995.

Beyond Ourselves

When the legendary Alonzo Stagg was a student at Yale, he was so poor that for a time he lived on twenty-five cents a day. Even so, this small man—five feet six inches tall—made Walter Camp's first All-American football team.

This splendid athlete considered the ministry; he attended Yale Divinity School, but concluded that his voice was inadequate for the pulpit. Consequently, he devoted himself to the training of American youth. He coached football until he was about ninety years old.

While Stagg was head football coach at the University of Chicago, a phenomenal event occurred. In a game with the University of Illinois, an official sustained an injury and Alonzo Stagg was asked to step in and referee. This was not unlike asking an attorney to judge her own case, or a farmer to determine price support for his crops, or a parent to evaluate his or her child's examination. Stagg possessed such undisputed integrity that the rival coach trusted him to make impartial calls.

Stewardship

Sensitive Human Being

Chris Gross, twenty-six, of California, was on his way to work when he first heard about the 1995 Oklahoma City bombing. He was so affected by the news that he felt compelled to respond. After sharing his feelings and discussing options with friends, he concluded that the most compassionate action would be to help provide some degree of financial security for the children whose parents were killed.

This caring young man started an educational scholarship fund. His idea was authenticated by pledging his full year's salary, $54,000, to the fund. Other individuals and corporations have also contributed.

What a sensitive and sacrificial human being!

Enviable Example

Rush Limbaugh writes about the remarkable Marine Corps Scholarship Fund in his book, *The Way Things Ought to Be*. This fund provides for the education of the children whose fathers or mothers die as Marines in the line of duty. Since the Gulf War, they have broadened their compassion to include children of parents killed in all branches of the service.

The Marine Corps Scholarship Fund is a model of efficiency. Charitable organizations often spend 10 to 50 percent of their income to achieve their objectives. The Marine Fund stands apart: 95 percent of the dollars donated reach the intended beneficiaries.

God's Tithe

The tithe was commonly practiced among the Phoenicians, Arabians, Carthaginians, Chinese, Greeks, and Romans. It is important to note that many cultures other than those within the Hebrew tradition were dedicating their tithes. Aristotle, the famed Greek philosopher, referred to the tithe as "an ancient law."

When we examine the Hebrew Bible, we find that the principle of the tithe runs through it like a golden thread. Malachi summed it up: "Bring the full tithe into the storehouse, so that there may be food in my house, and thus put me to the test, says the LORD of hosts; see if I will not open the windows of heaven for you and pour down for you an overflowing blessing" (3:10).

Tithing was expected of the ancient Jew. Jesus declared that he came not to destroy the law and the prophets, but to fulfill them. If tithing was an ancient law, then Jesus confirmed it. In fact, he said, "Woe to you, scribes and Pharisees, hypocrites! For you tithe mint, dill, and cummin, and have neglected the weightier matters of the law: justice and mercy and faith. It is these you ought to have practiced without neglecting the others" (Matthew 23:23).

Converted in the Car

A splendid churchman and friend shared this experience.

"Years ago four good friends and neighbors from a small southern town were driving to a football game in an adjoining state. After a hundred miles or so of sports chatter, the conversation turned to family budgets. The four compared costs of the necessities of life, insurance, automobiles, and other items. They all had young children and modest incomes, so they found that they had much in common in stretching their dollars to provide the most for their families. One of the foursome quietly stated that the *first* item in his family budget was the tithe. A second, and then a third indicated that they also gave the first tenth of each dollar to the Lord's work. The fourth man in the group sat in silent shock. He had thought of himself as a pretty good churchman since he was president of his Sunday school class and fairly regular in worship attendance. He had heard sermons on tithing all of his life, but it did not occur to him that 'regular fellows' like these friends and neighbors—

football fans even—were tithing. He would have wondered how they could afford it, when he was straining to give one percent. Now he was hearing their matter-of-fact statements that their family financing was working *better* because of these gifts, not in spite of them. At that moment in his life, he felt the presence of God in his three companions, and he resolved to become a tither.

"I was that fourth man, and on that football Saturday I learned how the power of God is revealed through Christian witness."

The Widow's Mites

In August 1995, President Aubrey Lucas of the University of Southern Mississippi, in Hattiesburg, announced another major do - nation to the school. Yet the circumstances of this particular gift "overwhelmed" him. The donor was neither wealthy nor a graduate. Although the person lived near the school, the benefactor had never been on the campus. Furthermore, this gift was the largest ever given to Southern Mississippi or any of the state's predominantly White universities by an African American.

The donor was eighty-seven-year-old Oseola McCarty. She quit school in the sixth grade to take care of a sick aunt and worked seventy-five years washing and ironing for some of Hattiesburg's oldest families. She never married, never had children, and never learned to drive an automobile. She lived in her family home and spent next to nothing, cutting the toes out of shoes and binding her ragged Bible with Scotch tape. And over the decades she saved one-quarter of a million dollars.

McCarty signed an irrevocable living trust giving the university $150,000 to endow a scholarship with "priority consideration" to be given to Black students who demonstrate financial need. "I thought it would be nice to try to help (deserving students)," she said. "I thought that was the right thing to do. Everybody is calling for an education nowadays." McCarty plans to donate another $100,000 to her church and to some cousins.

Bill Pace, the executive director of the University of Southern Mississippi Foundation, remarked, "This is the first time I've experienced anything like this from an individual who simply was not affluent, did not have the resources and yet gave substantially. In fact, she gave almost everything she has."

"And Jesus sat over against the treasury, and beheld how the people cast money into the treasury: and many that were rich cast in much. And there came a certain poor widow, and she threw in two mites. . . . And he called *unto him* his disciples, and saith unto them, Verily I say unto you, That this poor widow hath cast more in, than all they which have cast into the treasury: For all *they* did cast in of their abundance; but she of her want did cast in all that she had, *even* all her living" (Mark 12:41-44 KJV).

Community Compassion

Four dozen college students who lost one or both parents in the April 19, 1995, terrorist bombing of the Alfred P. Murrah Federal Building in Oklahoma City were back in school the next fall, thanks in part to college grants provided by a generous outpouring of community compassion. The financial assistance was part of a larger, collective effort by charitable foundations, state and local officials, and universities around the country to assist dependents of blast victims in continuing their education.

Officials at the State Regents for Higher Education, who coordinate the program, stated that an additional 126 children, whose parents died in the bombing or who themselves were injured, will be eligible for support. The last anticipated payment will be made in 2018 when the youngest dependent—a child born two months after the bombing—is expected to graduate from college.

In only four months, more than $20 million in private money has been raised from across the country, by eighty funds, to help blast victims pay their day-to-day expenses, medical bills, and uninsured property damage, as well as education costs.

The Stewardship of Suffering

Rose Fitzgerald Kennedy died on January 22, 1995, at the age of 104. This matriarch of one of America's most prominent families was a remarkable woman: daughter of John F. Fitzgerald, Boston mayor and congressman; wife of Joseph Kennedy, a United States ambassador; mother of a president and two U.S. senators. She had every right to be proud. Her monetary fortune, social connections, and political instincts converged to create a powerful, influential person at home and throughout America.

Few mothers have had to endure more suffering and sacrifice than Rose Kennedy. Four of her nine children were killed: two died in plane crashes and two were assassinated. And Rosemary, her daughter, has lived in a home for the retarded for over fifty years. As if this were not enough, a grandson died from a drug overdose. And then, there was the Chappaquiddick incident involving Senator Edward Kennedy and Mary Jo Kopechne. What a mountain of human pain! Mrs. Kennedy once referred to her life as living through "a series of agonies and ecstasies."

An ardent and faithful Roman Catholic, she demonstrated again and again an enviable Christian faith. "God wants us to be happy," she once said. "Birds sing after a storm. Why shouldn't we?"

You Never Know!

The president of Eureka College, Dr. George A. Hearne, told me this intriguing story.

Back in the 1980s when the college was creating a scholarship program to honor its distinguished alumnus Ronald Reagan, a mailing list of some of Mr. Reagan's friends was purchased.

Subsequently, a direct mail, promotional letter was sent to selected persons. A small percentage responded with modest gifts of $10 to $25. However, a Mr. H. J. "Harry" Casey sent a check for $13,000, explaining that it would help a student for the first two years and that he would make plans to cover the final two years. Such stewardship caught the attention of the president, who conducted a quiet, discreet inquiry.

Information revealed that Harry Casey was born and reared in Seattle, where he and his brothers started a delivery service on bicycles.

Mr. Casey moved to Portland, where he became the first Ford dealer in town. Meanwhile, he provided his brothers back home with additional transportation for their delivery service. From this mod - est beginning emerged the United Parcel Service.

Through thoughtful attention, George Hearne became a trusted friend who visited the Caseys several times a year, especially on anniversaries. Mr. Casey lived to be 101 years old. At the time of his death, cumulative gifts to Eureka College from him and his sister, Marguerite Casey, ran to over $2 million.

Is Your Will Christian?

People have different attitudes about wills. The average person is allergic to the idea of a will. Some feel the drawing of a will is so personal that no one should talk to them about it. Others seem to think writing a will is so simple that they need no assistance. Still others feel that a will is only for the well-to-do.

While a will is a legal instrument and one of the most important ones an individual can draft or cause to be written, it is more of a record of a person's faith than a declaration of one's possessions. It is the individual's effort to extend influence and stewardship into the future beyond death. It is, therefore, one's legal and spiritual resurrection. Though being dead, one continues to speak—and act.

Wills, of course, can be very foolish, ambiguous, and costly. Back in 1817, Nathaniel Wilson created a presidential graveyard near Lancaster, Ohio. The will is perfectly legal and each president is comforted by the fact that he has a place to go. Yet it accomplishes very little.

In Williamstown, Kentucky, a seventy-five-year-old widow who seldom attended church bequeathed virtually all of her estate, $76,000, to forty-three churches in Grant County, Kentucky. While this is a generous amount, one can think of better ways of helping the church than distributing $76,000 among forty-three congrega -

tions! But at least, as one relative said, "she didn't wear her religion on her sleeve."

As Christians, we are challenged not only to believe in the future, but to provide for it in every way possible; to experience the eternal *now*.

Whatever your accomplishments, whatever your provisions for the church, make a will and strive to live under the admonition: "Well done, good and trustworthy slave; you have been trustworthy in a few things, I will put you in charge of many things; enter into the joy of your master" (Matthew 25:21).

Speaking After Death

Good stewards not only use their talents and resources wisely while living, but they also anticipate future needs by using proper legal instruments to continue their Christian witness after death. No one is compelled to draw a will, but if you do not declare your intentions, the state will execute its own plan. You may not approve of their decisions, but it will be too late to protest.

Church members frequently neglect to prepare wills. Experts estimate that seven out of ten Christians have no will.

Celebrities also neglect the privilege of speaking after death. Pablo Picasso is a case in point. He wrote, "When I die it will be like a shipwreck." And it was! His son Paulo was his only legitimate heir. Claude, Paloma, and Maya were illegitimate children by two mistresses. When he died in 1973 without a will or testament, his estate was appraised at $260 million.

On the day of the funeral, Paulo's son, Pablito, swallowed a container of bleach and later died. In 1977, Maya's mother, Marie Theresa, hanged herself. Jacqueline, Picasso's second wife, carefully selected paintings for a 1986 show, then shot herself.

In contrast, when Malcolm Forbes died, he left all employees a week's salary and forgave all personal debts up to $10,000.

Television

Our Choice with Television

In 1938 E. B. White, the distinguished man of letters, sat before a strange looking electronic box that continuously belched out pictorial images. He is reported to have said, "I believe television is going to be the test of the modern world, and that in this new opportunity to see beyond the range of our vision we shall discover either a new and unbearable disturbance of the general peace, or a soaring radiance in the sky."

After six decades, the words of Mr. White sound more like those of a prophet than those of a literary giant.

This technological marvel has the capability to entertain, instruct, and inspire; it also possesses the seductive powers of addiction, distraction, and defiance. The choice is ours!

Commercials

In his book *Who Will Tell the People? The Betrayal of the American Democracy*, William Greider addresses issues related to television. He says, "The American audience is now overwhelmed by random bursts of advertising—300 messages a day for the average consumer; 9,000 a month; 108,500 a year."

Tethered to the Tube

According to the June 1995 *U.S. News*/CNN poll, children ages three to eighteen watch television, on the average, eighteen hours per week (*U.S. News & World Report*, July 3, 1995). One-third average ten hours or less per week, while 11 percent exceed thirty hours per week. One-half of the parents surveyed think their children watch more television than they should; one-quarter of the parents believe their children watch more TV than they admit; and one-quarter let their children watch as much TV as they want.

An Internal Compass

Ed Joyce, former president of CBS, has written a book entitled *Dan Rather: Off Camera*. With convincing clarity, Joyce profiles this multimillion-dollar-a-year man who lives under national, ongoing scrutiny. He describes Rather's abrasive, combative nature and cites the time he walked off the set in New York when the U.S. Open tennis match ran overtime and his shouting match with then Vice President George Bush.

Acknowledging Mr. Rather's abilities as well as the difficulties of being a television news anchor, Joyce, nevertheless, concludes, "Rather lacks a sense of who he really is. He lacks an internal compass—a standard that other people in times of crisis are able to follow."

Irrespective of the accuracy of the accusation, most of us struggle with the same issue to an extent seldom acknowledged.

There is a Chinese proverb that says, "There are five points to a compass: east, west, north, south and the point where we are."

When "Amen" Isn't Enough

There is an enormous difference between portraying a religious figure on television and being a religious person in life. Just ask Clifton Davis. You may remember him as the actor who played the Reverend Reuben Gregory on the NBC comedy *Amen*. Now he is vice-chancellor for planning and development at Elizabeth City State University, a historically Black university in Elizabeth City, North Carolina. Why the career change?

"I had to sacrifice my religious values for several TV shows," Davis explained, declining to name them. "I am no longer willing to do that. It is one thing to have fame and success. It is another to live with yourself."

Virtual Violence

The question of whether there is a causal connection between violence on television and violence in real life has been debated for decades. In 1952 a Senate subcommittee on juvenile delinquency, in response to children emulating Superman and jumping from roofs, warned against the effects of television violence on children. The 1968 Milton Eisenhower Commission on the Causes of Violence, created after the assassinations of Robert Kennedy and Martin Luther King Jr., concluded that there was a correlation between TV violence and violent behavior. In 1972 Surgeon General Jesse Steinfeld reported that a "causal connection is clear enough to warrant appropriate remedial action."

Despite these and other reports, violence on television continues at alarming rates. A recent study, funded by the National Cable Television Association, examined twenty-five-hundred hours of shows during the 1994–1995 season and introduced two new pieces of information. First, violence occurs in 57 percent of entertainment programs (excluding news and sports). Second, and more important, the report studied both the context and the consequence of the violence portrayed in shows. It found: 47 percent of violent confrontations show no harmful effects to the victims, 58 percent depict no pain, and perpetrators of violent acts go unpunished 73 percent of the time.

Not only are viewers of action shows desensitized to violence but they are also mental participants in "virtual violence." No harm, no pain, no consequences. They only enjoy.

The Success of Soaps

Although the origins of television soap operas are traced to fifteenth-century folktales, their name is derived from the soap companies that sponsored them on radio in the 1930s. Over fifty million viewers, one in every five Americans, watch soap operas each week. And 40 percent watch in the workplace.

A recent survey indicates that 62 percent of Americans say there is too much violence on TV; 41 percent say there is too much sex; but only 2 percent say there are too many soap operas.

Why are soaps so popular? Perhaps they are enjoyed because they speak to the needs of the human heart as satisfied by ongoing drama. They are our modern parables—our hopes and fears portrayed in everyday life.

Yet a fundamental difference exists between television and biblical parables. Soaps simply reflect cultural values while the parables of Jesus proclaim kingdom values. And that makes all the difference!

Turn Off the Television

Television stands alone as a blessing and a curse: a blessing when viewed wisely and a curse when allowed to control the home. No product of modern technology has influenced the family like television. Its visual images are powerful and seductive. Television truly epitomizes all that is desirable and undesirable in our society.

In her provocative book *Unplugging the Plug-In-Drug*, Marie Winn pleads with parents, civic groups, and schools to develop "TV turn-off" periods in their schedules. These controlled conditions should be democratically determined, and new activities substituted. Groups designed to help children "kick the TV habit" are also forming across the country. Their aim is not to bash television, but to help parents and others set priorities and monitor programs.

When children can rattle off the names of five alcoholic beverages but cannot name five United States presidents, it is time to turn off the television and turn children on to the library.

Who Will Save the Children?

Dr. Neil Postman, a professor of communications at New York University, has written a disturbing book, *Amusing Ourselves to Death*, which deals with genuine communication in an age of media hyperbole. Professor Postman asserts that the most obvious cultural fact of our day is the decline of the "Age of Typography" and the acceleration of the "Age of Television." The entertainment center has replaced the bookcase. Television programming has become the motivating and manipulating engine of society.

Children, who spend significant time in imaginative worlds, are irresistibly drawn to this strange box that blurts out comical and serious sounds, along with luring and lurid images in living color. They are caught up in the extraordinary. Yet the average child between the ages of two and five, we are told, watches the "tube" seven hours and nineteen minutes a day, Monday through Friday.

If we are to save our children, their minds and souls, in this "Age of Television," adults must acquire new skills in parenting. In addition, they must introduce their children to the wonderful worlds of music, art, education, drama, and faith. Only adults can do it.

The Storyteller Knows Me

Although the popularity of television can be attributed to its seemingly infinite supply of stories, that ability also locates its Achilles' heel. This realization became clear when I read the following story in a church newsletter.

"People in an African village purchased a television set. For weeks all of the children and all of the adults gathered around the set—morning, afternoon, and night—watching the programs. Then, after a couple of months, the set was turned off and never used again. A visitor to the village asked the chief, 'Why do you no longer watch television?'

" 'We have decided to listen to the storyteller,' he replied.

"The visitor asked, 'Why? Doesn't television know more stories?'

"The chief replied, 'Yes, but the storyteller knows me.' "

Time

Twenty-four-Hour Gift

Each day bestows a twenty-four-hour gift of time. And the difference between promise and performance, possibility and productivity, is often the way we use it.

According to a 1995 market research survey (conducted by NPD Group Inc.) of the daily activities of three thousand people, work and sleep on the average consume about seven and one-half hours each per day. Parents of children spend an additional two hours in some form of child care.

Other endeavors that occupy our time include: watching television, 154 minutes; being on the move, 51 minutes; grooming, 49 minutes; preparing meals, 34 minutes; and worshiping, 15 minutes.

Some observations on time: We spend more time watching television than watching our children, and more time fixing ourselves than our food.

Touched by Time

On a visit to Saint Peter's Basilica in Rome, I was irresistibly drawn to the cast bronze statue of the patron saint, Peter, the vicar of Jesus Christ, in the nave of the church. Although scholars are unsure of the sculptor—some suggest Arnolfo di Cambio (1245–1308) who began the Duomo in Florence—tradition claims that this statue is the product of the early church.

Consequently, this depiction of Peter is particularly venerated by the faithful. Through the centuries pilgrims to Rome have touched Peter's extended right foot out of homage to him. Now it is noticeably smooth and concave.

The aggregate power of faith has left its indelible imprint on the statue. It has been touched by time.

Longevity

Some years ago this story appeared in the *Wall Street Journal*. A reporter was sent to a small, remote, Southern community to gather information on one of its citizens reputed to be 112 years old.

"Tell me," the reporter inquired of a native, "how do you account for your neighbor living all these years?"

"Well," came the reply, "I guess it's because he's never done anything else."

The Passage of Time

The annual ritual of preparing and receiving holiday greeting cards marks not only the passage of time, but it also affords an occasion to reflect on the meaning of time. Our family received a letter that began: "I vividly remember sitting in my fifth-grade classroom thinking there had to be at least 100 hours in a day and 2 million days in a year—either that scenario or all the clocks around the world were simultaneously slowing down to a crawl! Now that I have too many places to go, too many things to do, and too many people that I want to see, it appears those same clocks are in a race—a day now occurring in less than 10 hours. My, how one's perspective skews reality! I constantly think of how many people I had planned to call, write, or visit during the year—and now the year is drawing to a close."

What Year Is It?

Have you made your party plans for the millennium? Better hurry. The Savoy in London is booked, the Space Needle in Seattle is rented, and Disney World is full.

But wait a minute . . . or more. What year is it?

Although purists argue that the twenty-first century, and thus the third millennium of the common era, does not officially start until January 1, 2001, most people will celebrate millennium eve on December 31, 1999.

The argument over time is not new. Calendars are neither accurate nor uniform. For example, the Western or Gregorian calendar is a revised version of the Julian or Roman calendar. When Pope John I, in the sixth century, asked the mathematician and monk, Dionysius Exiguus, to design a method for calculating the date of Easter, the monk also renumbered the years of the calendar, focusing on the birth of Jesus instead of the founding of Rome. However, Dionysius mistakenly placed Jesus' birth in the 753rd year of the old Roman calendar. Scholars generally agree that Jesus was born a few years before Herod's death and that King Herod died in the 750th year of the old calendar. Thus, our present calendar may be off by as much as six years.

Moreover, when Great Britain and the American colonies adopted the Gregorian calendar, eleven days were skipped in 1752 to ensure uniformity. Tremendous problems resulted. For instance, on George Washington's twentieth birthday, his date of birth changed from February 11 to February 22.

Confused? So was Washington. But not to worry. America cleared up that confusion by creating Presidents' Day.

Digging Up the Past

In 1642, civil war broke out in England and ended with the defeat of Charles I in 1645–1646 and the disestablishment of the Church of England. After the "Rump Parliament" initiated proceedings against Charles, he was found guilty of high treason and beheaded on January 30, 1649.

Eleven years later Charles II was victorious on the battlefield and restored the monarchy. On gaining the throne, the new king immediately arrested the men who had signed his father's death warrant. Although fifteen of the signatories had already died, Charles ordered their bodies exhumed so that they could be hanged alongside the forty-four others still living.

American Ghosts

In September 1995, ghosts haunted the New Globe Theatre in London, an authentic reproduction of the Elizabethan playhouse. Two of the invited ghosts were Americans—Edwin Booth, one of the most successful Shakespearean actors of his day, and his younger brother, John Wilkes Booth, also an actor but better known as the assassin of Abraham Lincoln.

The play, *Booth, Brother Booth*, written and performed by John Ammerman, an associate professor of drama at the University of Georgia, revolves around the trunk in which John Wilkes Booth had stored his costumes and props. Although it was confiscated by federal officials after the assassination, Edwin Booth retrieved it.

As the catalyst for both good and bad memories, the trunk's possessions permit the play to evoke Edwin Booth's life as well as his feelings about his brother and the assassination. According to Ammerman, Edwin's career was forever overshadowed by his brother's crime—"the nightmare of the memory he could not escape."

In the last scene, Edwin burns the trunk and all its contents, except for a photograph of his brother. As Edwin stares at the picture, he addresses his brother: "Johnny, comfort my soul with a sign of regret. Be the beautiful boy I remember so well."

Rock of Ages

Gravestones fascinate me, particularly their inscriptions. They not only inform us about the deceased—was the person pompous or plain, gracious or greedy—but they also instruct us about life.

What would you put on your tombstone? Do you have a favorite inscription? I like the one that simply said: "I told you I was sick."

Perhaps the least asked, but equally important, question pertains to the material you should select for your headstone. Because illegible inscriptions defeat their purpose, the durability of the stone is crucial.

There are three basic types of rock: sedimentary, igneous, and metamorphic. Sedimentary rocks, like limestone and sandstone, erode the fastest and are, therefore, undesirable for gravestones. Although igneous rocks, like granite and basalt, are hard, metamorphic rocks, like marble and slate, are most resistant to weathering.

Although geologists are concerned with the ages of rocks, in the choice of tombstones metamorphic is the rock of ages.

On Waiting Too Long

In the December 1969 issue of *Atlantic,* Mitchell Wilson discussed Nobel laureates he has known—among them the brilliant Julian Schwinger. This remarkable man entered Columbia University's graduate program in physics at age seventeen in 1935. He became a full professor at Harvard when he was twenty-nine and later made significant contributions in World War II. Dr. Schwinger received the Nobel Prize in his field in 1965.

Through the years—in fact since age twelve   Julian Schwinger had wanted to meet Dr. Albert Einstein, who was then in residence at Princeton. Repeatedly, however, Schwinger declined invitations to visit the eminent scholar, waiting to see him on his own merit. Eventually Schwinger was recognized for his work on the electron. He was to be the first recipient of the Einstein Award, which carried a $10,000 cash prize. The award was to be made at Princeton.

Schwinger eagerly anticipated the occasion, when he was to meet the long-admired scholar, Einstein. He arrived just in time and Dr. I. I. Rabi made the presentation. Einstein rose slowly, waited for Schwinger to approach, and handed him the award. It was then that the brilliant teacher realized that Einstein was very old, that he had not understood a word said, and was confused.

Schwinger was greatly disturbed. "The man I had wanted to meet, the man I had revered, must have died quite a while before. As soon as I could, I got off by myself and just walked."

It was then that Schwinger realized the quickness and suddenness of life. Life was *now,* and he immediately went out and blew part of his prize money on a Cadillac convertible and exotic clothes.

What happened to the eminent physicist can happen to anyone who waits too long to do something he or she has always wanted or intended to do. Now is the time. Seize the now!

Footprints in the Snow

A letter from David, a son who lives in British Columbia, related the anguish associated with the sudden death of his father-in-law. He died in his sleep! The unexpected demise of this strapping man, highly successful in his business and disciplined in his personal affairs, shocked the family and the community of Stouffville, Ontario, Canada. Four different memorial services were held for this admired and beloved neighbor.

Days later, David drove up to his in-law's summer cottage. No sooner had inspection of the property begun than he encountered footprints, believed to be those of his father-in-law, in the snow. An eerie feeling! There were footprints but no visible person; he had been there, but now was gone. Everything seemed to be in order; the boat was tied and the house was secure.

Footprints of a dead man in the snow. They will soon disappear. But the memories, the relationships, and the influences of love will outlive us all.

The nineteenth-century American poet, Henry Wadsworth Longfellow, in his hortatory poem "A Psalm of Life," compares our days to "footprints on the sands of time." Whether in the sand or snow, visible or invisible, we all leave footprints; footprints that excite or frighten, challenge or condemn, advance or retard the reign of God.

Time to Stir

Many years ago there was a rabbi in Cleveland who would begin his classes by inviting questions from his students.

One day the students asked, "Rabbi, what makes coffee sweet— the sugar or the stirring?"

Temporarily stymied, the rabbi replied that he would have an answer for tomorrow's class.

The next day the students immediately repeated the question: "What makes coffee sweet—the sugar or the stirring?"

The rabbi replied, "The stirring."

Quickly the students asked, "Then why add the sugar?"

"Because," the rabbi said, "the sugar tells you when to stir."

Violence

"Collateral Damage"

On a stop in Vukovar, a small town in Croatia, Madeleine Albright, then U.S. Ambassador to the United Nations, visited a farm. There, beneath a pile of rubbish and broken down equipment, was a shallow grave containing the bodies of two to three hundred human beings. According to the guide, it was "collateral damage." Ambassador Albright went on to say that they were "massacred, not because of what they had done, but who they were."

Civilian Carnage

Although World War I (1914–1918) inaugurated global conflict, it was fought traditionally. Military action was limited primarily to opposing armies. The ratio of military to civilian dead was ninety to ten.

But that changed with Adolf Hitler. Targeting both military and civilian populations, Hitler redefined warfare by initiating civilian genocide. In World War II, sixty-seven civilians died for every ten soldiers.

By 1995, writes David Rieff in *The New Republic* (January 29, 1996), civilian carnage had reached alarming proportions. The ratio worldwide was the exact opposite of what it was for World War I—ninety civilians killed for every ten soldiers killed.

Base-Brawl

Anyone who has ever watched minor league baseball knows that the quality of play is characterized more by excitement and enthusiasm than by execution and etiquette. Therefore, the bench-clearing brawl in the bottom of the third inning in a game between the Durham Bulls and the Winston-Salem Warthogs on May 22, 1995, was not especially unusual. And the fact that ten players were ejected and one was taken to the hospital after being knocked unconscious was not altogether uncommon.

What distinguished this brawl from other baseball fights was this irony: it occurred on "Strike Out Domestic Violence" night at the Durham Bulls Athletic Park. Baseball had imitated life. Antiviolence had struck out.

Violence Against Children

On October 1, 1993, twelve-year-old Polly Klaas was abducted from her home in Petaluma, California, by a bearded intruder. She had been hosting a slumber party for two friends. Two months later, her body was found and the alleged killer captured.

As her accused murderer went to trial in a San Jose courtroom in early February 1996, Polly's father, Marc Klaas, was more concerned about apathy outside the courtroom than the inside proceedings. The trial lasted six weeks. It has been estimated that, during any six-week period 115,000 children will disappear in America. According to Justice Department figures, about 45 percent will be runaways, 35 percent will be abducted by a family member, about 13 percent will be thrown out by their families, and almost 7 percent will be lost or missing for different reasons. In the same six-week period, fourteen thousand children will experience failed kidnapping attempts and thirty-five will be abducted by strangers. More than half of those kidnapped will be killed. Moreover, 350,000 children will suffer physical or sexual abuse.

"Children have no rights in our society," says Klaas, who is now a full-time advocate for programs to protect children. "We have no national policy to protect them. A million children disappear in this country every year. What would happen if a million corporate executives disappeared? There would be immediate action. But kids have no voice, and it just goes on."

Juvenile Arsonists

For the first time ever, juveniles account for a majority of all arson arrests in the United States. According to the 1994 National Fire Protection Association report, children and teenagers make up 55 percent of arson arrests. In that year, one-third of all those arrested for arson were under fifteen, while nearly 7 percent were under ten.

The agency claims that these statistics are not inflated by children who play with matches and accidentally start fires. "These are strictly kids who know what they're doing," declared John Hall, a NFPA researcher.

From the White House to the Wheelchair

On March 30, 1981, at about 2:30 in the afternoon, John Hinkley Jr. whipped out a handgun near the entrance to the Washington Hilton Hotel and shot President Reagan and his press secretary, James S. Brady. Two police officers were also injured.

Following extensive surgery, treatment, and therapy, Mr. Brady now has to use a wheelchair, and he continues to battle pain and the National Rifle Association.

Although subject to intense NRA pressure, Congress finally passed the Brady Bill; it requires a waiting period before one can purchase a handgun. However small, it is a significant beginning as well as a victory over the powerful gun lobby.

Through their Center to Prevent Handgun Violence and through educational programs, Sarah and Jim Brady do not advocate the banning of guns but rather the development of a licensing process designed to keep guns "out of the wrong hands." According to a Gallup poll, 77 percent of our citizens favor such a plan.

Why are Americans so obsessed with guns? It would seem that guns are in our genes. Romantically, it may be true. But the days of the Wild West are over. Yet there are those who feel they must have a handgun. I have a friend well into her eighties who keeps a gun in the glove compartment of her car.

Statistics indicate that people who live in homes where firearms are available are six times more likely to kill loved ones than those in homes without guns.

We so-called civilized Americans lead the world in handgun killings. According to FBI Uniform Crime Reports, in 1992 handguns were used to murder 13 people in Australia; 33 in Great Britain; 36 in Sweden; 60 in Japan; 97 in Switzerland; 128 in Canada; and 13,495 in the United States. Every day, fifteen American children, aged nineteen and under, are killed with guns.

However, no amount of political pettifogging and posturing or bills passed in Congress will restore Jim Brady, a splendid public servant, to his former self; neither will these efforts resurrect gun victims from the dead.

Murder at Harvard

"Harvard Student Kills Roommate, Self" was a frightening head-line Monday, May 29, 1995. According to reports, during the early Sunday morning hours on the twenty-eighth, Sinedu Tadesse, twenty, of Addis Ababa, Ethiopia, stabbed to death twenty-year-old Trang Ho, her Vietnamese roommate. Then Tadesse ran into the bathroom and hanged herself.

A visitor was injured, but not seriously.

Motivation for the killings was unclear.

Violence in Sports

Violence in professional football is not limited to the playing field. St. Louis Rams running back Ron Wolfley explains, "Wherever you go in the NFL, fans are all alike. The only thing that separates them is what they throw. On the West Coast, they throw food. The farther east you move, the larger and harder the objects become. In Midwest cities like Chicago, it's an AA battery. When you get to Philadelphia, it's a D battery."

Who's Behind Bars?

According to the Bureau of Justice statistics, as reported in *Parade Magazine* on August 12, 1995, "On June 30, 1994, there were 1,012,851 inmates in 1,291 state and 70 Federal prisons—950,979 men and 61,872 women. The majority of them—68%—are from 18 to 34 years of age. Although they constitute about 12% of the American population, 45% of all prisoners are black. Moreover, 54% of all inmates have been incarcerated before.

The cost of keeping a person in prison varies from state to state: In Arkansas it runs about $7,557 a year, while in Minnesota it is said to cost $30,302. Studies show that "the average cost of imprisoning an inmate over the age of 50, with health problems, is $60,000 a year."

Maintaining our prison system is a costly, harsh business. We need to put more resources into preventing crime; we must work for literacy, employability, sobriety, and citizenship.

School Uniforms

When children are shot for their designer shoes and jackets, what's a school principal to do? According to a survey of fifty-five hundred administrators attending the National Association of Secondary School Principals convention in San Francisco on February 26, 1996, 70 percent of the principals believe school uniforms will reduce violence.

In 1994, the Long Beach (California) Unified School District was the first public system in the nation to require uniforms in elementary and middle schools. After one year, the number of fights was down by one-half and suspensions were down by one-third. During the same time, academic performance improved.

"(School uniforms) obviously won't solve all the problems," admits Michael Casserly, executive director of the Council of the Great City Schools. "But it's a step in the right direction."

Women's Issues

Two Women Who Changed the World

They came from totally different worlds: one knew the opulence of British "royalty," the other the austerity of Albania and India; one wore designer clothes, the other a simple white and blue sari of her Missionaries of Charity order; one had a palace for a home, the other was at home in any slum. Their differences were most apparent in a photograph taken of them during their last meeting in New York City. The diminutive, frail nun was literally dwarfed by the tall, elegant princess.

These dissimilar yet exceptional women departed this world within five days of each other in the summer of 1997. Princess Diana, thirty-six, died on August 31 in a horrible automobile accident in Paris, while Mother Teresa, eighty-seven, died on September 5 of multiple health complications on her bed in a simple room in Calcutta.

In a rare public statement on the eve of Princess Diana's funeral, Queen Elizabeth II referred to the Princess of Wales as "a remarkable person. . . . No one who knew Diana will ever forget her."

This icon of beauty and grace inspired media obsession. Diana survived an embarrassing marriage and divorce. She bore the weight of history and the expectations of the aristocracy. She emerged as "England's rose." More than 1 million people lined the three-mile funeral route to view the cortege as it moved from Kensington Palace to Westminster Abbey, while an estimated 2.5 billion people watched the funeral on television or listened on the radio.

Beyond political correctness, celebrity culture, and personal safety, Diana's commitment to the disadvantaged and dying impelled her to mingle with and minister to the homeless, lepers, AIDS patients, and victims of land mines. She was truly the "people's princess."

Half a world away, Mother Teresa spent her life working with the "poorest of the poor" in the slums of Calcutta, India. Recipient of the Medal of Freedom from the United States and the 1979 Nobel Peace prize, she never wavered in her commitment to Jesus Christ. Her gift to the world was her extraordinary ability to see the face of God, as she often described it, "in its most distressing disguise."

Prime Minister Inder Kumar Gujral of India, after visiting St. Thomas Church where Mother Teresa's body lay, declared: "Just as India had Mohandas Gandhi to lead the fight against poverty, hunger and injustice in the first half of the century, so it had Mother Teresa to carry on that fight in the latter half."

The death of these two women caused the world to stop, weep, and pray. To what extent and duration their impact will endure, no one knows. But this we do know: Each made a profound difference in the world.

What attracted these contrasting personalities to each other? Why were their special memorial services global, dramatic, and inspiring? Was it not because each demonstrated contagious compassion for human beings?

Women Around the World

Fifty thousand women from 189 countries convened in China in late summer of 1995. Despite the weather and rather harsh hospital-ity, both the United Nations–led group and the nongovernmental organizations (NGOs) made bold to report on the status of women in the world as well as their proposals. Five thousand delegates hammered out a document known as a "Platform for Action." It will be widely distributed and read.

The impact of the Beijing Women's Conference will be significant. As Hillary Rodham Clinton said in her speech, "Women's rights are human rights."

Girls' Education Initiative

At the "Women, Poverty and Population" conference, held February 9-10, 1996, in Washington D.C., Joan Brown Campbell, general secretary of the National Council of the Churches of Christ in the USA, proposed an interfaith effort to promote at home and abroad education for girls, including sex education. Two previous conferences, the 1994 United Nations' World Conference on Population and Development, in Cairo, and the 1995 World Conference on Women, in Beijing, were deeply divided by passionate debates and differences over abortion and family planning. Campbell's initiative not only seeks common ground, it also addresses common concerns.

"[The education of girls] is a common-ground issue that can engage both opponents and supporters of abortion," Campbell told the conference. "It is a common-ground issue that can engage the support—and the political clout—of the entire religious community."

Quoting United Nations statistics, Campbell indicated that women's wages rise by 10 to 20 percent for each year they remain in school. "In Asia, Africa and Latin America," she said, "women with seven or more years of schooling have two to three children less than women with only three years of schooling."

Mother Doesn't Know Best

On May 6, 1996, Nancy Lieberman-Cline, thirty-seven, became the first woman inducted into the Basketball Hall of Fame. While a teenager in Far Rockaway, New York, she rode the subway to Harlem in search of the best pickup games in the city. That strong competitive urge enabled her to earn unprecedented honors.

In 1975, at age seventeen, she helped lead the USA to a gold medal in the Pan American Games. The next year, she became the youngest basketball player in Olympic history to win a medal when the U.S. women's team captured the silver. While a student at Old Dominion University, she twice won the coveted Wade Trophy, awarded to the women's national Player of the Year. When Lieberman-Cline signed a contract in 1986 with the Springfield Fame of the United States

Basketball League, she became the first woman to play in a men's pro league.

According to Lieberman-Cline, her mother deserves the credit. When Lieberman-Cline was ten, her mother informed her that "little girls don't play sports."

"I got up," remembers Lieberman-Cline, "and put my hands on my hips and said, 'I'm going to make history.' "

Women and Preaching

A funny thing happened on the way to the conservative takeover of the seminary. On April 27, 1995, only a week after trustees of Southern Baptist Theological Seminary in Louisville, Kentucky, specified that future professors must believe that women are *not* called to preach, the school announced that the top three recipients of the annual Clyde T. Francisco Preaching Awards were women!

This was the first time in the history of the awards that all the top prizes went to women. All the judges—six students and two faculty members—were men. Even more important, the field of twenty-eight entries was reduced to three by a "blind" review: written manuscripts were identified neither by name nor gender. Only after the three finalists were chosen did the selection committee hear audiotapes of the sermons to determine the order of finish.

Fit to Lift

According to a 1995 study conducted by the Army Research Institute of Environmental Medicine, women, given proper strength training, can also "tote that barge, lift that bale."

At laboratories in Natick, Massachusetts, researchers studied forty-one women volunteers, all but one of them civilians and many who had never exercised regularly. Before the start of the program, only 24 percent of the women qualified for Army jobs whose lifting requirements were considered "very heavy," such as lifting one-hundred-pound loads. However, after spending ninety minutes a day, five days a week for twenty-four weeks performing supervised

255

strength-building exercises designed to simulate specific military tasks, 78 percent of the women qualified.

Army scientist Everett Harman, who headed the study, concluded that it proved "women are capable of being trained to perform most very heavy military tasks."

Queen of the "Second Oldest Profession"

On April 22, 1996, the world lost a wonderful woman. For years, readers of Erma Bombeck's syndicated newspaper column and numerous books delighted in her humorous insights into the ordinary events of life. Although nothing escaped her wit, she focused primarily on what she knew best: being a housewife and mother—"the second oldest profession," as she liked to say. Most important, Bombeck reminded forgotten heroines that raising children was just as significant as sitting in the boardroom of a Fortune 500 corporation.

Even through her bout with breast cancer and kidney failure, Bombeck found the lighter side of life. When she was told that a kidney transplant was her only hope for survival, she refused to use celebrity status to her advantage. She endured dialysis four times a week for three years before a kidney became available.

Erma Bombeck inspired both women and men to look for the good in life and to keep a smile on their faces as well as on the faces of those we meet. When she died, we lost a perceptive commentator on life and a trusted friend.

Equal Opportunity Violence

The gender revolution hit television in the 1970s when female action heroes first appeared in shows like *The Bionic Woman* and *Charlie's Angels*. A quarter of a century later, L. Rowell Huesmann, a psychologist at the University of Michigan, has concluded the first long-term study of how violent heroines on TV may affect women's aggression over time. Huesmann reported that "girls get desensitized to violence just like guys, and when heroines' aggressive acts are portrayed positively, girls conclude it's a good way to solve problems." The study also discovered that the more young women watched violent shows in the 1970s, the more physically aggressive they became, and the more violent they remain even as women in their twenties.

Robert Lichter of the Center for Media and Public Affairs lamented, "Going from Barbie to *Thelma and Louise* is not necessarily progress. We have equal-opportunity media violence now. . . . This shows parents have to worry about effects of TV violence on kids regardless of gender."

Clean It Up

Regardless of the space, some people still think it's women's work to clean it up. In April 1996, fifty-three-year-old American biochemist Shannon Lucid joined two Russian cosmonauts aboard the Russian space station *Mir*, orbiting 250 miles above the earth's surface. After completing the five-day hookup with the United States space shuttle *Atlantis*, earthbound Russian General Yuri Glazkov declared that *Mir*'s cleaning ventilation fans "will be taken care of in a more timely manner because we know that women love to clean."

Lucid replied, "That kind of thinking doesn't bother me. We all work together to keep the place pretty tidy."

When Dr. Lucid returned to earth in August, she had broken the record for the most time spent in orbit of the earth by an American astronaut.

Comet's Legacy

It was the biggest bang ever witnessed by the human eye. On July 16, 1994, NASA's Hubble Space Telescope transmitted pictures of a comet named Shoemaker-Levy 9 colliding with the planet Jupiter. A "bruise" more than half the size of Earth marked the crash site.

At NASA's daily news conferences, the media and the public met the people behind the telescopes. Many were women, even though a 1990 survey of the American Astronomical Society identified only

13 percent of North America's 6,300 professional astronomers as female.

Carolyn Shoemaker, along with her husband, Eugene Shoemaker, and colleague, David Levy, discovered the comet in March 1993. She has tallied thirty-two comets, more than any other living person. Heidi Hammel, a principal research scientist at MIT, and Melissa McGrath, an assistant astronomer with the Space Telescope Science Institute in Baltimore, were two of six "team leaders" for the Hubble telescope observations. Reta Beebe, a professor of astronomy at New Mexico State University, is one of the world's top experts on the cloud structure of Jupiter. And Lucy McFadden, who at the time was a visiting professor of astronomy at the University of Maryland, helped to coordinate worldwide observations of the comet collision.

The educational legacy of this cataclysmic crash is considerable. Today's young people imagine themselves observing the outer limits of our solar system. In a letter to Dr. Hammel, a seventh-grade student, a young woman, wrote: "When I saw you on the news, I began to realize that there is so much more out there to see and know . . . I would like to experience first-hand the thrill of discovery someday."

The Power of Women

In *The Color of Water: A Black Man's Tribute to His White Mother*, James McBride, a saxophonist and award-winning composer, chronicles the powerful and purifying love of his mother. Through constant adversity and hostility, Ruth McBride Jordan created a caring world for her twelve children.

When she was a baby, her orthodox Jewish family emigrated from Poland to America to escape anti-Semitism. Yet rural Virginia introduced them to a new form of prejudice—the Ku Klux Klan. After marrying Andrew Dennis McBride, a Black violinist who later became a Baptist minister, her family sat "shiva" for her—the Jewish seven days of mourning. Although devastated when her husband died from cancer, leaving her with seven children and pregnant with James, she persevered. In time she married Hunter Jordan, also Black, and had four more children.

"Music and art and thought," McBride explains, "those were the distractions that Mommy used to manipulate us into not thinking about our whole mixed-race problem."

When asked why he wrote the book, James McBride responded, "One of the things that makes her story so unique is it shows how much power women have, because women absorb the shock of life's punishments with so much more willfulness and so much more strength than men do."

Work

Pay Attention to Your Dreams

Perfecting a shore-to-shore, bow-loading-and-unloading boat has long challenged marine engineers. Although many crafts of this kind have been constructed and launched over the years, none met more success than the one designed and built by the Eureka Tug Boat Company of New Orleans, under the supervision of Andrew J. Higgins.

His twenty-eight-foot R-boat combined seaworthiness with beaching capabilities. The U.S. Marine Corps accepted the design. From this accomplishment evolved the thirty-two-foot Eureka known as the Higgins boat. It was first used in American exercises in 1941. Eventually a fifty-foot MK3 was developed and 8,631 were built. Not only did the MK3 prove to be the most successful landing craft of World War II, but it was also instrumental in securing D-Day victory.

It is reported that during the stressful days of experimentation, Mr. Higgins had a dream, and in that dream he saw the image of the desired boat. After sharing his vision with his colleagues, the dream was translated into working drawings. The Higgins boat emerged.

Pay attention to your dreams!

Humble Creativity

Having been to St. Petersburg, Russia, I was fascinated by this story told by the twenty-year veteran of Church World Service, the Reverend Terry Grove.

During the early days of designing the capital city, the planners encountered a troubling problem—a huge rock occupied a pivotal place on the landscape. It had to be removed. Local contractors were asked to submit cost estimates. All bids came in too high; all were rejected.

Learning of the city's dilemma, a humble man from a neighboring village offered to relocate the stone for considerably less than previous proposals. Although skeptical of the stranger's skills, authorities awarded him the contract.

On the appointed day, the low bidder arrived with his crew. The men were carrying picks and shovels, and pushing wheelbarrows. The agrarian artisan started the project by driving heavy stakes around the base of the stone. The laborious job of digging out and removing the dirt from much of the circumference of the rock began. At last the workmen created a gaping cavity into which they pushed the rock. Then the condemned boulder was covered with the dirt that was salvaged from the excavation.

Humble creativity!

Career or Calling

William Sloane Coffin, former chaplain of Yale University and pastor of Riverside Church in New York, makes significant distinctions between a career and a calling in his book *A Passion for the Possible.*

"A career," he writes, "seeks to be successful, a calling to be valuable. A career tries to make money, a calling tries to make a difference. . . . A career . . . demands technical intelligence to learn a skill, to find out how to get from here to there. A calling demands critical intelligence to question whether 'there' is worth going toward."

Humanity, Not Technique

Michael Moschen is one of the finest jugglers in the world. His creativity, innovation, strength, and speed set him apart. He is variously referred to as an "illusionist," "movement artist," and "dancer-physicist."

This remarkable performer grew up in Greenfield, Massachusetts, the son of a stonemason, and now lives in Cornwall Bridge, Connecticut. As a youngster, he participated in sports; he was especially fascinated by the ability of a person to direct a golf ball with a club. As a beginning juggler, he would practice six hours a day, six days a week—a discipline he continues. This hard worker has been known to spend as much as eight years perfecting a single act. A typical show runs about two hours and, during it, he does not speak a word.

Although Michael Moschen is the only "juggler" in history to receive a MacArthur "genius" grant, he is humble and modest. After a performance he is accommodating, especially to aspiring jugglers who seek advice. "Try to find the humanity in the magic and maybe you'll come up with something of your own. It's the humanity that gets you there, not techniques."

A Glimpse of Grace

Vytautas Kabelis emigrated from Lithuania to the United States in 1989. He was trained in classical music; he taught and was a director of considerable stature.

Because of age—he's in his sixties—and language problems, he had difficulty finding employment in the United States in his field of music. So, for the past five years, this splendid gentleman has spent his days serving tables in a retirement center and his evenings delivering pizzas. What a contrast between the formalities of a concert hall and the common attire and atmosphere of a dining room for older adults!

This smiling man has made the difficult transition with enviable humility and grace.

Are You Comfortable in Your Work?

After serving twenty-two years as basketball coach at Vashon High School in St. Louis, Missouri, Floyd Irons resigned in the fall of 1995 to become the school's principal. He was the epitome of success: 537 career victories, 12 final four appearances, and 5 state titles. And now, selected as principal. However, after only a few months as principal, Irons resigned and returned to coaching for a reported $15,000 decrease in salary.

According to the *St. Louis Post-Dispatch,* "Irons never stopped wanting to coach . . . he's comfortable now."

The Retirement Paradox

Betty Friedan, founder of the National Organization for Women and the National Women's Political Caucus, discusses many of the illusions of young and older adults in *The Fountain of Age*. The author sees aging as a social, as well as a physical phenomenon. Individuals' performances differ, not only because of physiology, but also because of experience and environment. One reason that Supreme Court justices live longer than many, says Friedan, is because they are forever facing and responding to new challenges.

Justice William Brennan, who sat on the Court for thirty-three years, continued to grow. In fact, he chose cases that were difficult and challenging. As a so-called "old man," he brought new insights to the Fourteenth Amendment. He conquered throat cancer and a mild stroke, and was the life of the party at age eighty-three.

Justice Potter Stewart was a very different individual. He retired at the age of seventy, and it is said that he "deteriorated like a bullet hit him when he left the Court." Soon, there appeared symptoms of Hodgkin's disease. Justice Stewart would return to the Supreme Court Building from time to time "looking disheveled" and bent over. His appearance affected the Justices: it was like "seeing a ghost."

Beyond Retirement

Hans Archenhold retired from the Hallmark Company at age sixty-five, which was at that time mandatory. He had been corporate vice president for graphic arts, but after retirement he accepted the job of managing a printing company.

In due time, this active retiree was called back to Hallmark to take his old position. However, it was not the same. Competition in the greeting card industry was keen, but Archenhold had an idea as to how to gain an edge. He would expose managers to new cultures, the great art of Europe. "I decided to expand their brainpower." Some were having difficulty making the jump from yesterday to tomorrow. He wanted to make his colleagues dissatisfied with their work. He succeeded.

Hallmark created a learning center that cost $35 million. There, selected persons from diverse professions and different backgrounds lived in the same community, and managers of the company stayed on-site within the special residences for several months at a time. Together they discovered new ways of seeing and creating things. This innovation greatly increased effectiveness and profits.

Mr. Archenhold ran this program for seventeen years after his first retirement.

From Pioneer to Proofreader

Born in 1895 in Newman Grove, Nebraska, Audrey Stubbart lived on the Wyoming prairie for twenty-eight years and reared her children there. After moving to Independence, Missouri, she worked for eighteen years as a proofreader for Herald House, a local religious publisher, until mandatory retirement at the age of sixty-five.

Endowed with a strong work ethic, she soon found employment as a proofreader for the local newspaper, the *Examiner*. Still working full time at the age of one hundred, each year she makes the same speech at the newspaper on the occasion of her birthday: " 'Thank you for keeping me alive. If I couldn't come to work, I'm sure I would have died.' I've got too much energy, too much ambition, too much get up and go. I have to have something to do" (*U.S. News & World Report*, August 28/September 4, 1995).

Prayer in the Workplace

Corporate downsizing and mergers frequently devastate employ - ees. Many workers who once felt that their well-ordered lives were securely locked into an organization are facing painful adjustments in careers and lifestyles.

Anticipating problems in the workplace, some communities are turning to religion for answers. According to *The Wall Street Journal* (October 19, 1995), Pittsburgh is home to an informal ministry known as "The Experiment." A small group of men and women come together once a week in a designated place, perhaps in a restaurant, to share the large and personal problems of the week. They quietly unburden themselves. They listen to one another; they pray for one another. There are forty active groups in Pittsburgh. The operation is carried on by word of mouth, no advertising.

The Reverend Gregory S. Hammond, a former small business - man, says, "With the gap that exists between employee and manage - ment, where does one turn? One must turn outside the corporation." Leaders would like "to make Pittsburgh as famous for God as it is for steel."

Trainees!

We were queued up in the bank waiting for the next available teller. At last a vacancy occurred directly in front of our line. The customer ahead of me approached the window and asked the teller, "Are you a trainee?"

"Yes sir, I am."

Whereupon, the customer stepped to the side and waited for the next vacancy to occur.

The young teller was obviously embarrassed. I was then served by the trainee and found him to be courteous and efficient. When I complimented him on his demeanor, he replied, "Oh well, it's Mon - day."

Are we not all trainees?

Who Calls the Shots?

Considering the present culture of corporate America, perhaps it is time to reread Antony Jay's *Corporation Man* (1971). From a background of business, British television management, and television production, this provocative writer compares corporate managers to primitive hunting bands.

After some fifteen million years, the "genetics of history" continues to play a remarkable role in human groupings and responses. We see this phenomenon emerging again and again in our well-calibrated, controlled society. By design and desire, a relatively small number of persons in multinational corporations control the business community. As the noted economist Kenneth Galbraith has asserted, the consumer no longer controls the marketplace. Rather, it is the manufacturer, together with advertising.

World

"Get Along Without It"

In Ralph Waldo Emerson's day there was excitement over prophecies concerning the collapse of the world. One day when an unexpected person burst into his office hysterically exclaiming that the world was coming to an end, Emerson calmly replied, "We can get along without it."

Too Close to See

When Charles Lindbergh sighted the southern tip of Ireland, nearing the end of his first transatlantic flight, he remarked, "I haven't been far enough away to know the earth before. For twenty-five years I have lived on it, and yet not seen it until this moment."

This is true for most of us. Irrespective of age, gender, or status, we are so close to our blessings that we frequently fail to see them.

The First Universal Nation

A 1996 Census Bureau report forecasts profound demographic changes in the United States for the next half-century. The current population of 264 million is projected to reach nearly 400 million by midcentury. Although that sounds huge, it actually reflects an all-time low growth rate. Aging baby boomers will die faster than new Americans will be born.

Most important, by the year 2050, the United States will become a "majority minority" nation with non-Hispanic Whites accounting for barely half of the population. The population of Hispanics and Asians will grow fastest, on average, while the number of Blacks will nearly double, and the number of non-Hispanic Whites will increase slightly. In percentages, from 1995 to 2050: Hispanics will increase from 10.2 percent of the population to 24.5 percent; Asians will increase from 3.3 percent to 8.2 percent; Blacks will increase from 12 percent to 13.6 percent; and Whites will decrease from 73.6 percent to 52.8 percent. Ben Wattenberg of the American Enterprise Institute claims that these demographic changes will make America "the first universal nation in human history."

The Direction of Progress

George Bernard Shaw, the Irish dramatist, critic, and novelist, saw history from a fresh perspective when he said, "The reasonable man adapts himself to the world; the unreasonable one persists in trying to adapt the world to himself. Therefore all progress depends on the unreasonable man."

Jurassic Ark

When Karl Barth implored Christians to read the Bible and the newspaper with the same pair of eyes, he could not have anticipated the proposed creationist museum in Florence, Kentucky, near heavily traveled Interstate 75. Sponsored by an organization called "Answers in Genesis," the museum will display life-size dinosaur models alongside models of Adam and Eve as a means to refute the theory of evolution and promote a literal interpretation of Scripture.

Although scientists estimate that the earth is 4.6 billion years old, the exhibit will claim that the earth's age is only 10,000 years. Although the scientific community believes dinosaurs died out tens of millions of years before human beings appeared on earth, the exhibit will claim that dinosaurs were aboard the ark (the ones that didn't get aboard became fossils) and became extinct only a few hundred years ago. A conservative Christian newspaper declared that when the museum is constructed, "Kentucky just may be Jurassic Park's greatest nightmare."

Despite public ridicule, this declaration parallels the findings of the latest Gallup poll to ask about "creation." According to this 1993 survey, when Americans were given three statements and asked which came closest to their views:

Eleven percent chose "Human beings developed over millions of years from less advanced forms of life. God had no part in the process."

Thirty-five percent chose "Human beings have developed over millions of years from less advanced forms of life, but God guided this process."

Forty-six percent chose "God created humans all at once and pretty much in their present form within the last 10,000 years or so."

We Have Become God

At precisely 8:15 A.M. on August 6, 1945, the nuclear age began when an American B-29, piloted by Lt. Col. Paul W. Tibbets, and named for his mother, Enola Gay, dropped a fifteen kiloton atomic bomb on Hiroshima, Japan. Three days later, the world's second atomic bomb was dropped on Nagasaki. The initial blasts and fires killed 140,000 in Hiroshima and 70,000 in Nagasaki.

On the occasion of the fiftieth anniversary of the apocalyptic advent of the nuclear age, Mitsuo Okamoto, professor at Hiroshima's Shudo University, said, "Before, the destruction of the world was the work of an angry god. Now we know that we are capable of bringing about our own finality. We have become god."

On the Road

At the conclusion of the conference championship football games on January 14, 1996, the road to Super Bowl XXX became unexpectedly littered with verbal potholes.

In postgame network television interviews, several players used profanity. While holding the AFC championship trophy, Pittsburgh Steelers all-star linebacker Greg Lloyd exclaimed, "[This trophy] belongs here, and let's see if we can bring this damn thing back here next year, along with the (expletive) Super Bowl." Four hours later in Dallas, Michael Irvin, who caught two touchdown passes for the triumphant Cowboys, spoke in defense of his beleaguered coach: "Nobody deserves it more than Barry Switzer. He took all of this (expletive)."

Reactions were swift. A spokesman for the National Football League said he regretted the profane language but planned no disciplinary action. Players have been fined for making obscene gestures on the field, but there is no precedent for fining players for using obscene language on television.

Former Education Secretary William Bennett, a crusader for clean-ing up television, watched the games with his sons and had this reaction: The incidents show that swearing is "in the mainstream. Now it's over the . . . airwaves. (It's not) the end of the world, that . . . jocks use dirty language," Bennett claimed. "It's one more notch. . . . Civili-zations don't collapse all at once, they do it one degree at a time."

New Self, Old World

Determined to make good on her New Year's Eve resolution to become a new person, the woman visited her local beauty parlor on the second of January. After a facial, a manicure, a pedicure, a perm, and a tan, she felt and looked brand new. With supreme confidence the woman strolled from the shop to the sidewalk, ready to greet the world. But no sooner had she emerged than a car turned the corner and splashed her with mud and a mugger stole her purse. Under her breath she was heard to mutter, "I may be a new self, but it's the same old world."

Salvation may be personal, but it is never private. Because the external structures of sin reinforce and intensify the internal, re-demption necessarily includes the self *and* the world.

The Eyes of Faith

In his book *From Beirut to Jerusalem*, Tom Friedman, a *New York Times* reporter, describes his ten years in the Middle East. His expe-rience in Beirut, Lebanon, is particularly revealing.

You recall that Beirut is a city split in half. East Beirut has basically been controlled by Christians; West Beirut by Muslims. In the middle is a burned-out, torn-out section of the city that is no one's land. It is called the Green Line. And in the middle of the Green Line is located the Beirut National Museum, which houses priceless Egyptian statues, bas-reliefs, and stelae bearing early Phoenician writing. Because the Lebanese civil war jeopardized the museum's safety, the aged director, Emir Maurice Chehab, had wooden frames built around the immovable pieces and then filled those frames with poured concrete. Each object is literally encased in a foot of protective concrete that would repel any bullet or shell.

When Friedman entered the museum and the Gallery of Ramses on the ground floor, all he saw were huge square pillars of cement reaching up from the floor to various heights. Chehab, who knew every piece by heart, greeted him and began the tour. He pointed to a massive column of concrete and described in intricate detail a spectacular Egyptian statue found at Byblos. Then he walked to the next identical block of cement and identified the salient features of that object as well.

Friedman summarized his tour with these words: "After about an hour of this I started to believe I could actually see the objects he was describing."

One of the primary purposes of the church, positioned between the garden of Eden and the Second Coming, is to describe the world as it was once intended by God and once more can be. The eyes of faith see hope in the midst of a fallen world.

Living in Two Worlds

In his book *Where Do We Go From Here: Chaos or Community?* Martin Luther King Jr. reminds us that every person lives in two realms simultaneously: the internal and the external. The internal realm includes ideas, art, literature, moral values, and religion; while the external realm includes the world of competition and conflict, manipulation and management. In this latter realm, the so-called real world, the bottom line is often governed by arrogance and greed.

Dr. King concludes: "Our problem today is that we have allowed the internal to become lost in the external. We have allowed the means by which we live to outdistance the ends for which we live."

Worship

"Letters from God"

"I find letters from God dropped in the street," said Walt Whitman, "and every one is signed by God's name."

Worship is a letter from God. We are encouraged to open and respond in thankful praise.

Rituals of Meaning

Why do we treasure the watch that was given to our father by his father? Why do we wear lace from grandmother's dress at our wedding? Why do we want Uncle John to carve the Thanksgiving turkey? Why do we get teary eyed when Aunt Jane sings "Amazing Grace"?

The past and its rituals are the vehicles for meaning in our contemporary lives. The watch that we pass on, the lace that we wear, the family rituals that we enact, and the songs that we sing form the interior walls of our house of meaning. They evoke the influential past—those beliefs that structure our lives and those people who endow us with purpose.

Christian worship is the ritual of meaning for the church.

Preaching

The story goes that one day St. Francis of Assisi laid his hand on the shoulder of a young monk and said, "Brother, let us go into the town and preach." They went, and walked several streets and alleys before turning back to the monastery. Finally, his companion asked, "When shall we preach?" St. Francis replied, "My son, we have been preaching. We were preaching while we were walking. It is no use to walk anywhere to preach unless we preach as we walk."

A Lifetime

Following an especially well-received sermon, a parishioner asked the preacher, "How long did it take you to prepare that sermon?"

The preacher replied, "A lifetime!"

Like a Dove

"Come, Holy Spirit—Renew the Whole Creation" was the theme of the World Council of Churches' 1991 assembly in Canberra, Australia. Appropriately, one of the worship services was patterned after the Pentecost story.

As the delegates gathered in a big tent, a gusty breeze, right on cue, reminded the worshipers of "the rush of a violent wind." When it was time for the epistle reading from Acts 2, a single person read the first four verses. The next nine verses, 5-13, were read simultaneously by thirty-five to forty people, each one in his or her own language while standing in the midst of the congregation. Then a single person read the concluding verses, 14-21. The confusion of languages was visually as well as aurally experienced by the assembly.

At the point in the service when the people were invited to share what the Spirit "had poured out" to them, a "dove" suddenly appeared in the tent, circled over the heads of the worshipers, and then exited with a spectacular loop.

After the service, a delegate approached one of the members of the worship committee and expressed appreciation for the detail with which the committee had replicated the Pentecost story—complete with a dove!

Per Harling, worship leader at the assembly, commented that the " 'dove' was a very local and very lost Australian magpie, but who could tell?"

Clash of Conscience

Five minutes before the start of the worship service the organist informed me that she refused to play one of the hymns I had selected. Another was hurriedly chosen.

The disputed hymn was John Newton's "Glorious Things of Thee Are Spoken," which uses imagery from the day's epistle lection, Revelation 7:9-17, and appears in at least five denominational hymnals. I thought my selection, suggested by a popular lectionary resource, was both appropriate and "safe."

Although I had neglected to read the notation at the top of the hymnal page, which identified Franz Joseph Haydn as the composer, it would not have told me what the organist knew: This tune is most familiar as the setting for the words of the German national anthem, *"Deutschland, Deutschland über alles."* And that day was the fiftieth anniversary of the surrender of the Third Reich! On that day, General Dwight D. Eisenhower, commander of the Allied forces in Europe, had sent this simple telegram to field officers: "The mission of this Allied Force was fulfilled at 0241 local time, May 7, 1945."

Because music functions like a tattoo on the subconscious, our organist had had a clash of conscience.

Human-Centered Worship

While researching the history of the original Seventh Street Christian Church in Richmond, Virginia, G. Edwin Osborn uncovered a startling fact about the worship space. When he first viewed the church in the 1930s, massive organ pipes located behind the central pulpit and above the choir dominated the interior space and formed the focal point for worship. Then he discovered that the first sanctuary, built in the late-nineteenth century, had had no pipe organ. A tall, stained glass window, depicting Holman Hunt's "The Light of the World," occupied the back wall behind the pulpit and choir.

Further investigation revealed that the window was still in place. However, the exterior wall was bricked over by an adjoining structure constructed later, and the interior window was hidden by the organ pipes.

Osborn concluded that human-made devices had "reversed the divinely intended direction of worship."

The Word and Worship

The church is a "story-formed community" that is rooted in the crucifixion and resurrection of Jesus the Christ. This dual yet insepa- rable event functions for Christians as both the normative self-disclosure of God in history and the means of redemptive transformation. The Bible serves, then, as the primary witness to this originating event for the church.

In order for the community of faith to endure through time and to withstand the threats of enculturation, the story of what God has accomplished for the Hebrew people and the Christian community must be continually retold in corporate worship. And this narration occurs primarily through the service of the Word.

Traditionally, the Word refers to that portion of Christian corpo- rate worship where the reading of Scripture and the preaching of the sermon (or homily) are located. On the one hand, the Christian Scriptures record the story of God's saving acts for humanity; espe- cially the life, death, and resurrection of Jesus. On the other hand, preaching recounts the salvific revelation of God to which the Bible testifies so that the community may be *included* in the continuing story of God's redemptive activity in the world.

Lost in Worship

If little boys are made of "snips and snails and puppy dog tails," does that apply to Jesus as well? What was he "made of"? Did he play tricks on his sisters and brothers? Did he make imaginary figures from the wood scraps in his dad's workshop? Did he com- plain about his chores?

Although we know very little about the boy Jesus, we do know that he went to worship. At the age of twelve, Jesus' parents took him to Jerusalem for the Passover. And when they departed, he became separated from his family. Assuming that Jesus was with others in the group of travelers, his parents were not immediately concerned. But after a day, they returned to Jerusalem to look for him and eventually "found him in the temple, sitting among the teachers, listening to them and asking them questions" (Luke 2:46).

And Jesus responded to his parents' frantic inquiries with these words: "Why were you searching for me? Did you not know that I must be in my Father's house?" (Luke 2:49).

Enthralled by the wonder of worship and intoxicated by the intellect of the rabbis, Jesus got "lost" in the temple. If only our worship were so captivating!

In-Difference

While meeting with a consultant to discuss a new church brochure that would be designed specifically for prospective members, our pastor was asked a basic question: "Who is your competition?"

He replied, "The Sunday newspaper and the coffeepot. That is, indifference. Many people do not think that attending corporate worship makes a difference in their lives."

The more I reflected on his comment, the more convinced I became that he was right. "*In*-difference" is the key!

Christians are "called out" of the world by God *(ekklesia)* and grafted into the body of Christ through the power of the Holy Spirit at baptism. As new creations *"in* Christ," Christians are *different*. And, through corporate worship, redemption becomes a present reality in the hearing of the Word and the partaking of the sacraments.

Appendix A

Sermon Sparks

Preaching effectively on the high days of the church is a challenge. It is also difficult to address celebrations with vitality and freshness year after year. Here are some suggestions for sermon topics that address special days for both the Christian and national calendars.

Christian Calendar

Advent	Prerequisites for Peace: Luke 19:41-43
	Paradise Regained: Isaiah 11:6-8
Christmas	Christmas Savings: Luke 2:19
	Grace Upon Grace: John 1:14-16
Epiphany	Expecting the Lord: Luke 3:15-17
	Going Home Another Way: Matthew 2:12
Lent	He Too Was Tempted: Luke 4:1-13
	"The Wounded Healer": Isaiah 53:4-6
Palm Sunday	"Who Is This?" Matthew 21:10-11
	The Unforgettable Parade: Luke 19:36-38
Easter	Himself He Could Not Save: Mark 15:31
	He Is Risen! Luke 24:1-5
Pentecost	Winds of God: Acts 2:1-2
	Living Stones: 1 Peter 2:4-10

National Calendar

New Year's Day	Beginning Again: Revelation 21:1-5*a* Forward by Forgetting: Philippians 3:12-16
Martin Luther King Jr. Day	Worrisome Walls: Ephesians 2:13-14 One God—One Family: Acts 17:26-27
Mother's Day	Your Mother and Mine: John 19:26-27 The Language of Love: 1 Corinthians 13
Memorial Day	Nothing Separates Us: Romans 8:31-39 Weapons of Our Warfare: Ephesians 6:10-17
Independence Day	Concerning America: Psalm 33:12 Freedom Is Not Free: Galatians 5:13-14
Labor Day	While It Is Day: John 9:4 Do You Work in Gloves? Exodus 4:2
Thanksgiving Day	Growing in Gratitude: Luke 17:15-16 Lest We Forget! Psalm 107:1

Appendix B

Quotations Worth Quoting

Words, well-chosen words, powerful words, whether spoken or written, frequently ignite ideas and elicit suggestive images. The mind soars in playful imagination. The creative process begins.

"A mind stretched by a new idea can never return to its original dimension." Anonymous

"To live alone, one must either be an animal or a god." Aristotle

"I preached as never sure to preach again, and as a dying man to dying men." Richard Baxter

"A human being without faith, without reverence for anything, is a human being morally adrift." William J. Bennett

"The best helpers are those who tend their own vineyards first." Eugene Brice

"Forgiveness restores our hearts to the innocence that we knew—an innocence that allowed us the freedom to love." Robin Casarjian

"We are not human beings having a spiritual experience. We are spiritual beings having a human experience." Teilhard de Chardin

"Happiness is not the end of life: character is." Henry Ward Beecher

"In God there is minimum protection, but maximum support." William Sloane Coffin

"Character, my father used to tell me, is what you're like when no one's watching you." Robert Coles

"Total power leads to total vulnerability." Norman Cousins

"In relationships, the little things are the big things." Stephen R. Covey

"Without inner peace, it is impossible to have world peace." The Dalai Lama

"Like Israel in exile, we all live in constant danger of assimilation." Ellen F. Davis

"The most beautiful thing we can experience is the mysterious." Albert Einstein

"We must not cease from exploration. And the end of all our explor-ing will be to arrive where we began and to know the place for the first time." T. S. Eliot

"Shallow men believe in luck." Ralph Waldo Emerson

"The past is not dead; it isn't even past." William Faulkner

"Those things that hurt, instruct." Benjamin Franklin

"Becoming parents makes you sense your responsibility to another soul." Billy Graham

"No one else can grow for us." Linda B. Irwin

"I have sworn upon the altar of God, eternal hostility against every form of tyranny over the mind of man." Thomas Jefferson

"Those who see God must gird for service." Rufus M. Jones

"We Christians have much to learn about conversion and inner peace, and we should pray every day to pass through new doorways of understanding." John Killinger

"The idea that God gives people what they deserve, that our mis-deeds cause our misfortune, is a neat and attractive solution to the problem of evil at several levels, but it has a number of serious limitations." Harold S. Kushner

"Love's as warm as tears / Love is tears." C. S. Lewis

"When death destroys an important relationship, it is essential that someone be found partially capable of replacing that relationship." Joshua Liebman

"Our problem in the inner cities is not just economic poverty. It is a poverty of values." Rush Limbaugh

"Be kind, for everyone is carrying a heavy burden." Ian MacLaren

"God is God or we are nothing." Archibald MacLeish

"For there is a pendulum to all life and the sweat you deliver, if not rewarded today, will swing back tomorrow, tenfold." Og Mandino

"Everything that lives, lives only by running the risks of living." Carlyle Marney

"Procrastination is the art of keeping up with yesterday." Don Marquis

"We live in proportion to our ability to respond to and correlate ourselves with our environment." Charles H. Mayo

"We can only give ourselves to God when Christ, by his grace dies and rises again spiritually within us." Thomas Merton

"The mind is its own place, and in itself can make a Heaven of Hell, a Hell of Heaven." John Milton

"The essence of life is change, panoply of growth and decay." M. Scott Peck

"We live in the ruins of inherited moralities whose authority is gone." Gene Qutka

"Our goal as Christians is not to win a popularity contest but to serve a Master." Gary C. Redding

"It isn't working that's so hard, it's getting ready to work." Andrew A. (Andy) Rooney

"We are human in so far as we are sensitive." John Ruskin

"It doesn't take a hero to order men into battle. It takes a hero to be one of those men who goes into battle." General H. Norman Schwarzkopf

"I picked up the book of Job today by chance and found my own history there, precisely." George Bernard Shaw

"Time is a glutton that devours life." Red Skelton

"Nothing is sure that grows on earthly ground." Edmund Spenser

"This world's time dies, but the Lord remains." Helmut Thielicke

"I believe that the reason of life for each of us is simply to grow in love." Leo Tolstoy

"The best prayer is seldom a hit-and-miss matter, but grown by the glad acceptance of discipline, which, far from being its antithesis, is the price of real freedom." Elton Trueblood

"Time is a tailor specializing in alterations." Dale E. Turner

"Peace is always beautiful." Walt Whitman